# THE WHEEL OF TIME AND PHILOSOPHY

## The Blackwell Philosophy and Pop Culture Series
*Series editor: William Irwin*

A spoonful of sugar helps the medicine go down, and a healthy helping of popular culture clears the cobwebs from Kant. Philosophy has had a public relations problem for a few centuries now. This series aims to change that, showing that philosophy is relevant to your life—and not just for answering the big questions like "To be or not to be?" but for answering the little questions: "To watch or not to watch South Park?" Thinking deeply about TV, movies, and music doesn't make you a "complete idiot." In fact, it might make you a philosopher, someone who believes the unexamined life is not worth living and the unexamined cartoon is not worth watching.

**Already published in the series:**

**Alien and Philosophy: I Infest, Therefore I Am**
*Edited by Jeffery A. Ewing and Kevin S. Decker*

**Avatar: The Last Airbender and Philosophy**
*Edited by Helen De Cruz and Johan De Smedt*

**Batman and Philosophy: The Dark Knight of the Soul**
*Edited by Mark D. White and Robert Arp*

**The Big Bang Theory and Philosophy: Rock, Paper, Scissors, Aristotle, Locke**
*Edited by Dean A. Kowalski*

**BioShock and Philosophy: Irrational Game, Rational Book**
*Edited by Luke Cuddy*

**Black Mirror and Philosophy**
*Edited by David Kyle Johnson*

**Black Panther and Philosophy**
*Edited by Edwardo Pérez and Timothy Brown*

**Disney and Philosophy: Truth, Trust, and a Little Bit of Pixie Dust**
*Edited by Richard B. Davis*

**Dune and Philosophy**
*Edited by Kevin S. Decker*

**Dungeons and Dragons and Philosophy: Read and Gain Advantage on All Wisdom Checks**
*Edited by Christopher Robichaud*

**Game of Thrones and Philosophy: Logic Cuts Deeper Than Swords**
*Edited by Henry Jacoby*

**The Good Place and Philosophy: Everything is Fine!**
*Edited by Kimberly S. Engels*

**Star Wars and Philosophy Strikes Back**
*Edited by Jason T. Eberl and Kevin S. Decker*

**The Ultimate Harry Potter and Philosophy: Hogwarts for Muggles**
*Edited by Gregory Bassham*

**The Hobbit and Philosophy: For When You've Lost Your Dwarves, Your Wizard, and Your Way**
*Edited by Gregory Bassham and Eric Bronson*

**Inception and Philosophy: Because It's Never Just a Dream**
*Edited by David Kyle Johnson*

**LEGO and Philosophy: Constructing Reality Brick By Brick**
*Edited by Roy T. Cook and Sondra Bacharach*

**Metallica and Philosophy: A Crash Course in Brain Surgery**
*Edited by William Irwin*

**The Ultimate South Park and Philosophy: Respect My Philosophah!**
*Edited by Robert Arp and Kevin S. Decker*

**The Ultimate Star Trek and Philosophy: The Search for Socrates**
*Edited by Jason T. Eberl and Kevin S. Decker*

**The Ultimate Star Wars and Philosophy: You Must Unlearn What You Have Learned**
*Edited by Jason T. Eberl and Kevin S. Decker*

**Terminator and Philosophy: I'll Be Back, Therefore I Am**
*Edited by Richard Brown and Kevin S. Decker*

**Watchmen and Philosophy: A Rorschach Test**
*Edited by Mark D. White*

**Westworld and Philosophy: If You Go Looking for the Truth, Get the Whole Thing**
*Edited by James B. South and Kimberly S. Engels*

**Ted Lasso and Philosophy**
*Edited by Marybeth Baggett and David Baggett*

**Mad Max and Philosophy**
*Edited by Matthew P. Meyer and David Koepsell*

**Taylor Swift and Philosophy: Essays from the Tortured Philosophers Department**
*Edited by Catherine M. Robb and Georgie Mills*

**Joker and Philosophy**
*Edited by Massimiliano L. Cappuccio, George A. Dunn, and Jason T. Eberl*

**The Witcher and Philosophy**
*Edited by Matthew Brake and Kevin S. Decker*

**The Last of Us and Philosophy**
*Edited by Charles Joshua Horn*

**The Wheel of Time and Philosophy**
*Edited by Jacob M. Held*

For the full list of titles in the series see www.and philosophy.com

# THE WHEEL OF TIME AND PHILOSOPHY

## A PORTION OF WISDOM

Edited by Jacob M. Held

WILEY Blackwell

# Contents

## The Web Can Be Woven Many Ways

# List of Contributors

**Steve Bein** is True Blade of Southwest Ohio, Bearer of the Holy Gradebook, Defender of the Wall of Students Writing Their Own Papers Instead of Letting AI Do It, Translator of Watsuji, Kyoshi of Bujin Bugei Jutsu, Lord of Stately Bein Manor, and Associate Professor of Philosophy at the University of Dayton. His research interests include Japanese philosophy, Buddhism, environmental ethics, applied ethics, and philosophy and science fiction. Steve has contributed chapters to fourteen volumes on pop culture and philosophy on topics ranging from LEGO to Wonder Woman. The big philosophical question that drives him these days is, if duty is as heavy as a mountain, then why is it so easy to put off unwanted tasks until the last minute?

**Jeremy Christensen**, a doctoral candidate in English at the University of South Dakota, has taught rhetoric, argumentation, composition, public speaking, and literature for twenty years. His research interests are in Appalachian folklore, rhetoric, and critical theory. His affection, however, is reserved for his three children, his wife, and many, many good friends, who are the source of the One Power in his life.

**Roderick Cooke** teaches French literature and culture at Villanova University. He is the author of *The Dreyfus Affair's Literary Politics* (2023), and works on literature from the United States, United Kingdom, and Japan, in addition to France. He is interested in how philosophical ideas are used in works of fiction, and is writing a book that examines this topic in the French tradition from the Enlightenment to the present day. He first discovered *The Wheel of Time* as an excuse not to revise properly for high school exams in 1990s England, and never imagined that one day he'd get credit from his job for writing about it.

**Benjamin B. DeVan** is the Chair and Associate Professor of Ethics and Organizational Behavior at Palm Beach Atlantic University. He has taught Asian philosophy, philosophy of moral leadership, philosophy of social science, psychology of cultural diversity, marriage and family, and the Bible. Compared to Robert Jordan and Brandon Sanderson, his writing output is incredibly slim, hovering around seventy-five articles, chapters, reference entries, poems, and reviews such as "Do Not Look Up? Four Views on Heaven," "High Rule? Vintage Virtue in *The Legend of Zelda*," "Royal Righteousness in the *Ramayana*? Faithful Leadership in India's Mythic Masterpiece," and "Love Is Universal: AI, Angels, and Astrobiology at the Ends of Space and Time."

**Caitlynn Fletcher**, an undergraduate student at Augustana University in Sioux Falls, South Dakota, graduating in spring of 2025, is a biology major minoring in philosophy and classical philology. Long enamored with *The Wheel of Time*, she is always willing and able to discuss ideas, plot elements, and details from the series.

**Tobias T. Gibson** is a Professor of Political Science and Security Studies at Westminster College, in Fulton, Missouri. He was introduced to *The Wheel of Time* in the early 1990s, and it immediately became his favorite book series. He has published three coedited volumes, including the recent *International Security Studies and Technology* (2024). He has also written about the philosophy of *The Princess Bride* and *Better Call Saul*.

**Maja Griem** is Science Manager for the Center for Mind and Cognition at Ruhr-University Bochum. Her doctoral dissertation focused on animal social cognition, especially empathy, play, and attention guidance. Her fascination with communication across species motivated her dive into the research area of human–animal studies. Alas, the ever-spinning Wheel of Time did not see her fate as a Wolfsister with the ability to telepathically communicate with her pets—yet. However, she never gave up trying to understand them. Finishing the animal psychology course at the ATN (Academy for Applied Animal Psychology and Animal Behavior Training) is the closest she has come to telepathically connecting with animals possible in our mundane world without the One Power.

**Jacob M. Held** is Professor of Philosophy and Assistant Provost for Academic Assessment and General Education at the University of Central Arkansas in Conway, Arkansas. He's a philosophical generalist who works primarily at the intersection of philosophy and popular culture. He has published over fifty articles or essays and edited or coedited ten books, including *Wonder Woman and Philosophy: The Amazonian Mystique* (2017), *Stephen King and Philosophy* (2016), and *Dr. Seuss and Philosophy: Oh, the Thinks You Can Think!* (2011). When he began his career as a philosophy professor, he envisioned a life resembling that of an Aes Sedai joyfully laboring in the White Tower. Most days, however, he feels more like one of the Forsaken.

**Eric Holmes** is an instructor of writing and public speaking. His primary scholastic interest is horror and he has published works on EC comics, monster lore, and chapters in *Stranger Things and Philosophy* (2019), *Neon Genesis Evangelion and Philosophy* (2022), and *Anthony Bourdain and Philosophy* (2024).

**Tim Jones** is Course Leader of City College Norwich's BA (Hons) in psychology with sociology, where he also teaches access to higher education. He is reminded each day that, much like the turning of the Wheel of Time, there are neither beginnings nor endings to the marking workload.

**Dean A. Kowalski** is a Professor of Philosophy and Associate Dean of Academic Affairs in the College of General Studies at the University of Wisconsin-Milwaukee. He regularly teaches philosophy of religion, Asian philosophy, and ethics. He has authored, edited, or coedited a dozen books, each with a connection to popular culture, including *Joss Whedon as Philosopher* (2017), *Indiana Jones and Philosophy* (2023), and the *Palgrave Handbook of Popular Culture as Philosophy* (2024). Although he can neither sing, dance, juggle, nor play an instrument, he fancies himself as a fantabulous gleeman.

**Julie Loveland Swanstrom** is an Associate Professor of Philosophy, Religion, and Environmental Studies at Augustana University in Sioux Falls, South Dakota. She received her PhD in philosophy from Purdue University and teaches a range of courses spanning philosophy, theology, ethics, and environmental culture. She also uses philosophical and theological methods and ideas to explore science fiction and fantasy works. Her work on medieval theories of causation made her a strong Aes Sedai candidate to join the Browns—you can find her in the library looking up odd and curious cases of causation in order to explore presumptions people hold about causation.

**Steven Michels** is a Professor of Political Science at Sacred Heart University and the author of *Sinclair Lewis and American Democracy* (2017) and the editor of *Scenes from the American Working Class: This Hard Land* (2025). Like Thom Merrilin, he enjoys performing songs, but unlike the gleeman, he does not do much traveling or have much in the way of talent.

**Traci Phillipson** is Assistant Professor of Philosophy at Loras College in Dubuque, Iowa. She specializes in the history of philosophy with a focus on medieval philosophy in the Arabic and Latin traditions. She also works and teaches in ethics and the philosophy of religion. She has a burgeoning interest in public philosophy and philosophy in pop culture, having contributed to two past volumes of the Blackwell Philosophy and Pop Culture series.

**Kenneth R. Pike** is Assistant Professor of Philosophy and Law at the Florida Institute of Technology. His research applies moral and political theory to technology, family, and law. Among his publications are "The Doctrine of Sufficiency as a Contractualist Principle" (in *Moral Philosophy and Politics*, 2024) and "*Secher Nbiw* and the Child's Right to an Open Future" (in *Dune and Philosophy*, 2023). As a teenager he memorized poetry from *Lord of Chaos*; in college he studied creative writing with Brandon Sanderson. Today Kenneth spends most of his time imagining ways to prevent *gholam* from slipping under his office door.

**Kenneth Silver** is an Associate Professor at Trinity College Dublin. He works within the philosophy of action and business ethics, and his central focus is on corporate moral responsibility and corporate personhood. Though an American possessing a doctorate in philosophy, Dr. Silver finds himself employed by a business school abroad because the Wheel weaves as the Wheel wills.

**Andrew D. Thrasher** is an Adjunct Professor of Religious Studies at George Mason University and in the Virginia Community College System. He is the lead coeditor (with Austin M. Freeman) of *Theology, Fantasy, and the Imagination* (2023), where he contributed an interreligious analysis of *The Wheel of Time*. He is also author of *An Advaitic Modernity? Raimon Panikkar and Philosophical Theology* (2024), and *Post-Christian Religion in Popular Culture: Theology Through Exegesis* (2024). He has been fascinated with religious and philosophical dimensions of *The Wheel of Time* since high school, and though he relates with Mat's phrase of being lost in his own mind, he is far more like Perrin in build and demeanor. While not a wolf-brother per se, he has repeatedly been compared to a bear, both in his grizzly demeanor and how much he sleeps in *Tel'aran'rhiod*.

**Michel-Antoine Xhignesse** is an Instructor of Philosophy at Capilano University. He specializes in the aesthetics/philosophy of art and the philosophy of literature, and is the author of *Aesthetics: 50 Puzzles, Paradoxes, and Thought Experiments* (2023), the translator of *On the Ideal in the Pictorial Arts*, by Antoine-Chrysostome Quatremère de *Quincy* (2024) and, with James O. Young, of *the Causes of the Corruption of Taste*, by Anne Le Fèvre Dacier (2025). He'd really, really like to get his hands on a copy of *Mirrors of the Wheel*, so he can read more about the Portal Stones and the dinosaurs lurking behind them.

# Acknowledgments

First, I would like to thank series editor Bill Irwin. Since the beginning of my professional career—with my chapter in *Buffy the Vampire Slayer and Philosophy* (edited by James B. South)—he has been a constant in my academic life, and I have benefitted greatly from our relationship. He has also been incredibly patient with the production of this volume.

I'd also like to thank all the contributors. They produced wonderful essays that will hopefully broaden the reader's appreciation for both Robert Jordan's work and the history of philosophy.

# Introduction "A Part of What We Know"

The *Wheel of Time* series is vast. My first complete read-through took approximately five years, but I had kids and a job so free time was a rare commodity. But that's about the same amount of time it took me to finish my PhD program. Maybe someone should grant me an honorary degree in Robert Jordan studies. (Such a program probably exists in the recesses of some well-funded liberal arts college out east.)

I abandoned my reread of the series as I was developing this book when I realized that every page of *The Wheel of Time* I reread foreclosed the possibility of reading a page of some other work new to me. No offense to Robert Jordan, but when you write a series whose word count is equivalent to that of five-and-a-half Bibles, the opportunity cost of a reread, calculated in terms of missed opportunities to read new content, quickly outweighs the modicum of additional enjoyment generated by revisiting *The Wheel of Time*. There is just so much out there to read, and although I am sure I'd have enjoyed *The Wheel of Time* another time round, as do many fans, I just couldn't justify it.

But the *Wheel of Time* series is incredibly rich. It's hard to imagine a trope, theme, idea, or concept not introduced at some point in the series. These themes cover far-ranging ideas, from metaphysics and religion to ethics and politics. One can scarcely scratch the surface of *The Wheel of Time*, or the history of philosophy for that matter, even after years of study. So, I can imagine that some who revisit Jordan's *oeuvre* time and time again do wrest new insights from it. I am sure for these readers this book will omit things they perceive as essential to the series. And I am sure at some point we got a detail wrong, or interpreted an example or scenario inaccurately or inadequately, from their point of view. Given the vastness of the series there are bound to be many things left unsaid. For example, there are no mentions, to my chagrin, of the Aelfinn and Eelfinn. The idea of luck, whether as metaphysical chance or moral luck, is left mostly unmentioned. We failed to include a chapter on madness and mental health. These are just a few omissions I'd expect any fan of the series to notice, if not lament.

But what we did include, what my fantastic collaborators have provided for you, are engaging introductions to some foundational concepts, traditions, and major thinkers throughout the history of philosophy with reference to, and in appreciation of, the rich world of *The Wheel of Time*, both Jordan's series and the Amazon Prime show. From Arad Doman to the Aiel Waste you'll travel with these authors as they discuss just-war theory, existentialism, the philosophy of literature, and the nature of free will. You'll do so while pondering the Aes Sedai and the nature of truth telling, the Dark One, Darkfriends and nihilism, and Rand's love life. Although there are bound to be lacunae the devoted fan will notice, the richness of what is present should delight not only the casual reader or viewer, but even the most devoted fan. Lan is wise to note: "You can never know everything, and part of what you know is always wrong. Perhaps even the most important part. A portion of wisdom lies in knowing that. A portion of courage lies in going on anyway."[1] You hold in your hands a portion of our collected wisdom, a part of what we know. Is the opportunity cost of vesting time in this volume worth it? ... Read and find out.

Jacob M. Held

# Note

1. From Robert Jordan, *Winter's Heart*, chap. 32, at https://wot.fandom.com/wiki/Winter%27s_Heart/Chapter_32 (accessed November 24, 2024).

# STORIES HAVE POWER

# 1

# Tolkien's Influence and the World of *The Wheel of Time*

## *Michel-Antoine Xhignesse*

Some people complain that *The* Wheel of Time (*WoT*) is similar to Tolkien's Lord of the Rings (*LotR*). The implication is that *WoT* is somehow *derivative* of *LotR*. But while this is a popular criticism, it reflects fundamental misunderstandings about (i) the nature of *WoT*'s worldbuilding, (ii) the function of influence, and (iii) the formation and development of genre conventions. My hope, in this chapter, is to go some way toward rectifying all three of these misunderstandings.

It is certainly true that the two series have a lot in common, especially structurally (and especially where *WoT*'s first three books are concerned). And that is not to mention *WoT*'s many thinly disguised allusions, ranging from Trollocs (Troll-Orc hybrids), Ogier (Elves with a hint of Ent), Myrddraal and The Forsaken (each inspired by different aspects of the Nazgûl), Padan Fain (Gollum), and Ba'alzamon (Sauron[1]). Or, indeed, its penchant for *LotR*-related placenames like Andor or the Mountains of Mist, or the similarity between The Blight and Gorgoroth, Thakan'dar and Mordor, or Shayol Ghul and Mount Doom (indeed, *WoT* even has the Mountains of Dhoom!).

All these parallels, and many, many more, are there to be found. Indeed, Robert Jordan himself made no bones about Tolkien's influence:

In the first chapters of *The Eye of the World*, I tried for a Tolkienesque feel without trying to copy Tolkien's style, but that was by way of saying to the reader, okay, this is familiar, this is something you recognize, now let's go where you haven't been before.[2]

This helps to explain why Jordan's allusions to Tolkien are thinly veiled: readers are *meant* to catch them, so that they can feel at ease with the story. Astute readers will also spot many more allusions to other familiar stories: vampires (Draghkar), werewolves (wolfbrothers), Norse mythology (particularly Mat, who is a clear analogue of Odin), Arthurian legend (especially Rand, who is an analogue of Arthur), contemporary(ish) science

*The Wheel of Time and Philosophy*, First Edition. Edited by Jacob M. Held.
© 2025 John Wiley & Sons, Inc. Published 2025 by John Wiley & Sons, Inc.

fiction (Loial reading *To Sail Beyond the Sunset* in *The Great Hunt*), and even the Cold War (the tale of the giants Mosk and Merk), among many, many others. Here again, Jordan was crystal clear about his intentions. Concerning his plans for the series, Jordan wrote, in a note to his publisher sent with the typescript for *The Eye of the World*, that

> The story will take in parts not only of the most obvious myths (Arthur and Thor) but others, as well. Parts of the Arthurian legend will be blended with Norse myth, Greek myth and others. These will not be taken whole, however. What will be done is to show occurences [sic] which could, over thousands of years, be distorted into the sources of these myths.[3]

And here, we come to the crux of the matter: *The Wheel of Time* is deliberately chock full of stories we know and love. Not accidentally, and not as the result of incidental borrowing, but because Jordan wanted to use his novels to tell the story behind these other stories, the founding myth for all human cultures. And for that reason, something very philosophically interesting is going on in *WoT*. But to see just what that is, we first need to establish the basic building blocks of modern philosophy of literature. So: RAFO![4]

## A Gleeman's Tales, the *So'feia*'s Words

The first thing we need to remember is that authors are gleemen—story*tellers*. But *how* do they tell their stories? By writing them down, of course—but *what*, exactly, do they write down? At a first pass, it is tempting to say that authors write everything that they want us to imagine is true in their stories. Jordan wanted us to imagine that five young men and women from a rural backwater will grow up to save the world from evil, and so that's what he wrote down; he wanted us to imagine that Rand has red hair, so he said so; and so on. But although this much is clearly right, it does not get us as far as we might like, because there are lots of other things which must be true in the story if it is to make any sense. Rand, Nynaeve, Thom, Logain, Lanfear, and all of the other characters, for example, are obviously human beings—but we are never explicitly told as much. If they are human beings, then they must have a certain genetic profile, but we never hear about that, either. Perhaps more importantly, the law of gravity is clearly true in the story, otherwise its most basic physics would not make much sense—but again, we are never told as much. These are just some of the many pieces of information that we take for granted.

For philosophers of literature, this just shows that stories are necessarily incomplete: there are lots of details which must be true, but which the author was simply unable to tell us about.[5] Sometimes this may be because of author error (e.g. is Bela alive or dead?), because they neglected to tie up a loose end (e.g. what is up with the portal stones, the Mad Lands, and Shara?), or because they deliberately left it ambiguous (e.g. who is Nakomi? What happened to the pipe?). Speaking more broadly, no author can hope to tell us everything that happens in their story—at least, not in finite time. There are simply too many details—How many hairs are on Perrin's left forearm? How many times has Nynaeve tugged her braid?—most of which are too boring and irrelevant to include. There is an obvious reason we are not told every time Rand has to void his bowels: doing so would not be of much interest to most readers. Conversely, if we *did* have a scene in which he poops, we would expect it to be important to the story in some way (e.g. by contributing to the horror of the atmosphere inside Sevanna's box). Good storytelling requires authors to tell us what they think we need to know, or what will enhance our experience of the story, and to trust us to fill in the rest when and where appropriate while ignoring what is irrelevant or uninteresting.

One important consequence of this is that more is true in a story than just what we are explicitly told: a lot goes unsaid—including things of which there is no doubt that they must be true—if the story is to make sense. Similarly, often what we are explicitly told in a story is unreliable evidence for the story's content: we are often told, for example, that Stilling cannot be Healed. So if we want to know what is true in a story, we need to look at more than just what we are explicitly told; we need to also consider how reliable what has been said really is, and what has gone unsaid. With that in mind, philosophers of literature commonly draw a distinction between what stories *explicitly* tell us ("primary" story truth), and what they *implicitly* tell us ("secondary" story truth). Some things implicit in a story are just the consequences of other things that are true in the story. For example, the last we hear of Aldieb has her stabled at the Sun Palace in Cairhien after Moiraine disappears, so presumably she is still there in *Winter's Heart*. And some of what is implicit is what philosophers of literature call the story's *background*.[6] Background is just the set of beliefs we have about the real world that inform our understanding of the story world; think of it as the baggage you take with you on your journey into the story world, things like the law of gravity, English grammar, and so on. Background helps to fill in some (but not all) of the gaps left by an author, especially when we are talking about facts whose presentation would detract from the story in some way.

Not all background comes from the real world, although plenty of it does; sometimes, it comes from other stories. So, for example, we can be confident that the events of *New Spring* are part of the past in *The Eye of the World* and *A Memory of Light*, even if they're not explicitly mentioned or alluded to. Even genre conventions can inform a story's background: a story might be about a dragon, for example, but say nothing about whether it breathes fire; if it's appropriately situated in the Western tradition of fantasy tales about dragons, then we can rest assured that this dragon also breathes fire. (*WoT*, of course, has only one Dragon, and he is human—though he does weave balefire. Here again, we see the potential historical inspiration for a piece of real-world mythology.) This kind of background is called carry-over content, because it is carried over from other stories.[7]

The best way to think of background content is just as the set of facts (from the real world, or from other stories) that we take with us into a story world. As we read on, some of our background assumptions will be challenged by the facts on the ground; once we discover that is the case, we let go of that assumption and carry on reading. Most of the time, we do not even notice we are bringing these assumptions into the story until it becomes clear that the story is inconsistent with some assumption we were making. So, for example, you probably assumed that Randland was a fantasy realm distinct from the real world until you encountered the reference to the Apollo space program (the story of Lenn and Salya) in *The Eye of the World* (chapter 4), Mosk and Merk in *The Shadow Rising* (chapter 20), or the artifacts in the Panarch's Palace in Tanchico. Ultimately, what is true in a story is a function of both the story's explicit content and its background content, along with whatever additional facts these might entail.

Although philosophers have suggested several different ways of determining a story's secondary content given its primary content (so-called *principles of generation*[8]), we do not have the space to explore them in this chapter. Instead, I want to direct your attention to an assumption that lurks behind all of these principles. It has been called many things in the past, but most recently it has been articulated as the *Reality Assumption*:

*Reality Assumption*
Everything that is true in the real world is also fictionally true, unless excluded by the work.[9]

Straightforwardly, the Reality Assumption has us assuming that whatever is true in the real world is also true in the story, unless we are told otherwise. It is a defeasible *assumption* about story-content, and it is easily defeated: it can be defeated by explicit content (e.g. *WoT* is a world containing the One Power), or by genre conventions (e.g. satire is not to be taken literally), by carry-over content, or any number of other factors. What is important is just to notice that this is a commonly assumed starting point for determining story truth.

These are the basic building blocks of contemporary philosophy of literature, and they are necessary in order for us to see and understand Robert Jordan's uniquely ambitious creative achievement in writing *The Wheel of Time*, and to appreciate just why it is so philosophically rich.

## The World of *WoT*: *Tia mi aven Moridin isande vadin*

We saw, earlier, that Jordan explicitly conceived of the series as a kind of crucible in which the myths and legends of the real world were forged: that is why we can recognize in it so many elements of these stories from around the world. The conclusion we should draw from this fact is that *our world is part of WoT's world*. Yes, Randland has the One/True Power, a Creator and a Dark One, Trollocs, Myrddraal, and To'raken; these are significant differences, to be sure. But we can see elements of our world in each of these: magic, for example, was long believed to be real (and, as Arthur C. Clarke reminds us, "sufficiently advanced technology is indistinguishable from magic"[10]), good and evil deities are a feature of many world religions throughout human history, trolls are ubiquitous in Scandinavian folklore, *The Lord of the Rings* popularized the image of the dark rider, and a number of Seanchan beasts bear a striking resemblance to Earth's extinct megafauna. *The Wheel of Time* is presented to us as a possible configuration of our world, as its once and future state. The world as we know it is part of *WoT's* story, as is the world in any number of ways in which we do not know it.

If you are reading this book, then I expect that none of this is news to you. You might have missed a throwaway detail like Mosk and Merk or the Mercedes-Benz hood ornament in the Panarch's Palace, but the series wears its design on its sleeve. In fact, readers will doubtless be struck by another clear parallel to Tolkien: Tolkien likewise conceived of himself as creating (or "sub-creating," to use his own term[11]) a new, real-world mythology which, as Charles Mills put it, "[chronicles] the true feigned history of mythic creatures who 'reflect a splintered fragment' of the truth."[12] Tolkien himself was quite clear about his aims:

> Middle-earth is *our* world. I have (of course) placed the action in a purely imaginary (though not wholly impossible) period of antiquity, in which the shape of the continental masses was different.[13]

*WoT* and *LotR* are thus very much alike in conception, although *WoT's* real-world borrowings are perhaps easier to see than *LotR's*. But *WoT* takes things a step further than *LotR*: it incorporates the story of *The Lord of the Rings* into its own background. In other words, it is not just the case that *LotR* influenced Jordan; rather, *it is true in WoT* that there was once (or will one day be?) a dragon called Smaug, a race of hairy-footed hobbits, a flaming eye in the sky,[14] and so on.

This may seem like an extravagant claim. After all, *WoT* features no dragons, hobbits, or big flaming eyes in the sky. So what could possibly make this claim true? Two interrelated things:

1.  Our world is in *WoT's* background, and *LotR* features prominently in our world.
2.  The frequent allusions to *LotR*, especially in *The Eye of the World*.

We know that Jordan wanted to recreate the basis for the myths and legends we find in the real world; and we know that the allusions to *LotR* are no accident or lazy borrowing: Jordan deliberately structured *The Eye of the World* along the same lines as *The Fellowship of the Ring*, deliberately introduced references to Underhill, the nine rings, and so on. One perfectly charitable way of explaining this is just as a kind of homage to Tolkien, much as George R.R. Martin paid homage to Jordan by introducing house Jordayne of the Tor in *A Song of Ice and Fire*. But such an interpretation does not seem equal to Jordan's ambitions, nor does it satisfactorily explain why there are *several* allusions to *LotR* sprinkled throughout the novels. A more likely explanation is that just as Tolkien wanted to use *LotR* to create a mythology for England, so is *LotR* part of *WoT*'s mythology. To see that this is the case, we will have to consider Jordan's worldbuilding, an issue we will return to below.

But first, let us take stock of where things stand. We said that stories are *told*, and that authors tell us what they think we need and want to know; we said that stories are told against the background of the real world, which allows us to fill in additional details as needed; we saw that *LotR* is supposed to be a story from our own world's distant past; and we said that *WoT* is a story from our distant past/future as well. Putting these together, we arrive at the surprising claim that the events of *LotR*—in some shape, at any rate—likewise lie in *WoT*'s distant past/future, just as the Cold War and dinosaurs do. This shows why Jordan's allusions to Tolkien are so interesting: they are part and parcel of a broader mytho-poetic project that he shared with Tolkien, though the scale of its ambition was much larger. By incorporating a fictional mythology into his own fictional mythology,[15] Jordan played with storytelling norms in a new and interesting manner.[16]

But our friendly neighborhood *WoT*-skeptic may not yet be convinced. Jordan, after all, was clearly *influenced* by *LotR*—in fact, he was even more influenced by it than we initially suspected, since it turns out that he took on the same project of mythologizing the world! Does that not show that *WoT* is *derivative* of *LotR*, and isn't derivativeness an artistic defect? Not at all, and now let me tell you why.

## Influence: *Sa souvraya niende misain ye*

Philosophers of art and other art theorists have not had very much to say about the concept of influence, as such. Still, it is worth considering the little they *have* said, because it sounds a note of caution concerning our tendency to dismiss through influence.

The art historian Michael Baxandall, for example, famously argued that "'Influence' is a curse of art criticism" because it reverses the roles of agent and passive subject: the underlying grammar of "Tolkien influenced Jordan," for example, suggests that Tolkien did all the work, while Jordan simply received his wisdom (and perhaps also the credit).[17] But, Baxandall argues, this obscures all of the hard and interesting work that the person who is influenced does to assimilate and transform the insights of their predecessor into something new—at least where good artists are concerned.[18] When we conceive of the influenced party as the agent in the relation, we gain access to a new and richer critical vocabulary, allowing us to say things like "Jordan drew on Tolkien," "Jordan adapted Tolkien," "Jordan subverted Tolkien," and so on. In other words, as Baxandall puts it, "To think in terms of influence blunts thought by impoverishing the means of differentiation."[19]

There is something to this insight, particularly with respect to the tendency to "[impoverish] the means of differentiation." Every artist is influenced by a host of things, after all, including art's prior history. Abstract artists working today can only do what they do because artists like Wassily Kandinsky and Kazimir Malevich opened the conceptual space that made that sort of art possible, but to call that influence tends to paper over the real and significant artistic achievements of later artists, including such titans of modern art as Jackson Pollock, Salvador Dalí, and Frida Kahlo. The reason influence has a tendency to flatten the (non-) representational palettes artists draw from, according to Baxandall, is that it masquerades as a causal relationship: when $x$ influences $y$, we think of that as $x$ *causing* $y$'s actions—while in point of fact, it is $y$ who sees, in $x$, something that they must respond to, elaborate on, and so on.[20] Influence does not really proceed from $x$ to $w$, $y$, and $z$; it is established in retrospect, when we see that $w$, $y$, and $z$ all latched on to something in $x$, and made it their own.[21]

To say that someone's work is influenced by another is, too often, to suggest that it is in some way derivative; and to say that it is derivative is to suggest that it is in some way imitative, that the artist fails to make it their own, and so pales in comparison to its original. Oscar Wilde, for example, wrote in *The Portrait of Mr. W.H.* (1889) that "influence is simply a transference of personality, a mode of giving away what is most precious to one's self, and its exercise produces a sense, and, it may be, a reality of loss."[22] In *The Picture of Dorian Gray* (1890), he adds that

> to influence a person is to give him one's own soul. He does not think his natural thoughts, or burn with his natural passions. His virtues are not real to him. His sins, if there are such things as sins, are borrowed. He becomes an echo of someone else's music, an actor of a part that has not been written for him.[23]

This seems to be the substance of the complaint so often leveled at *WoT*: *WoT* looks a lot like *LotR*, and so it is less original, less aesthetically valuable.

In fact, we now have the resources to meet this charge against *WoT*. After all, the fact that Artist$_2$ was influenced by Artist$_1$ does not entail that Artist$_2$'s work is less creative or original than Artist$_1$'s—on the contrary, it often allows Artist$_2$ to be *more* original.[24] Yes, *WoT* was influenced by

*LotR*—but what work of epic fantasy isn't? *LotR* was a seminal, ground-breaking work that shaped the structure of modern fantasy literature, pushing it out of the realm of children's fairy tales and into the realm of respectable adult literature.

What matters is that these influences are not incidental and unthinking: they were deliberately chosen by Jordan and put to work toward certain ends. Most prominently, Jordan wanted to ease readers into his world by giving them a sense of familiarity, and he opted to do so by structuring the first novel in ways that echo *The Fellowship of the Ring*. But he also wanted to (i) extend Tolkien's mythologizing project beyond England to the rest of the world, and the rest of human history, and (ii) incorporate *LotR* itself into his own mythologizing. This project is distinct from Tolkien's; clearly, it is much more ambitious than Tolkien's (and that helps to explain why it took fifteen novels [counting *New Spring*] rather than five [counting *The Hobbit* and *The Silmarillion*]). But, yes, it is a project that was made possible by Tolkien first attempting to create a mythology for England.

Finally, it is worth raising something of a pedant's quibble against the charge that *WoT* is derivative of *LotR*. Jordan's influences were broad, spanning the entire globe, its history, its myths, and its legends. As Jordan himself put it, "I gathered together a lot of legends, fairy tales, and folk tales from around the world and stripped away the cultural references, so that just the bare story was left. Then I reverse-engineered them."[25] Already, this is far more intricate—and interesting—than wholesale borrowing.

But Jordan's notes reveal that far and away the biggest influence on *WoT*'s content is not *LotR* but rather Arthurian legend, especially as told in Mallory's *Le Morte d'Arthur* (1485).[26] This influence ranges from simple names (e.g. Morgase/Morgan/Morgawse, al'Thor/Arthur, Merlin/Amyrlin, sa'angreal/sangreal, etc.) to character arcs and plotlines (although these have often been recombined or ascribed to several characters). The most obvious case here is Rand himself: like the once and future king, Lews Therin died but is prophesied to rise again; Rand is acclaimed as the Dragon when he pulls Callandor (Excalibur/Caledfwlch) from the Stone (of Tear), his mother was Tigraine (Igraine), he is supposed to marry Egwene al'Vere (Guinevere), he dies at the Battle of Caemlyn (Camlann), and so on. But we can also see elements of Lancelot's story in Lan, of Galahad in Galad, of Morgawse and Morgan in Morgase, and so on.


## Genre: Sure as Peaches Are Poisonous


Alternately, we can think about influence's influence in terms of the mechanics of genre creation. A genre is, essentially, a collection of narrative elements that are typically associated with particular kinds of stories.[27] Fantasy, for example, canonically features magic and an array of mythical creatures from elves and trolls to dragons, and typically occupies a late medieval or early Renaissance technological and political setting. As more and more stories are written which feature similar collections of narrative elements, a genre coalesces around them. Such collections of properties are said to be a genre's *standard* properties, the kinds of properties you'd expect to find instantiated in a typical work falling within that genre.

Because genres are identified by reference to their standard properties, we can also easily articulate properties that are *contra-standard* for some genre: the kinds of properties which are so unusual in the genre that their presence tends to count as evidence against classifying the work in that genre. So, for example, a story that features futuristic technology or action in outer space/on other planets is more properly associated with science fiction than fantasy. Alternately, as Orson Scott Card so succinctly put it, "science fiction has rivets, fantasy has trees."[28] In other words, rivets are standard for science fiction, while an emphasis on trees is contra-standard; conversely, the emphasis on trees is standard for fantasy, while rivets on anything other than mail are contra-standard. And some properties, of course, are *variable* for a genre: they don't count much toward one classification or another. The properties we take to be standard (or contra-standard) for a genre depend, in large part, on the kinds of properties that genre's founding members are taken to have. It is no accident that so much fantasy looks like *LotR*: *LotR* is the text that founded the genre, and so it acts as a reference point for subsequent fantasy readers and writers.

Now, this is not to say that there is never any overlap—quite the contrary! The fact that medieval/Renaissance settings are standard for fantasy does not mean that they are necessary, and plenty of fantasy boasts different settings. Urban fantasy, for example, features contemporary(ish) urban settings; even *WoT* itself, a paradigmatic work of fantasy, features a setting simultaneously from our past and future (recall, e.g., that the Age of Legends, Randland's future, lies three thousand years in its past, while our own age lies buried in even deeper time). The point is not that a given story cannot deviate from the properties that are standard for its genre. The point, rather, is that it cannot deviate *too much* and still be classed in that genre. If someone starts out to write a fantasy novel but sets their story on a ship light years from earth, with no magic except advanced technology … Well, it will look a lot more like science fiction than fantasy.[29] Stories are classified into a genre when they possess a sufficient number of standard properties for that genre, and do not feature too many contra-standard properties.

Just what the precise threshold is, is a matter for readers and writers to determine collectively through their discourse and practices. A genre is built up over time, as authors return to certain key properties over and over again. Once they are robustly established in the community of readers, genre classifications can survive the introduction of contra-standard properties. Indeed, so long as the new contribution does not feature too many contra-standard properties, these can actually help to cement the centrality of the genre's standard properties by highlighting both the kind of story it is trying to be and the ways in which it is departing from standard narratives.

This also explains why and how genres may change over time: if enough people glom on to a particular contra-standard property in their contributions to a genre, it can become standard for the genre over time. This is what happened with cozy mysteries, for example: they started out as male-led stories (think of Sherlock Holmes, Hercule Poirot, and Arsène Lupin), but quickly became dominated by female protagonists (e.g. Miss Marple, Mrs. Bradley, and Miss Fisher), to the point where that is what we expect from them now. This is essentially what Harold Bloom means when he argues that great writing is a matter of misreading one's predecessors:[30] writers are also readers, and as such they are engaged in a kind of conversation with one another, and with the works that precede them. Their own work helps to extend the boundaries of a genre in different directions by taking slightly different clusters of properties as standard for the genre, introducing new clusters of properties as contra-standard, and so on.[31]

This does offer one last refuge for the defender of originality: if *LotR* was a pioneering work of the fantasy genre, such that subsequent fantasy was and is very much written in its mold, does that not mean that it is more original, more creative, than the works which followed it, such as *WoT*?

It does not. While it is certainly an achievement to produce a pioneering work, this is no guarantee of the work's independent quality. Many of the pioneering works of science fiction, for example—from the heady days of pulp "scientifiction" to Cold War titans like Asimov and Arthur C. Clarke—are simply unreadable by today's standards (e.g. the "science" is not very scientific, the plots are trite, the characters are cardboard cutouts, the misogyny is unbearable, etc.). Even at its worst, of course, *LotR* is nothing like that; the point is just that pioneering status is no guarantee of quality. But more importantly, we should not ignore the fact that pioneering works are themselves influenced by the history of works which precede them. *LotR*, for example, is heavily indebted to Arthurian legend and Celtic, Greek, and Norse mythology, including for its cast of critters—dragons, dwarves, elves, goblins, trolls, and so on are all drawn from mythological traditions, and *LotR* is no less creative or impressive for it. What matters is not their presence in the story, but what Tolkien *did* with and to them.

## Of Rockets and Hobbits

Putting it all together, we can see that:

> The Wheel of Time turns, and Ages come and pass, leaving memories that become legend. Legend fades to myth, and even myth is long forgotten when the Age that gave it birth comes again. In one Age, called the Third Age by some, an Age yet to come, an Age long past, a wind rose ...[32]

So begins every book of *WoT*. It is natural not to pay too much attention to it, although by the time Rand steps through the rings in Rhuidean most readers will have gathered that the story is built around a cyclical understanding of time, so that events in the story world are endlessly repeated (though the details may vary from one iteration to the next). This opening is our first clue that we are reading something special. It is a story that resembles many of the stories with which we are already intimately familiar—*LotR*, certainly, but also Arthurian legend, the life of Alexander, Norse mythology, and much, much more. But far from these narrative elements marking *WoT* out as derivative, a work of hackneyed borrowings and imitation, instead they serve to showcase just how rich the world of *WoT* really is. It is every bit as layered with meaning as our own cultural history, and more.

As we have seen, the complaint about Jordan's debt to Tolkien actually *understates* Tolkien's influence: if all it amounted to were several allusions to *LotR* and the narrative structure of *The Eye of the World*, then it would not amount to very much. But Jordan borrowed something much more significant from Tolkien, and the results are far more philosophically interesting and give us a very different story: he borrowed and expanded Tolkien's method of worldbuilding. As Michael Livingston puts it, "Jordan has applied philological principles to material culture, something Tolkien never dared in quite the same way."[33] Tolkien influenced Jordan insofar as Jordan's project is Tolkien's writ very, very large indeed, but the story itself is far from derivative. *WoT* represents the natural extension of Tolkien's mytho-poetic project, its enlargement to a scope far beyond what he envisaged. Jordan's project is singularly philosophically interesting because of how it weaves subsidiary fictional worlds into its own; *WoT* is a philosophical tour de force. Randland, like Middle-Earth, is *our* world, and if we unpick the threads of its history we will find both rockets and hobbits.

## Notes

1. It may be tempting to identify Shai'tan (The Dark One) with Sauron, but *LotR* fans will recall that although Sauron is the current "Dark Lord," he merely took up the mantle after his master Morgoth was defeated by the Valar. This story closely parallels that of Ba'alzamon (Ishamael), who was only partially sealed by the Hundred Companions and so was able to periodically sow chaos in the world.
2. Robert Jordan, quoted in Michael Livingston, *Origins of the Wheel of Time: The Legends and Mythologies That Inspired Robert Jordan* (New York: Pan Macmillan, 2022), 46.
3. Livingston, *Origins of the Wheel of Time*, 93.
4. "Read and Find Out," Jordan's stock answer to plot-related questions about *WoT*.

5. It is worth noting that there is some disagreement as to whether the incompleteness is *epistemic* or *ontological*: do we just not *know* what the pertinent details are, or is there no fact of the matter in the first place?

6. David K. Lewis, "Truth in Fiction," *American Philosophical Quarterly* 15 (1978), 37–46, David K. Lewis, "Postscripts to R. Woodward 'Truth in Fiction,'" in J.L. Austin ed., *Philosophical Papers, Volume 1* (New York: Oxford University Press, 1983), 276–280.

7. Lewis, "Truth in Fiction," 42.

8. Kendall Walton, *Mimesis as Make-Believe: On the Foundations of the Representational Arts* (Cambridge: Harvard University Press, 1990), 145.

9. Stacie Friend, "The Real Foundation of Fictional Worlds," *Australasian Journal of Philosophy* 95 (2017), 29.

10. Arthur C. Clarke, "Clarke's Third Law on UFO's," *Science* 159(3812) (1968), 255.

11. J.R.R. Tolkien, "Faerie Stories," in Christopher Tolkien ed., *The Monsters and the Critics, and Other Essays* (London: Harper Collins, 1997), 132.

12. Charles W. Mills, "The Wretched of Middle-Earth: An Orkish Manifesto," *Southern Journal of Philosophy* 60(S1) (2022), 108.

13. Humphrey Carpenter, *Tolkien: A Biography* (Boston: Houghton Mifflin, 1977), 91.

14. Technically, this owes more to the films than the books, where the eye is Sauron's symbol. But we should not let the facts get in the way of a good image!

15. Granted, all mythologies are fictional, but some, like Norse mythology, were once presented as real-world truth (or, at least, as closely allied to it), whereas others (such as *LotR*) never were.

16. Though perhaps not as novel as we might think; what is fanfiction, after all, if not a smaller-scale ambition of the same kind?

17. Michael Baxandall, *Patterns of Intention: On the Historical Explanation of Pictures* (New Haven: Yale University Press, 1985), 58, Harold Bloom articulates a similar feeling as the "paradox of poetic influence," according to which it is later poets who determine the nature and extent of previous poets' influence. See Harold Bloom, *The Anxiety of Influence: A Theory of Poetry*, 2nd ed. (New York: Oxford University Press, 1997), 42–43.

18. Baxandall, *Patterns of Intention*, 59.

19. Baxandall, *Patterns of Intention*, 59.

20. Baxandall, *Patterns of Intention*, 59.

21. Baxandall, *Patterns of Intention*, 60. Jerrold Levinson, on the other hand, argues that the relationship is causal—but a special kind of cause which cannot be known until some time after the fact. See Jerrold Levinson, "Artworks and the Future," in *Music, Art, and Metaphysics: Essays in Philosophical Aesthetics* (New York: Oxford University Press, 2011), 209–210.

22. Oscar Wilde, quoted in Bloom, *The Anxiety of Influence*, 6.

23. Oscar Wilde, quoted in Bloom, *The Anxiety of Influence*, 6.

24. Bloom, *The Anxiety of Influence*, also makes this point, 7.

25. Livingston, *Origins of the Wheel of Time*, 67.

26. See e.g. Livingston, *Origins of the Wheel of Time*, 64–65, 76–80, 84–85, 100–103.

27. The following observations on the nature and development of genres—especially as articulated in terms of standard vs. contra-standard properties—originally come from Kendall Walton, "Categories of Art," in *The Philosophical Review*, Vol. 79 (, 1970), 334–367, although his concern is with categories of art more broadly (e.g. music, painting, sculpture, etc.). They were first articulated for genre by Stacie Friend, "Fiction as a Genre," *Proceedings of the Aristotelian Society* 112 (2012), see esp. 188.
28. Howard Mittelmark, "Interview: Orson Scott Card," in *Inside Books* (, 1989), 38–39.
29. Though even then, extra-textual considerations may impact our classification—Iain M. Banks's *Inversions* (1998), for example, features a straightforwardly medieval setting, with nary a whiff of science fiction about it—save that it is a novel in his Culture series, one of the jewels of science fiction.
30. Bloom, *The Anxiety of Influence*, xix, xxiii, 5, 30. Bloom calls this "poetic misprision."
31. See alsoBaxandall, *Patterns of Intention*, 60–61.
32. Robert Jordan, *The Eye of the World* (New York: TOR Books, 1990), 21.
33. Livingston, *Origins of the Wheel of Time*, 56.

**2**

# *The Wheel of Time* and Authorship: The French Connection

*Roderick Cooke*

In 1968 France's foremost literary critic, Roland Barthes, published an essay which has bothered many an undergraduate in the years since: "The Death of the Author." I'll return to what Barthes meant in a philosophical sense later on, but as any reader of *The Wheel of Time* after 2007 knows, the death of the author can be quite literal, and have major implications for the status of his work. Reading the fifteen books that make up the series challenges us to think about the concept of authorship in many different ways, and French literary history offers a range of insights to help in the task. I'll concentrate on two of them in this chapter. The first will come from the Middle Ages, and the epic storytelling tradition which Jordan helped to extend into the third millennium. The second will come from the late twentieth century and the work done by philosophically minded literary critics like Barthes who challenged existing ideas about what it meant to be an author, and especially the role that authorship should play in guiding how we read.

## King Arthur Connections

Robert Jordan was often rather irritated by the common assumption that *The Wheel of Time* was set in some equivalent of our own Middle Ages: "this is not the medieval period, not a fantasy with knights in shining armor. If you want to imagine what the period is, imagine it as the late seventeenth century without gunpowder."[1] But despite this distinction, Jordan still drew on the stories that fascinated medieval readers and listeners for many of the founding concepts of *The Wheel of Time*. As many readers know, three of the members of the "Emond's Field Five" have names drawn from Arthurian legend. Rand al'Thor's name refers to King Arthur (as does Artur Hawkwing, his fellow powerful *ta'veren*), Egwene

*The Wheel of Time and Philosophy*, First Edition. Edited by Jacob M. Held.
© 2025 John Wiley & Sons, Inc. Published 2025 by John Wiley & Sons, Inc.

al'Vere namechecks Arthur's queen Guinevere, and Nynaeve al'Meara echoes the Lady of the Lake (who goes by many different names in the different Arthurian stories, most commonly Nimue but sometimes a variant of Nineve). The parallels keep going in the royal house of Andor, where the friends and lovers of the Emond's Fielders include Gawyn Trakand (who never fights a Green Knight in Jordan's version), Galad(edrid) Damodred (no Holy Grail for him), and Morgase Trakand (who avoids incest in her *Wheel of Time* incarnation).

But it is not these specific connections between Jordan's books and the stories of King Arthur that really stand out. Instead, it's another character with an Arthurian name who provides the clearest insights into how Jordan viewed the relationship between storytelling and tradition. If the individual you have in mind is "Thomdril Merrilin," you are way ahead of me (and bonus points for remembering all of his first name). From very early on in the series, which is to say the first few chapters of *The Eye of the World*, Jordan uses Thom to encourage the reader to see *The Wheel of Time* as something more than "just" the sprawling story and detail-rich fictional world being laid out for us on the page. Alert readers (and many often miss this until they get around to rereading the series) can spot as soon as Thom appears outside the Winespring Inn to meet Rand, Egwene, Mat, and Perrin that there is something lurking behind his entertainments:

> "You want stories?" Thom Merrilin declaimed. "I have stories, and I will give them to you. I will make them come alive before your eyes." A blue ball joined the others from somewhere, then a green one, and a yellow.[2]

And when Egwene asks for tales of "Lenn … How he flew to the moon in the belly of an eagle made of fire," Thom replies that they are "Stories from the Age before the Age of Legends, some say. Perhaps even older." Others from the same period are: "tales of Mosk the Giant, with his Lance of Fire that could reach around the world, and his wars with Elsbet, the Queen of All. Tales of Materese the Healer, Mother of the Wondrous Ind."[3]

John Glenn, the Apollo missions, the USSR's atomic bomb, Queen Elizabeth II, and Mother Theresa are all folded into a distant past to Jordan's world. He invites the reader to imagine themselves part of Rand and the others' universe, with the late twentieth century as another moment in the same Wheel's turning that spawned myths that would endure long after the specifics had been lost to history. A few books later, rather than talk about the particular stories he knows, Thom instead muses to Elayne Trakand about how stories come to be in the first place:

> My epic, if I compose it … will be no more than seed. … Those who know the truth will die, and their grandchildren's grandchildren will remember something different. Two dozen generations, and you may be the hero of it, not Rand …

"Or even myself." He grinned at her, warming his weathered face. "Thom Merrilin. Not a gleeman—but what? Who can say? Not eating fire, but breathing it. Hurling it about like an Aes Sedai."[4]

Thom plans to compose an epic poem telling the end of the Third Age of his world, but has no faith that it will be remembered the way he wrote it, because stories change in the telling from one generation to the next, and no individual version of the tale can hope to survive intact. What matters is the transmission, the storyteller's participation in the tradition, keeping the chain unbroken into the future. One of the reasons the Breaking of the World, which marked the end of the previous Age, was such a catastrophe was not just the massive loss of life, although that would of course have sufficed. It was also that so much *knowledge* was lost; only a few bits of stories are available to the professionals, like Thom, and the amateurs who tell tales around campfires and hearths.

## A Few Matters

A common complaint first-time readers have about *The Eye of the World* is that it "rips off" J.R.R. Tolkien's *The Fellowship of the Ring*. The parallels are indeed everywhere: naive villagers swept up by a mysterious magic-wielder to fight an ancient dark lord who has returned to threaten civilization itself; an uncrowned king of a fallen kingdom who hesitates to claim what is his as war engulfs the land (Lan and Aragorn); a dangerous, obsessed pursuer who hates the dark lord as much as he does our protagonists (Padan Fain and Gollum); and so on. But, the subsequent books prove that Jordan was not short of ideas that Tolkien never had. The American chose to model his opening volume, in part, on the Englishman's not because he was struggling for inspiration, but as a commentary on the nature of authorship. No one storyteller should claim to be truly original; instead, they should aim to innovate within a tradition to which they pay their respects in the act of storytelling. Both the Arthurian names that so many characters bear, and Thom's commentaries on the past and future tales of his world, underline the worldview that Jordan was trying to advance in *The Wheel of Time*.

And this is a worldview that would have been immediately recognizable to his European predecessors of the Middle Ages. The epic and chivalric poets of the eleventh and twelfth centuries have often been forgotten, with only their stories surviving to us. Even when we do have a name, such as Chrétien de Troyes, we often know little more than that. In France, the poems are typically divided into three (subject) "matters," each of which is associated with a place (and time): the "Matter of Britain," "Matter of France," and "Matter of Rome." "Britain" here means not only the Celtic myths of Great Britain (*Grande Bretagne* in French), but also their transmission to Brittany (*Bretagne*), in what is now northwestern France, through which they were adopted into the Old French-speaking world and its narrative traditions. The Matter of Britain deals with more than Arthurian legend alone. However, tales of the Round Table are a central part of it, and so we find poems such as Chrétien's *Perceval, the Story of the Grail* being written in France in the late twelfth century. It was important to these writers to, as a scholar of medieval literature puts it, "define their authorship by representing, in various ways, their relationships to their predecessors—thus portraying themselves as sensitive and sometimes critical readers of established authorities such as Ovid, Aesop, and Jerome."[5]

Robert Jordan's concern with his relationships to his predecessors makes him close intellectual kin to the likes of Chrétien de Troyes. It is not just the fact that they both chose to use the Matter of Britain in their very distinct ways to tell popular fictions that reached a wide audience in their own times. But more broadly, more philosophically, they share an approach to the work that does not hold originality as the supreme virtue, and which sees stories as lacking in value if they do not acknowledge those which went before, and which made the current story possible. When Jordan's villagers learn about Lan's backstory, fittingly enough, it is through a story told by Lord Agelmar Jagad. Agelmar tells them a brief historical epic which reveals both to the Emond's Fielders and to us, the readers, how the kingdom of Malkier fell through treachery, and how Lan received his life's mission as a baby from his doomed parents:

> Then did al'Akir and el'Leanna lead the Malkieri out to face the Shadow one last time. There they died, at Herot's Crossing, and the Malkieri died, and the Seven Towers were broken. … The oath sworn over his cradle is graven in his mind. There is nothing left to defend, but he can avenge. He denies his titles, yet in the Borderlands he is called the Uncrowned, and if he ever raised the Golden Crane of Malkier, an army would come to follow.[6]

This is known as a framed tale, or embedded narrative (you may also know it as a "story within a story"). The literary theorist Gérard Genette refers to this type of story as "intradiegetic,"[7] because it takes place within another act of storytelling, in this case Robert Jordan's. But behind Robert Jordan's story and the one he places in his character Agelmar's mouth, as we have already said, lies *The Lord of the Rings*, and behind *The Lord of the Rings* lay Tolkien's own passion for the ancient epics of the Anglo-Saxon, Norse, and Celtic worlds, which he taught at Oxford for over thirty years. So, it is not just that Jordan and Tolkien alike were interested in the subject-matter of those ancient periods; they also absorbed the idea that awareness of past tales is what breathes life into one's own writing, and worked to make those resonances audible to the reader.

## Barthes and the Death of the Author

Barthes's essay has been called "the most overrated article of all time,"[8] but despite this (or perhaps because of it), it has been a fixture of college literature courses ever since it came out, and shows no sign of disappearing any time soon. What does Barthes intend by his title, and why does it help us to think about *The Wheel of Time*? The French critic was not referring specifically to the case in which the author passes away before completing the work. Rather, Barthes argued that a fixation on the author as a source of authority in fixing the *meaning* of a story was wrong-headed, and should die off in order to liberate readers. He claimed that "we must reverse the myth: the birth of the reader must be requited by the death of the author."[9] Why does the reader need this death to come into their own? Because, for Barthes, "writing is the destruction of every voice, every origin."[10] In other words, it is a fiction to believe, as many readers instinctively do, that we can deduce what a book means by knowing what the author's life story was, or perhaps something about their political or philosophic beliefs. Instead, for Barthes, the democratization of literature can only be achieved by returning power to the people, that is, the people who read books, rather than those who write them. In this framework, authors appear as some sort of aristocracy or oligarchy, unfairly monopolizing the economy of meaning the same way that economic oligarchs monopolize industries to the detriment of the wider society.

Whatever we may think of the merits of this argument, there are many ways in which it can provoke us to reflect more deeply on *The Wheel of Time*. On one level, the death of James Oliver Rigney Jr. (as Jordan was known in everyday life) on September 16, 2007, which forced his wife and editor Harriet McDougal to find another writer to finish the series, combines the literal meaning of "the death of the author" with Barthes's idiosyncratic take on it. For, when Brandon Sanderson took over to write the final three volumes, he did so initially as a reader, not a writer. In a series of blog posts between January and May 2008, in the wake of his hiring, he commented on each book in the series after rereading it, as a first step to becoming Jordan's successor.[11] Although Jordan left often extensive notes and voice recordings detailing how the series was to conclude, as well as early drafts of some key passages, Sanderson had to invent not only most of the text itself but also numerous plot points to fill in gaps in Jordan's record and make the ending coherent. As a result, what we see in those final three *Wheel of Time* books is one reader's interpretation of what Jordan meant both in books one through eleven, and in his unpublished notes.

We could even argue that, just as Robert Jordan was using myths from all over the world, including the Matter of Britain, to construct the world and plot of *The Wheel of Time*, Sanderson in turn was using the "Matter of Jordan" to write the final three volumes in the series. He had a set of characters, locations, magic systems, and plot points given to him, and was tasked with completing the narrative from these ingredients. This, too, creates an echo with a major work from medieval France, namely *The Romance of the Rose* (*Roman de la Rose* in French), which may have been the single most-read book of the two hundred years after it was written.

Despite the book's popularity, establishing the date of its composition is very difficult. Partly this is because of the lack of precise records that affects our knowledge of the thirteenth century more generally. But the really tricky part of dating the book comes from the fact that *The Romance of Rose* was written by two people, the first of whom died before his successor took over. Guillaume de Loris wrote his part around 1230, and Jean de Meun probably finished the poem around fifty years later. Jean's section is much longer than the initial segment produced by Guillaume (around 17,000 lines against the original 4,000), and the ideas contained within the two sections sometimes differ as much as their style does. As a result, *The Romance of the Rose* has perpetually fascinated theorists of authorship by asking us to answer not only the question of how we should apportion credit or responsibility for authorship when there is more than one author, but also for how to reconcile apparently conflicting meanings that seem to originate with these multiple authors.

Much the same is true of Sanderson's conclusion to *The Wheel of Time*. Sanderson is responsible for one of the most polarizing characters in the series (and there are many, as half an hour spent in any fan forum will confirm). The Asha'man Androl is mentioned in Jordan's books, and even gets a brief line of dialogue in the prologue to *Winter's Heart*. But it is only under Sanderson's stewardship, starting in *Towers of Midnight*, that he becomes a fully-fledged character, and arguably one of the most essential to the outcome of the Last Battle. Some readers are enthused by Androl, both for his channeling ability and his relationship with the Aes Sedai Pevara. Others, however, view him as an unwarranted intrusion by Sanderson into Jordan's well-defined world, and for allegedly "stealing" the glory that had long been foretold for his fellow Asha'man (and formerly false Dragon) Logain Ablar.[12] Did Sanderson enrich *The Wheel of Time* by adding Androl and other such modifications to what Jordan would probably have written if he had lived long enough, or did the younger author unjustifiably distort the tale? The wide range of views on the merits of the final three volumes tells us that sequential authorship, as observed in *The Romance of the Rose* and *The Wheel of Time*, adds a further twist to an already complex concept.

# Return of the Author?

But whether there is one author or a dozen, the process so dear to Barthes applies as usual; each of us responds slightly differently to a text once we encounter it, and we may well draw the opposite conclusion to what Jordan or Sanderson might have intended. However, as I mentioned, it is probably the default setting for the average reader that Jordan's intentions *do* matter, and set the baseline for what *The Wheel of Time* means. Or, and this is a related but distinct point, we can look for transformed versions of events the author lived through as a source of meaning. How might this apply in Jordan's case? The most commonly cited event(s) would be his participation in the Vietnam War. Rosamund Pike, who plays Moiraine in the ongoing TV adaptation of the series, is a celebrity example of someone who reads *The Wheel of Time* this way. Speaking to the *Radio Times* while promoting season 1, she commented that "When I found out that Robert Jordan had been a helicopter gunner in Vietnam, I thought, oh, that's where this big fantasy world originates. That's why he's interested in men who had power and abused it and broke the world."[13] In this reading, both Lews Therin in the Age of Legends and the Asha'man at the end of the Third Age are directly descended from Jordan's experience as a young man firing heavy weaponry at the enemy in the jungles of Southeast Asia. More specifically, it is common to understand Rand's Altaran campaign against the Seanchan in *The Path of Daggers* as a direct adaptation of that style of combat to the plot of one of the books. The fog of war, constant rainfall, explosive and short-lived firefights, friendly-fire casualties, and finally the massive death toll inflicted and yet the inability to achieve the strategic aim of overthrowing the enemy government—these all echo the American experience in Vietnam.

All of which speaks against Barthes's hotly debated claims. There is a genuine hunger for meaning on the part of readers, whether famous like Pike or anonymous like those who have populated internet forums for decades to talk about *The Wheel of Time*, a hunger that for many of them can only fully be met by knowing more about Jordan's life, times, and ideas. To put it another way, readerly behavior seems to suggest that, even if authority is transferred from the author to the readers as Barthes wished, many of the latter will willingly return it right back to the former in exchange for what they believe is a more satisfying understanding of the book.

Ironically, Jordan sometimes referred to his political ideas as "Libertarian Monarchism,"[14] which may well have been a tongue-in-cheek mashup of two systems that seem about as far apart from each other as can be. And yet: combining the "death of the author" with the way that Jordan is often read does start to look a bit like libertarian monarchism. Libertarian, because if the author is no longer the starting-point for authority, readers are free to do as they like with no external regulation of their meanings. But monarchist, in that so many readers nevertheless assent to the singular, central authority of Jordan's experiences; perhaps an elective monarchy, then, in which the author-king governs not by divine right, but because he has been chosen by his "subjects" to guarantee stable meaning and ensure their minds are well-fed when they close the book's covers.

Why does this process occur? Perhaps because, as much as many readers like to debate meaning with their peers at conventions, online, or simply among groups of like-minded friends, most of them want that debate to be grounded in something that is not purely abstract or undefinable. Just as the term "anarchy" can be thrilling or essential for some people in the political sense, but is used as a synonym for chaos and disorder by others, so the implications of what Barthes argued for so strikingly in 1968 produce a wide variety of responses. Some of those who encounter his ideas take them as liberating, which was his intent. Other readers feel something is lost. For them, if "The Death of the Author" were accepted, the act of reading would become unstable, unreliable, or just plain unsatisfying. As a result, even the move from one author to two, with Sanderson's completion of *The Wheel of Time*, can produce anxieties and reluctance over the extent to which the younger man was able to uphold his predecessor's style, characterization, and worldbuilding principles. Characterization, in particular, stands out in the reader response to the final three *Wheel of Time* books. In a retrospective essay published later the same year *A Memory of Light* appeared, Sanderson acknowledged:

> My take on Mat is very divisive among Wheel of Time fans. A great number feel I did him poorly in *The Gathering Storm*. I've had a similar number approach me and tell me they like my Mat better than they did in previous books. Unfortunately, in doing so, these latter readers prove that the first readers are right. People do not come to me and say "I like your Perrin" or "I dislike your Perrin." They do not do it for Rand, Egwene, or any of the other major characters. While undoubtedly there are some who feel this way about those characters, there is not a consensus opinion among a large number of fans as there is that Mat was DIFFERENT in *The Gathering Storm*.[15]

In addition to plot changes such as those associated with Androl, discussed above, the characterization of Mat challenges the stability of meaning. Many, but not all, readers of *The Wheel of Time* seek stability of meaning that can be threatened by the death of the author, be it figurative or literal.

One retort to this takes us back from Barthes to the French Middle Ages. As I noted above, some medieval authors of major works are unknown to us even by name, and for others that is more or less all we have. For instance, the aforementioned Chrétien de Troyes was probably from the Champagne region of eastern France, hence his name, and seems to have worked for its countess at the time, Marie. More than that even specialists cannot say.[16] If these are major works, it cannot be because of anything to do with the author that is not contained in the text itself, in which case it does not matter where it came from since it is directly available to us.

This is one of the ways in which, despite its many links to medieval and epic storytelling, particularly in its insistence on tradition and retelling earlier material in a new style, *The Wheel of Time* ends up diverging from them. When we read Chrétien, all we have is the tale itself, and we must make sense of it how we can despite not having the author's life to inform us. When we read Robert Jordan, many among us choose to overlay his life on the pages of his books, despite the urgings of critics such as Barthes. When given the chance, it seems, the reader refuses to let the author die. Nynaeve al'Meara would surely approve.

# Notes

1. See https://www.theoryland.com/intvmain.php?i=114&utm_source=share&utm_medium=ios_app&utm_name=iossmf, from a March 2000 interview with *Locus* magazine.
2. Robert Jordan, *The Eye of the World* (New York: TOR Books, 1990), 43.
3. Jordan, *The Eye of the World*, 44.
4. Robert Jordan, *The Shadow Rising* (New York: TOR Books, 1992), 231.
5. Stephen Partridge, "Introduction: Author, Reader, Book, and Medieval Authorship in Theory and Practice," in Stephen Partridge and Eric Kwakkel eds., *Author, Reader, Book: Medieval Authorship in Theory and Practice* (Toronto: University of Toronto Press, 2012), 5.
6. Jordan, *The Eye of the World*, 597.
7. See Gérard Genette, *Narrative Discourse*, trans. Jane E. Lewin (Ithaca: Cornell University Press, 1980), 228.
8. Joshua Landy, "The Most Overrated Article of All Time?," *Philosophy and Literature* 41 (2017), 465–470.
9. Roland Barthes, "The Death of the Author," in *The Rustle of Language*, trans. Richard Howard (New York: Hill & Wang, 1986), 55.
10. Barthes, "The Death of the Author," 49.
11. These posts are still archived on Sanderson's website: https://www.brandonsanderson.com/blogs/blog/tagged/the-wheel-of-time-read-through. Since then, he has become one of the biggest-selling fantasy authors in his own right, so much so that many new readers now come to *The Wheel of Time* because they have read his other works and are curious about his contribution to the series.
12. A Dragonmount.com forum post after the release of *A Memory of Light* by Joshua Mark Humphrey sums up this perspective in a more balanced way than most: "And though I would not want to get rid of them and their scenes, Androl and Pevara steal the spotlight away from Logain," at https://dragonmount.com/forums/topic/78499-logains-arc-full-spoilers (accessed March 3, 2024).
13. Quoted in Amelia Wynne, "'You See Many More Naked Men Than Women': Rosamund Pike Reveals It's 'Quite Pleasing' to Readdress the Nudity

Imbalance in Her New Feminist Fantasy Series *The Wheel of Time*," *The Daily Mail*, November 9, 2021, at www.dailymail.co.uk/tvshowbiz/article-10181743/Rosamund-Pike-reveals-naked-men-women-Wheel-Time.html.

14. Cited in Michael Livingston, *Origins of The Wheel of Time: The Legends and Mythologies That Inspired Robert Jordan* (New York: TOR Books, 2022), 28. The political self-description appears in the long, unpublished version of Jordan's author biography which features in the published books' dust jackets, along with references to such things as "the industrialization of space."

15. Brandon Sanderson, "*The Wheel of Time* Retrospective: *The Gathering Storm*: What I Learned," at https://www.brandonsanderson.com/the-wheel-of-time-retrospective-the-gathering-storm-what-i-learned (accessed June 30, 2024).

16. Karl D. Uitti discusses Marie's role in commissioning Chrétien's *Lancelot* in "Background Information on Chrétien de Troyes's *Le Chevalier de la Charrette*: Chrétien de Troyes and Some Poetic Issues," January 22, 1997, at https://www.princeton.edu/~lancelot/romance.html. Another irony is that Brandon Sanderson found himself in a very similar position to Chrétien de Troyes in late 2007. Both Marie de Champagne and Harriet McDougal Rigney were wealthy patronesses who were hiring the author to produce a new work (*Lancelot, the Knight of the Cart* and *A Memory of Light* respectively) based on the storytelling tradition they loved. In both cases, the writer gave his patroness immense and public credit for helping to shape the final work and inform its meaning.

**3**

# "We Call Ourselves Gleeman Because a Silly Name Makes Us Less Frightening:" Artists, Marginality, and Epistemic Privilege

## *Traci Phillipson*

We meet Mat and Rand as they are walking through cold and desolate mountain terrain after a harrowing escape from the corrupted city Shadar Logoth. Just as Mat is starting to complain, they come upon a town where they take refuge at an inn. The town is rather unwelcoming, with a caged corpse on the outskirts and with streets populated by locals who eye our friends with suspicion. Thankfully, the interior of the inn is more inviting, bustling with patrons and staffed by a kindly innkeeper, Dana. What's more, there is another newcomer to town—a gleeman who is about to perform. The viewer, perhaps like Rand and Mat, expects, or at least hopes, that this will be an opportunity for some merriment and raised spirits after the darkness of the first two episodes of *The Wheel of Time*—glee is in the performer's job title, after all. Instead, however, the inn's patrons are treated to a slow, sad, mesmerizing song.

The song is a subtle reference to Lews Therin Telamon, the Dragon who broke the world and indirectly caused the tainting of *saidin*. But, while we might expect a bard's song to focus on the Dragon's power and early successes during the War of Power, or, more likely, his hubris and resulting fall from grace at the end of the war, the lyrics focus on the inescapable pain and sadness he feels seeing what he has done. In the last stanza the gleeman sings: "He caused the whole world's breaking / That tortured soul I met / In a prison of his making / The man who can't forget." Despite the unexpectedly empathetic nature of the song, the gleeman is able to enrapture the entire bar, which falls into utter stillness and quiet, only broken when Dana exclaims, "all right. We all gonna cry, or do we want another round?"

This first encounter with Thom Merrilin, the gleeman, is an excellent example of the way that artists and storytellers are able to bring their audience to unexpected emotional and epistemic places. Even if it was only for a moment, Thom was able to help an entire room full of rowdy people empathize with the Dragon and understand something of the pain that could be felt by someone who caused so much damage. How does he do it? Thom turns a disadvantage into an advantage. As a gleeman, he is marginalized from the larger communal structures of society, but this helps him to understand people in unique ways and convey that knowledge to the masses.

We have entered the land of epistemology, the branch of philosophy concerned with how we know things. As we'll see, Thom the gleeman supplies an interesting example for standpoint epistemology, according to which being an outsider can actually be helpful in understanding some things more accurately.

## "He Was Murdered by Cowards Who Feared Something They Didn't Understand"

After their initial meeting at the inn, we next see Thom interacting with one of the main characters when he confronts Mat, who has gone to loot the caged corpse he and Rand encountered on their way into town. As Mat is looking at the gem at the corpse's side, Thom comes up behind him and asks what he's doing. This leads to a brief, tense standoff, as Mat immediately draws his dagger in response. Mat says he doesn't want to hurt Thom, who responds that Mat would bleed out before he could lay a finger on him. Mat retorts that "I've not survived Trollocs to die at the hands of a singer." Thom is surprised that a person from the Two Rivers would have had occasion to encounter a Trolloc. When Mat asks how he knew where he was from Thom responds, "it's written all over you. Your speech, your dress, your asinine attitude. Stubborn as a mule." This exchange hints at the power dynamic involved between the two: Mat seems to have a low opinion of the gleeman, while Thom hints at an unexpected level of physical power. It also gives us a first glimpse into the wide-ranging knowledge that Thom has gained as a person who wanders among various societies rather than staying in one place; he is able to correctly place Mat's origin after only a short interaction.

This point is more strongly presented in the exchange that follows about the corpse. Thom states that he isn't there to hurt Mat but to bury the body, which is that of an Aiel man. He says that the killing of the man was not justice and that he heard the townspeople bragging about killing an Aiel, suggesting that the man was not executed for a crime but simply for being Aiel. Mat shrugs, saying "the stories say they're as bad as Trollocs."

Thom counters, "Mine don't. They're fighters, yes. But they're honor-bound ones ... he was murdered by cowards who feared something they didn't understand." Thom is implying that he, unlike most people in their society, understands the Aiel and does not fear them; the cultural details he provides Mat lend credence to this claim. If we think about knowledge and knowers through the framework of standpoint theory, we can see why a gleeman might have such knowledge.

Contemporary philosopher Heidi Grasswick explains that social epistemologies in general hold "that experiential differences lead to differences in perspective, and these perspectival differences carry epistemic consequences."[1] Regarding standpoint theory in particular, she notes that "standpoint theory also represents one of the more thorough attempts to ground epistemology and, correspondingly, a view of knowers in a social theory. It ties social location very closely to epistemic position, arguing that social locations not only vary from an epistemological point of view, but that some social locations offer the potential to be more epistemically reliable than others."[2]

Essentially, standpoint theories of knowing hold that a person's social position provides a certain level of epistemic privilege, granting them access to knowledge that is inaccessible to those who do not inhabit the same social position. Further, it is generally thought that holding a marginalized social position corresponds to a more privileged epistemic position. Speaking within the context of feminism, Grasswick notes that, "the activities of women that place them in a socially underprivileged position can form the basis of a privileged epistemic standpoint, through which a deeper understanding of patriarchal institutions and ideologies can be reached."[3] This can be translated to the position of the gleeman within the context of *The Wheel of Time* fairly easily. Gleemen occupy a socially underprivileged position in society; the societies in the world of *The Wheel of Time* are highly localized within tight-knit towns, villages, or provincial communities. We see this in episode 1 when all the women of the town come together for Egwene's Women's Circle ceremony, and the whole town comes together for Bel Tine. Gleemen exist on the margins, able to travel through and among various towns and cultures, even going into the Aiel Wastes, which is generally forbidden to outsiders. They are able to see these societies and cultures from the outskirts, largely free from the pressures of the status quo and the prevailing ideologies and institutions. Viewed within the context of this epistemic theory, Thom's ability to see beyond the cultural hatred of the Aiel is explained by the ways his position as a gleeman has allowed him to access knowledge that was simply inaccessible to those in more stable social positions within Andoran culture.

Thom's special epistemic position is further on display as his interaction with Mat continues. When Mat admits he needs money to get home and thought the corpse might have some, we expect Thom to be offended and prevent it, especially given his view that the man was treated unjustly in life. Instead, the gleeman sees the embarrassment on Mat's face and steps away, saying, "We've all had desperate moments. Tell me when you're finished." As a person who exists not only on the social margins but also on the economic margins, relying on "donations for the gleeman" to make his way, it is no surprise that Thom can understand Mat's desperation. Later we learn about Thom's nephew Owyn (who will be discussed below) and we can see that he likely also empathizes with the feeling of needing to get home to those who need us. Thus, instead of passing judgment on Mat for behavior worthy of judgment in Andoran culture, Thom is able to understand Mat's action from a different standpoint.

When Mat is done searching the body, he actually helps Thom bury it and Thom offers a culturally specific blessing, indicating he has some firsthand, experiential knowledge of Aiel customs. This lends further credence to the standpoint theorist's view that particular experiences allow people to gain knowledge of truths that are socially and experientially dependent. The combination of social identity and experience leads the knower to hold their particular epistemic perspective.

As a gleeman, Thom is removed enough from his own social systems, and accustomed to experience the cultures of others, such that he was able to see the Aiel for who they are as a people, rather than accepting the stories told about them. Additionally, although "standpoint theories have been controversial because by connecting epistemic perspective so closely to one's material and social location, they appear to posit chasms between knowers, suggesting knowers are unable to share knowledge across social locations,"[4] Thom, like many artists, seems to be able to avoid this potential pitfall. Through song and storytelling, the gleeman as artist is able to spread his knowledge to others. He can make sure that the stories he tells of the Aiel portray them as honorable rather than Trolloc-like. He can sing songs that highlight the pain and humanity of the Dragon and transmit his knowledge to others, helping them to see the world from a new perspective.

## "She's a Darkfriend, Boy"

Of course, the fact that Thom's marginal standpoint allows him to view the last Dragon and Mat with compassion and to understand something of Aiel culture does not mean he is totally free from social context and bias. After all he is still situated in a particular social context and he does not occupy every marginal standpoint, only one. For example, he does not seem to extend his openness and compassion to understanding Darkfriends. Indeed, Thom is quick to kill Dana once she is revealed to be a Darkfriend intent on bringing Rand and Mat to the Dark One. When the chase through town ends in a standoff, Rand and Mat ask her why she is willing to allow the Dark One to kill them. She responds with pain in her voice, "The Dark

One doesn't want to kill you, that's what the Aes Sedai want. He wants you to save us. Can't you see that? The Wheel keeps turning and people keep hurting … the Dragon has a chance to change all that. Break the Wheel. Make it stop." Her standpoint as an innkeeper allows her to hear the many sad and painful stories of people who pass through her inn, and she has come to see the Dragon and the Dark One's influence on the Dragon as a way to end their suffering.

We don't know how much of this conversation Thom overheard, but we do know that he heard enough to stab her in the back with a throwing knife. When Rand and Mat are shocked by his actions, he states matter-of-factly, "didn't you hear her. She's a Darkfriend, boy. Sworn body and soul to the Dark One." Perhaps Dana was not able to effectively convey her knowledge in the way the gleeman and other artists can; or, perhaps this was an epistemic gap that simply could not be traversed.

Or, the Dark One is simply evil and Thom already knows that. Yet the idea of an untraversable epistemic gap is the theory that seems confirmed when we hear the story of Thom's nephew Owyn in episode 4. Thom and Rand are discussing Mat's increasingly disturbing behavior. Thom sees in Mat a lot of Owyn, a young man who "spent half his life getting into trouble, the other half getting out of it, and a good part of mine helping him at both." Perhaps this is why it was so easy for Thom to see the good in Mat when he found him looting the Aiel man's body. Thom explains that Owyn was a good lad, on the whole, until "one day he went sour. Snapping at family and friends. Jumping at shadows. Animals had their hair up whenever he passed," all of which should sound familiar to us as we've seen similar signs from Mat. No one knew what was wrong with Owyn until one day he channeled in public, throwing a stone. Rand can't believe that Mat would hide it if he had accessed the Power; "he's not an idiot," after all. But Thom responds, "neither was Owyn. I'm a gleeman. Don't you think I told him the stories since he was a little boy? How at the end of the last Age the Dark One corrupted the One Power so men couldn't use it without going mad. And still he lied to me." Eventually, the Reds found Owyn and gentled him. Unable to live without the Power he took his own life a few weeks later. Thom doesn't want the same thing to happen to Mat. He tells Rand, "I'm going to stay with you as long as I can. Keep you safe. Whatever we do, we have to keep Mat away from those women." Rand is unsure, replying, "you know a lot for a simple gleeman." Thom says, "We call ourselves gleeman because a silly name makes us less frightening. Nothing is more dangerous than a man who knows the past."

From the perspective of standpoint epistemology, this exchange is notable in a couple of ways. First, it offers an example of Thom unable to effectively convey his knowledge to Owyn. Despite his epistemic privilege as a gleeman, and the close relationship they shared, Thom was unable to use stories, the special epistemic tool of the gleeman, to help Owyn avoid the fate of all men who channel the One Power. Not only did Owyn use the

Power when he found he had access to it, but he kept his abilities secret until the madness made it impossible to do so. Like Dana in the previous episode, Thom was unable to bridge the gap between himself and Owyn as knowers who occupied different epistemic standpoints. Even with all his "dangerous" knowledge of the past he could not save his nephew. But his knowledge and personal experience with the Aes Sedai may place him in a better position to save Mat. At the very least, his martial prowess is able to provide Mat and Rand with an opportunity to escape when they are found by a Fade soon after this discussion. Perhaps this lends further credence to the concerns some have about the seemingly inherent chasm between knowers in standpoint theory.

Second, we know that with respect to Mat, Thom is wrong. As a viewing audience we have the most marginal standpoint, being placed fully outside the world of *The Wheel of Time*. We know that Mat is not suffering from channeling madness; he is being corrupted by the darkness of Shadar Logoth, having ignored Lan's order to "touch nothing" by not only touching but taking a jeweled dagger from the ruins. We saw that the darkness began to wash over Shadar Logoth as soon as Mat touched the dagger in episode 2, and we see Mat puke out some of that same darkness just moments before Rand and Thom have the above conversation. Of course, Thom has no way of knowing this; Mat hasn't revealed what he did to anyone, and it does seem that the Dark corrupts in similar ways, whether it's imbued in a dagger or the Power. Being at the margins of society does not allow Thom to know everything.

## Is the Gleeman Epistemically Privileged?

We might say that these instances of error in understanding, or inability to covey knowledge, are unproblematic. After all, no one can be right all the time, and even when one is right, we know from our own social and political situation that people do not always listen to or understand those who try to share the truth. But, it might also be the case that these instances raise another concern that some thinkers have with standpoint theory—that it shows the limits of the concept of epistemic privilege as such, especially when paired with valuing social marginality for its own sake. The philosopher Bat-Ami Bar On (1948–2020) discusses these issues in her article "Marginality and Epistemic Privilege."[5] There she claims that "both the assumption of a single center from which the epistemically privileged, socially marginalized subjects are distanced and the grounding of their epistemic privilege in their identity and practices are problematic."[6] Claiming that epistemic privilege results only from distance from some social center risks assuming that distance is all that matters, epistemically. Whoever is further from the center is more able to know. In the context of the show, it seems evident that the Darkfriends are the most distant from the center of society. While gleeman live on the margins in the sense that they travel from community to community on their own and have access to various cultures, we see that they are still somewhat grounded in the culture—as Thom is grounded in the culture which understands the Dark One to be unequivocally evil, even if those who are unequivocally good are less clear. But, do we really want to say that Dana and others who support the Dark One, the entity who corrupted *saidin* and, at least indirectly, caused the breaking of the world, are to be trusted as knowers?

Further, we might point out that people are part of various social positions and can be marginal in some ways but central in others. The complexity and intersectionality of identity "make it hard to attribute epistemic privilege to just one of the many socially marginalized groups cohabitating in one society … even if it were possible to identify one socially marginalized group as special, it would be hard to make an attribution of epistemic privilege to this group that does not idealize its practices."[7] Thom is marginal as a gleeman, but fairly central in his cultural views of the Dark One. Bar On suggests the obvious solution to these difficulties is to "give up epistemic privilege,"[8] which she sees as a tool of oppressive structures and so ultimately ineffective in combating oppression. Perhaps if we view Thom's epistemic standpoint as not privileged but different we can retain some of the positive aspects of his special place as an artist with access to multiple social systems without having to take his view as always correct; perhaps this will also allow us to look more critically and openly at people like Dana. Of course, such openness can increase understanding without forcing us into acceptance or moral support of evil actions like those undertaken by the Dark One and the Darkfriends.

# Notes

1. Heidi Grasswick, "Feminist Social Epistemology," in *The Stanford Encyclopedia of Philosophy* at https://plato.stanford.edu/archives/fall2018/entries/feminist-social-epistemology.
2. Grasswick, "Feminist Social Epistemology."
3. Grasswick, "Feminist Social Epistemology."
4. Grasswick, "Feminist Social Epistemology."
5. Bat-Ami Bar On, "Marginality and Epistemic Privilege," in Linda Alcoff and Elizabeth Potter eds., *Feminist Epistemologies* (New York: Routledge, 1993), 83–100. Also see Grasswick, "Feminist Social Epistemology," for a brief discussion of this issue.
6. Bar On, "Marginality and Epistemic Privilege," 91.
7. Bar On, "Marginality and Epistemic Privilege," 94.
8. Bar On, "Marginality and Epistemic Privilege," 94.

# ALIVE, GLORIOUSLY ALIVE, TODAY

**4**

# The Anti-Natalist and the Aes Sedai

## Should Rand al'Thor Save the World?

*Kenneth R. Pike*

You and I have fought a thousand battles with the turning of the Wheel, a thousand times a thousand, and we will fight until time dies and the Shadow is triumphant!

—Elan Morin Tedronai to Lews Therin Telamon

## The Eye of the World

At the climax of *The Eye of the World*, the opening volume of Robert Jordan's epic *The Wheel of Time*, Rand al'Thor believes the "Dark One" to be an anthropomorphic (if suitably demonic) warlord whose army of monsters threatens to overrun civilization. Drawing on the titular "Eye," Rand "kills" his nemesis (he thinks!), but this is not the end of his journey—and not *just* because there are neither beginnings nor endings to the turning of the Wheel of Time. As Rand accrues martial and magical might in preparation for the true "Last Battle," he gradually arrives at the understanding that it is not ultimately the conflict that matters, but the *question*: Is the world worth saving?

If a heroically affirmative response seems obvious to you, consider the position of those whose lives are awash in credible apocalypticism. If you believed the world and its peoples were facing annihilation, but also that by giving yourself over to the service and advancement of the catastrophe you could improve your personal circumstances (maybe even to the point of surviving the cataclysm), what would you choose? After all, no less respected a thinker than David Hume (1711–1776) declared that it is "not contrary to reason to prefer the destruction of the whole world to the scratching of my finger."[1] The Forsaken and Darkfriends of *The Wheel of Time* seem to generally understand that they are behaving selfishly; they just don't see any reason to behave otherwise. Moridin makes this explicit

*The Wheel of Time and Philosophy*, First Edition. Edited by Jacob M. Held.
© 2025 John Wiley & Sons, Inc. Published 2025 by John Wiley & Sons, Inc.

when he insists to Rand that there is no "path to victory" over the Dark Lord, only the option to either struggle for indeterminate ages against the inevitable, or "follow the Great Lord and rule for a time before all things end."[2]

## Time to Be Gone

Indeed, some philosophers think that the end of all things has much to recommend it. This is particularly clear in the writings of "anti-natalists," scholars who regard procreation as morally impermissible and the extinction of humanity, perhaps *all* conscious beings, as optimal. To be clear, it is not my argument that contemporary philosopher David Benatar, the anti-natalist author of *Better Never to Have Been,* is a Darkfriend! Unlike Darkfriends, anti-natalists are deeply concerned with the alleviation of suffering, and so would not (if acting consistently with their ideas) selfishly inflict harm on others to bring about their ideal world. This is important because Epicurus (341–270 BCE) once argued that people who claim to wish they had never been born ought to either actually commit suicide, or admit they are being unnecessarily dramatic.[3] The anti-natalist response is that suicide sometimes inflicts unnecessary suffering on oneself and others; the belief that *bringing humans into existence* is necessarily harmful does not entail a belief that *continuing to exist* is additionally harmful.

*Is* it harmful to bring humans into existence? One argument for anti-natalism, sometimes called the "misanthropic" approach, points to the suffering that humans inflict on one another and on nature as evidence that it would be better if we did not exist. While the Forsaken of *The Wheel of Time* are not typically portrayed as committing horrors in service of a clear philosophical agenda, their actions are nevertheless often a demonstration by performance of the misanthropic view. From the petty (Asmodean maimed rival musicians) to the extreme (Semirhage delighted in torture, Aginor performed inhumane experiments), the deeds of the Forsaken run the gamut of vice—and yet it is unequivocally *human* vice, immediately recognizable to the reader as harms that humans often inflict in reality. Obviously, one needn't commit war crimes to fill the world with suffering; even when we merely "lie, steal, cheat, speak hurtfully, break confidences and promises, violate privacy, [or] act ungratefully, inconsiderately, duplicitously, impatiently, [or] unfaithfully,"[4] we make ourselves agents of substantial harm. But large or small, *no* such harms can exist in a world devoid of human consciousness—so perhaps we should strive toward a world devoid of human consciousness?

If misanthropy is the dragon's fang of anti-natalism, then philanthropy is its white flame. If the harm humans cause is an argument against our continued existence, then perhaps the good we accomplish is an argument in favor of continued existence. Even Arthur Schopenhauer (1788–1860), a philosopher whose pessimism is often associated with misanthropy, regarded philanthropic deeds as the virtuous response to the evils of the world.[5] But this response encounters at least two significant hurdles. First, much of the good accomplished by human hands actually exceeds the capacities of most humans. It would be difficult to establish a clear ratio of, say, murderers to Mozarts, but most people never make important discoveries, create amazing art, or otherwise transform the world for the better. Even setting aside accomplishments of particular uniqueness, most people (apparently!) can't bring themselves to do good deeds open to almost anyone. From serving the homeless to fostering orphans, staffing nonprofits to visiting the sick and elderly, opportunities to do good abound! How many people daydream (or worse, boast) of the philanthropic efforts *they* would undertake if only *they* were fantastically wealthy or politically powerful—of how much better a billionaire or politician *they* would be than the ones we actually have? But outside *Tel'aran'rhiod*, how many such people labor industriously at the good they are positioned to actually accomplish? How many strive diligently to increase their capacity for accomplishment? In my experience, the answer is very few indeed. Such envious imaginings can even be woven into the misanthropic argument: the Forsaken Sammael and Demandred swore allegiance to the Dark One specifically because they envied Lews Therin Telamon, even though it was well within their power to do great deeds of their own.

A second hurdle for philanthropic pro-natalism is that, even if we allot to not-so-good humans a share of the virtue their moral superiors accrue, Benatar thinks the *most* philanthropic thing we can do for other humans is to stop making them—because "coming into existence is always a serious harm."[6] In support of this claim, Benatar points to various asymmetries in the moral intuitions people tend to have concerning procreation.[7] The clearest of these is that it seems morally impermissible to procreate when there is good reason to believe that the resulting child would suffer tremendously, whereas almost no one thinks themselves morally obligated to procreate when there is good reason to believe that the resulting child would have an extremely good life. Even though humans often regard the total amount of good in life as outweighing the bad—Benatar thinks this is an evolutionarily implanted bias warranting skepticism—broadly shared moral intuitions demonstrate that humans feel greater moral weight in the creation or prevention of suffering than in the creation or prevention of pleasure, happiness, or other human flourishing. This is in part because the absence of suffering is good even when no one experiences that good, while the absence of pleasure or happiness is not bad unless someone who actually exists is being deprived of it.

So most of the Forsaken can be understood as embodying misanthropic depravity or a warped pursuit of human excellence—sometimes, both. The Forsaken Ishamael (or Elan, or Moridin, if you prefer) reflects a third approach to anti-natalism: its apparent *inevitability*. Most species that have existed on Earth are now extinct. The probability that humankind will also someday be extinct seems overwhelmingly high. Even if we don't (deliberately or accidentally!) kill ourselves off with nuclear weapons, bio-engineered plagues, or other anthropogenic disasters, some celestial accident (asteroid strike, gamma burst, solar weather) will eventually do the job. In most cases, the extinction process will involve a period of serious and possibly protracted human anguish. Benatar is not a nihilist; he treats the inevitability of extinction as a contextual defense of the philanthropic argument for anti-natalism. His idea is that, if we arrange for an orderly exit from existence *now*, we can arrange to minimize the suffering of those final humans whose existence stretches beyond the breakdown of extant social support structures.[8] But the inevitability of extinction is *also* a nihilistic argument for anti-natalism. After all: *What is the point?* Having children, like opposing the Dark One, constitutes a futile stand against the inevitable while inflicting unnecessary suffering on yet another hapless human. The tragedy is sufficient to keep Ishamael himself awake at night: in the Amazon adaptation, he tells Mat, "I lie there thinking about all the people in the world. All of them hurting. Whole universes collapsing from a shouted word. The stab of a dagger. So much pain."[9] That is precisely the kind of pain that anti-natalism seeks to prevent from ever happening.

## Care for the Living

In the grand analytic tradition, most philosophical critiques of anti-natalism reject one or more of Benatar's premises. Other critiques accept his premises but argue that his conclusion—the moral impermissibility of procreation—doesn't follow. What I would like to do here, however, is make the slightly skeptical, broadly meta-philosophical point that the way anti-natalists argue (as lawyers sometimes put it) "in the alternative" warrants a skeptical response.

"Argument in the alternative" is a common rhetorical technique, the point of which is to persuade the intended audience that no matter *which* premises they might accept, there is only one reasonable conclusion. For example, suppose you believe that the Forsaken Demandred, living under the pseudonym Mazrim Taim, killed Asmodean.[10] To argue against your conclusion "in the alternative," someone else might say, "Mazrim Taim plays no role in the story until after Asmodean's death. And if he *does* play an unnamed role in the story before Asmodean's death, it's not as Demandred. And if it *is* as Demandred, then he wasn't in Caemlyn. And if he *was* in Caemlyn, he wasn't the one who killed Asmodean." On one hand, this is admirably thorough! The anticipation of likely objections to one's position, and the ability to handle them in advance, may be taken as a sign of careful thinking.

On the other hand, the phenomenon of "confirmation bias" suggests that we tend to interpret evidence in favor of beliefs we already hold. As a philosophical matter, this makes argument in the alternative a risky proposition. While the outcome-oriented nature of law and politics often make *winning* a higher goal than *understanding*, philosophy is (at least ideally) more concerned with truth than with victory. Those who argue in the alternative may, by that fact alone, make themselves vulnerable to charges of motivated reasoning. After all, if there is *no* evidence that could possibly dissuade you from a particular belief, then what you have is more than just a belief; it is a *dogma*.

Dogmatism is precisely the accusation Benatar levels at his critics; he claims that anti-natalism is "a powerful argument, based on highly plausible premises, for a conclusion that if acted upon would reduce suffering without depriving the suffering person of anything, but which is rejected merely because of primal psychological features that compromise our judgement."[11] But Benatar's assertion that a "pro-natal bias" exists in humans both as the result of natural selection and as a fundamentally judgment-compromising trait is offered without evidence (beyond a vague appeal to certain intuitions from evolutionary psychology). So arguments for anti-natalism may, with minimal reductionism, be summarized in approximately this way: If you agree that suffering is bad and recognize that humans cause substantial suffering, you should agree to never create more humans. If you think some suffering is justified by the great good that humans can do, you're probably kidding yourself, likely as the result of evolutionarily implanted biases. And if you think nothing humans do ultimately matters either way, then you should relent to the inevitable and agree to never create more humans. Finally, if, after hearing these arguments, you still disagree with anti-natalism, then you're a dogmatist whose views can be safely dismissed as irrational.

It is remarkable how well the final confrontation between Rand al'Thor and the Dark One mirrors this struggle. In *A Memory of Light*, the Dark One first claims that he[12] will achieve victory in the Last Battle and fill the world with misery. In response, Rand imagines a future in which *he* has achieved victory in the Last Battle—and finds that while that possible world is a *less terrible* place, darkness remains in it, and so the Dark One has, technically, triumphed. Second, the Dark One claims that he will obliterate the Light entirely, filling the world with something worse than misery: absolutely callous indifference. To this Rand responds that he will obliterate the Dark One, and imagines a future in which the world knows only Light—but this, too, turns out to be a world of indifference and so the Dark One has, technically, triumphed again. Finally, the Dark One makes an *offer*: since he's going to win no matter what Rand does, why not take the option of oblivion? Instead of a world of horror, the Dark One offers a generous compromise: no world at all! Clearly, Rand would have to be some kind of irrational dogmatist to reject such an offer.

Just as Rand mirrors the Dark One's arguments, the arguments of anti-natalism can be mirrored. The inverted philanthropic argument is straightforward: Benatar claims that the net value of human life is negative, and that disagreement on this point can only stem from bias. But as Christopher Hitchens (1949–2011) once wrote, "What can be asserted without evidence can also be dismissed without evidence."[13] Many people think that it is at least possible for the net value of human life to be positive. Evolutionary psychology is interesting, but too often functions as a "just so" story. There is, for example, nothing in principle preventing evolutionary psychology from biasing *fit* specimens toward pro-natalism, while biasing *unfit* specimens toward anti-natalism. Persuading other people of the virtues of anti-natalism could also be an evolved strategy for preserving resources for one's own offspring. If something like this is true, then Benatar is just as guilty of dogmatism as his critics, rejecting pro-natalist arguments merely because of primal psychological features that compromise his judgment. To be clear—I do not know whether this is true! But my ignorance on the matter does not appear to be any greater than Benatar's.

Likewise, the misanthropic argument for anti-natalism suggests that humans should willingly go extinct because we are such a harmful species—but Benatar clearly claims that "although the process of extinction may be regrettable, and although the prospect of human extinction may, in some ways, be bad for us, it would be better, all things considered, if there were no more people (and indeed no more conscious life)."[14] What quicker, more effective way to achieve this aim than by rapidly increasing the human population, despoiling the environment so badly that the Earth becomes an uninhabitable wasteland—a Blight, so to speak—several million years ahead of schedule? This would spare *countless* conscious lives from ever coming into existence! Anti-natalist accelerationism thus manifests most clearly as strident pro-natalism.

Most interesting of all may be the argument from inevitability. Why would anyone believe that the extinction of the human race is inevitable? Because we, like the people of the Third Age, are marinating in apocalypticism—even those who don't subscribe to the eschatology of any particular religion. The fossil record suggests that all species come to an end. Weapons of mass destruction pose a genuine threat to our continued survival. If anthropogenic impact on the environment doesn't kill us all, a celestial event might. Anti-natalists offer the inevitability of our extinction as consolation, a reason to *accept* it. But the universe is vast! Our galaxy alone contains about a hundred billion stars orbited by some ten trillion planets; the observable universe contains hundreds of billions, possibly *trillions* of galaxies. At such mind-boggling scale, humanity likely represents an utterly insignificant percentage of all the conscious life in the universe. Given the *inevitability* of conscious life, then—why not simply accept it? Why *not* take the inevitability of conscious life as a reason to *accept* its continued existence, within our own local sphere?

This is, ultimately, Rand al'Thor's answer to the Dark One's final offer. The Dark One says, in effect, "I'm going to be here no matter what you do, so why not just *give up?*" Rand's response is, "if you're going to be here no matter what I do, why not just accept that you're part of the process and *keep on going?*" Oblivion ensures that nothing will ever get worse, and nothing will ever get better. But as long as the Wheel of Time continues to turn, there is always at least the possibility, at least the *hope*, of improvement. Thus it is that Ilyena Therin Moerelle's voice comes to the Dragon Reborn as he struggles with the fate of the world: "*We are reborn … so we can do better the next time.*"[15] Perhaps the best argument against anti-natalism is just this: however bad human existence or consciousness might be, extinction ensures that we will never get *better*. And even if we fail to improve, or to improve *enough*, Albert Camus (1913–1960) reminds us that there is value even in the attempt, in the *struggle*—no matter how apparently futile or absurd.[16]

## What Wise Ones Know

As resonant and moving as Rand's struggle might be, what I have offered here is not, in the end, a complete *refutation* of anti-natalism. In fact, I *agree* with Benatar that no one is under any ethical obligation to create lives, even when those lives are overwhelmingly likely to be good lives. I also think Benatar was broadly correct to recognize that people who regard life as worth living are likely to be positively disposed toward procreation, perhaps dogmatically so. What Benatar seems to miss is that he often commits to an equal, merely opposite sort of dogmatism. Nothing persuades him that life is genuinely a net-positive experience, so he is negatively disposed toward procreation. But of course—declining to procreate is always an option *for him*. And even if anti-natalism correctly recognizes that no life contains enough pleasure to justify the concomitant suffering, a failure to justify suffering does not imply a failure to justify existence. Rand al'Thor's heroic insight that "the Dark One was not the enemy"[17] is instructive. The Dark Lord's tempting promises could never amount to anything without the cooperation of villains like the Forsaken; likewise, bringing others into existence may be a necessary condition for their suffering, but it is almost never a *sufficient* one.

In other words, I think that procreation is permissible—neither obligatory nor blameworthy. Sometimes we have good reason to procreate, and often we have good reason to refrain. The total amount of goodness in a life, or in the world, might be such a reason, but it is not the only one. Other reasons will include facts about our own circumstances and values— facts to which generic philosophical arguments will naturally be insensitive—or even pre-rational commitments that are beyond evaluation. As the jurist Oliver Wendell Holmes Jr. (1841–1935) once wrote, "Deep-seated preferences cannot be argued about—you cannot argue a man into liking a glass of beer—and therefore, when differences are sufficiently far reaching, we try to kill the other man rather than let him have his way. But that is perfectly consistent with admitting that, so far as appears, his grounds are just as good as ours."[18]

So it is that each of us will at some point face our own personal Shayol Ghul, a moment in time when we decide for ourselves and others (including the hypothetical humans we ultimately create or do not create) what our contribution to the turning of the Wheel will be. Will we, like Darkfriends, selfishly seize our desires, no matter the cost? Will we, like anti-natalists, strive to alleviate suffering but also to break the Wheel? Or will we, like Rand al'Thor, decide that the hope of improvement is worth the price of persistence? Whatever we choose, it will not be the end of the argument, for there are neither beginnings nor endings to the Wheel of Time.

But it will be *an* ending.

## Notes


1. David Hume in L.A. Selby-Bigge ed., *A Treatise of Human Nature* (Oxford: Clarendon Press, 1896), 416.
2. Robert Jordan and Brandon Sanderson, *The Gathering Storm* (New York: Tom Doherty Associates, 2009), 238.
3. Epicurus, "Letter to Menoeceus," in Diogenes Laertius ed., *Lives of Eminent Philosophers*, trans. Robert Drew Hicks, Vol. 2 (New York: G.P. Putnam's Sons, 1925), 653.
4. David Benatar, "The Misanthropic Argument for Anti-Natalism," in Sarah Hannon, Samantha Brennan, and Richard Vernon eds., *Permissible Progeny? The Morality of Procreation and Parenting* (Oxford: Oxford University Press, 2015), 43.
5. Arthur Schopenhauer, *On the Basis of Morality*, trans. E.F.J. Payne (Oxford: Berghahn Books, 1995).
6. David Benatar, *Better Never to Have Been: The Harm of Coming into Existence* (Oxford: Oxford University Press, 2006), 1.
7. Benatar, *Better Never to Have Been*, 32–35.
8. Benatar, *Better Never to Have Been*, 196–200.
9. *The Wheel of Time*, season 2, episode 7, "Daes Dae'Mar," aired September 29, 2023.
10. According to Robert Jordan's personal notes, this is how Asmodean's death scene in *The Fires of Heaven* was originally plotted. Later, Jordan decided that Taim was not Demandred's alter ego after all, and even publicly denied that he *ever* intended the two characters to be one. Responsibility for the death of Asmodean was eventually narratively assigned to the Forsaken Graendal, and Jordan's original intentions did not become a matter of public knowledge until well after the series was completed. Terez, "Signings and Secrets," *Theoryland*, November 2015, at https://web.archive.org/web/20231201235629/http://www.theoryland.com/forums/discussion/8767.

11.  Benatar, *Better Never to Have Been*, 207.
12.  While Rand does eventually conceptualize the Dark One as a genderless "it," I here adhere to the pronoun most usually deployed by characters of *The Wheel of Time*.
13.  Christopher Hitchens, *God Is Not Great: How Religion Poisons Everything* (Crows Nest: Allen & Unwin, 2007), 150.
14.  Benatar, *Better Never to Have Been*, 164.
15.  Robert Jordan and Brandon Sanderson, *A Memory of Light* (New York: Tom Doherty Associates, 2012), 808.
16.  Albert Camus, *The Myth of Sisyphus and Other Essays*, trans. Justin O'Brien (New York: Vintage, 1959).
17.  Jordan and Sanderson, *A Memory of Light*, 891.
18.  Oliver W. Holmes, "Natural Law," *Harvard Law Review* 32 (1918), 41.

# 5

# Nietzsche's Test of Time: The Wheel as an Existential Imperative

*Steven Michels*

Time weighed heavily on Friedrich Nietzsche (1844–1900). Indeed, the high point of his philosophy is the "eternal recurrence" or "eternal return of the same"—that is, the notion that time is a circle within which all events and experiences occur over and over again and in the same way.

Although it was Nietzsche who gave the idea of eternal return its most developed and philosophically rich form, the notion that time is non-linear did not originate with him. The ancient Greek Heraclitus, whom Nietzsche liked quite a bit, suggested the idea of a cyclical nature of reality. Similarly, many Stoics, especially Marcus Aurelius, imagined a cosmos characterized by cycles of death and rebirth. And many Hindu and Buddhist traditions include the principle of reincarnation or *samsara*, where karma, or the good or bad that you do in this life, plays a key role in future lives.

In Nietzsche's philosophy, the eternal return has been interpreted as a metaphysical hypothesis about how time might operate. But it can also be, more to the point, a thought experiment to challenge what we value and the choices we make. In that sense, it is a test of sorts—that is, that the strongest people would be able to live their lives in a way that was the same for all eternity. Indeed, how would you react if a spirit came to you and said that you had to live your same life for all of eternity? "Would you not throw yourself down and gnash your teeth and curse the demon who spoke thus?" Nietzsche asks. Or would you say, "You are a god and never have I heard anything more divine"?[1] That time recurs eternally could force you to live your best life, or you could be crushed by what Nietzsche called "the greatest weight." Seeing time as a wheel or a circle should expand what we strive for and make us better, but that might not be true for everyone.

*The Wheel of Time and Philosophy*, First Edition. Edited by Jacob M. Held.
© 2025 John Wiley & Sons, Inc. Published 2025 by John Wiley & Sons, Inc.

In Bernd Magnus's phrasing, the eternal return functions as an "existential imperative," which Nietzsche intended as a counter to the self-denying perspectives offered by Christianity and modernity.[2] For Nietzsche, Christianity is too concerned with the afterlife, just as modernity is too concerned with truth as a value, rather than power and perspective. As Nietzsche puts it, "that everything recurs is the closest approximation of a world of becoming to a world of being."[3] In that way, he encouraged a life-affirming perspective based not on the resentment of what we cannot will, but the love of fate (*amor fati*).

This chapter examines the role that time plays in the first two seasons of *The Wheel of Time* series and compares it with Nietzsche's teaching. For example, what claims do the characters make about the movement of time? Is it welcomed or resisted? And how does this understanding affect the choices they make? Perhaps most importantly, what role does time play in the fight between good and evil and the hope that the world can be anything other than broken?

## The Breaking of the World

The simplest articulation of time and its effect on our actions comes in the opening sequence of first episode. As Robert Jordan writes in every book in the series: "The Wheel of Time turns, and Ages come and pass, leaving memories that become legend. Legend fades to myth, and even myth is long forgotten when the Age that gave it birth comes again." And in the opening narration, Moiraine tells us that "The world is broken"— that is, civilization as they know it is chaotic rather than ordered. Even so, the Wheel continues to spin, indifferent to how it affects humanity. In one form or another, this is the source of the tension that drives the drama.

This is also the episode in which Tam, Rand's father, explains to him what the turning of the Wheel means for how they should live their lives. The two of them are in the process of displaying a lighted candle in the hope that it will guide Rand's deceased mother back to them, when Rand asks about how long it typically takes for that to happen. "I wish I knew," Tam responds. "All we can do is the best we can with the life that's given to us." Whatever we face, we must press on and strive for better in future lives. Tam tries to be comforting, but he also seems amused by how absurd the lesson is. Rand takes some solace in this knowledge but also grasps the gravity of what this means for him.

In addition to accidents, there are also choices that are misguided or just plain bad. Consider the ferryman from the second episode who died in a vain effort to save his son. He ignores Moiraine's warnings about the likelihood that he will succeed and could not resist the natural impulse of a parent. Instead of recognizing that his son was already lost and taking comfort in the fact that the Wheel would eventually bring him back, he makes a poor decision in going back across the river. He could not bring himself to go on knowing there was a chance he could have saved his son—"If we have our own *why* of life, we shall get along with almost any *how*," Nietzsche teaches[4]—now he will need another turn from the Wheel and another chance to do better.

Yet, making choices is made difficult because no one can remember their previous lives. The Wheel does us a solid by bringing us back, but it's a life lived in the dark. Perrin, for example, would greatly benefit from the knowledge that he will accidentally kill his wife when the Trollocs attack the Two Rivers. In future lives, he will have no knowledge of his grievous error or how to avoid doing it again. In the meantime, he has to live with the pain of having killed someone he loves. Mat suffers a similar fate at the end of season 2 when he throws the spear tipped with the dagger from the cursed city of Shadar Logoth into Rand, which he did even after being forewarned by Min, a part-time bartender and full-time clairvoyant, that something like that was going to happen. Even knowledge of the future is not always helpful, especially if it cannot lead to different outcomes.

What's more, people can sometimes deceive us, complicating the decisions we make. Rand and company leave the Two Rivers with Moiraine because she convinces them that staying would put the village in harm's way. They've seen enough carnage, but still have much to lose. Moiraine earned a great deal of credibility for her role in saving the village, but even so, Rand is skeptical of her claims about one of them being the Dragon Reborn. "Who even knows what the truth is," Rand asks.[5] He wants the truth, but such a thing might not exist.

Nietzsche was more comfortable with ambiguities and contradictions. For him, absolute relativism and absolute truth are virtually indistinguishable in their hostility to life. He had a more functional view: if something served life, then it was good and (must be) true. If it did not, then it was of no use and did not much matter. Whatever the truth, the lesson is clear: there's no divine order or god with a plan. The burden is on us to do right or at least to do better. "The total character of the world … is in all eternity chaos," Nietzsche wrote.[6] In that sense, he would agree that the world is breaking or already broken. Finding a fix was at the heart of his project as a philosopher.

## Remembering and Forgetting

Nietzsche sketched out three different ways history can be used: the *monumental* view, in which we look to the greatest moments and examples in history for guides on how to live; an *antiquarian* view that finds affirmation in seeing history as a continual and rational chain; and the *critical* view, which is when we see history through an analytical lens. Because each mode has its own downsides, Nietzsche proposed a balanced view, such that history serves life, rather than the other way around.[7]

Moiraine too recognizes that history can be used and abused. Just after leaving the Two Rivers, Mat begins singing "Sing of Manetheren," which the villagers all know. As Mat has it, "It's just a song," which he thinks is about someone named Manetheren. Moiraine informs the group that "Manetheren" means "mountain home" in the old tongue of their people, which used to be the name of the Two Rivers.[8] The song tells of a battle that ruined the village, where only the children were saved. It's a tale of strength and courage—a lesson that has been lost on them. In the books, more so than in the series to date, the boys' history as children of Manetheren, especially Mat's as one of the old blood, inspires them to overcome challenges and become great men, perhaps exemplifying what Nietzsche described as *Übermensch*, often infelic-itously translated as "superman."

In contrast to Nietzsche's overman (*Übermensch*), the "last man" repre-sents the antithesis of human potential and vitality and embodies the qual-ities of mediocrity, complacency, and the rejection of higher aspirations.[9] Rather than using history in a deliberate and purposeful way, how Nietzsche instructs, it turns out that the villagers have forgotten much of the past and are living without the traditions that could give them focus and inspiration. As Moiraine tells them: "The old blood runs deep in you. Remember that. You'll need it in the days to come."[10] Moiraine wants them to develop a sense of history that will serve them going forward.

Yet, unlike animals, who are free to live in and enjoy the present, the ability of humans to remember and carry the past around can be a huge liability. In the section "On the Famous Wise Men" from *Thus Spoke Zarathustra*, Nietzsche criticizes philosophers and scholars who revere outdated and life-less ideas as if they were ghosts, rather than seeking knowledge that is vibrant and useful.[11] In the third episode of season 1, Thom, a gleeman, performs the tragedy of "The Man Who Cannot Forget." The character in the song is a man who did something horrible but simply cannot let it go. Unlike Mat and the villagers, who are not using history to guide them, this "tortured soul" has turned the past into "a prison of his making." But as Nietzsche explained, to thrive, humans need a certain amount of forgetfulness. Without forgetfulness, our development would be very much arrested.

Perhaps the best articulation of how to use history for life comes from Loial, an Ogier. In deciding to save Egwene at the end of season 2, he notes: "We are all the heroes of another age's legend ... I think it's time we started acting like it."[12] This sentiment places them rightly in the moment and with a specific goal. But it also elevates them into figures that could exist in his-tory as models for future generations to emulate. Loial also regularly chas-tises humans for living too quickly. Unlike the man in the song who cannot forget, Loial wants them to make what they do unforgettable, so they can be the subject of new and better songs.

## Becoming Who You Are

With chapter titles like "Why I Am So Clever," "Why I Am So Wise," and "Why I Write Such Great Books," no one has ever accused Nietzsche of humility. But Nietzsche had an incredible amount of self-awareness. One of his greatest statements on experience occurs in *Ecce Homo*, where he refers to the value of perspective in the context of his own growth as a philosopher. "To become what one is," he writes, "one must not have the faintest notion *what* one is."[13] This captures Rand's development and trajectory in the first season of the show. "It's me," he declares upon learning that he is the Dragon Reborn.[14] It's a mark not of ego or arrogance but based on the knowledge of who he is and the confidence that he can do what needs to be done. It's the point at which he transitions from immature skeptic to becoming one of the heroes we suspected he would become.

Rand is not the only one who struggles with becoming who he is. Mat is lost for most of the first two seasons, which leads him to make many terrible choices, especially abandoning his friends on their way to the White Tower. Perrin struggles with the fact that he is a wolfbrother. And Nynaeve and Egwene also lose sight of the task at hand. "The Wheel does not care if you are young or afraid, petty or weak," Siuan scolds them. "It certainly does not care what you want."[15]

The five have a bond that sometimes causes them to lose their purpose and let their emotions overwhelm their reason. This is why Nietzsche preached "the pathos of distance" and the virtues of solitude.[16] He went so far as to call people "a prison" and to claim that married philosophers belong "in comedy."[17] We see many strained and superficial relationships on the show. Selene (Lanfear), for example, wants to know who Rand thinks of when they are together. "Someone I wish I could forget," he responds, which we know is not true. Rather than be insulted by his honesty, she makes a deal with him: "You help me remember, and I'll help you forget."[18]

That's not to say that Nietzsche did not see a place for real relationships, provided they were among equals. For instance, in *Thus Spoke Zarathustra*, he suggests interactions among "overmen" would be based on mutual respect for each other's strength and self-created values.[19] Unlike the exploitative/manipulative relationship with Lanfear, what Rand has with Egwene is substantive and mutually beneficial. "Tell them I died here," he says to Moiraine, worried that men who can channel all go mad and kill everyone they love.[20] In effect, he makes the same sort of sacrifice that Egwene did, when she decides to leave the Two Rivers and train as a Wisdom, rather than pursue a relationship with Rand. It's one of the reasons they love each other as much as they do: their bond with one another, like each of their quests, is based on their sense of individuality and self-mastery. This, Nietzsche would endorse.

# Listening to the Wind

Nietzsche presented the will to power as the fundamental fact of nature, and Moiraine is very much a Nietzschean figure in that respect. Consider how she uses her power to do what is necessary to save civilization or rebuild it in a way consistent with nobility, strength, and greatness.

In the first episode, it's Moiraine who sees the ferryman's return as the threat that it is and creates the whirlpool to neutralize it. The ferryman could not live knowing that he did not try to save his son, but Moiraine could not live in a world where she does not take a life to save countless others. "I will let a thousand innocent people die, if there's an even chance that he will live," as she later explains her vow to protect the Dragon Reborn.[21]

Contrast Moiraine's unapologetic use of her power with what Nietzsche teaches about asceticism and the voluntary denial of instinct and nature, which we see in the ethos of the *Tuatha'an,* or traveling people. "What greater revenge against violence than peace," Ila asks. "What greater revenge against death than life."[22] This philosophy, called The Way of the Leaf, sounds like it's one with nature, but it's a naive view. The *Tuatha'an* preach nonviolence at any cost—it likely plays a part in why they are without land to call their own—and see the turning of the Wheel as an opportunity to be passive. But what good is reincarnation if your plan is to come back and let yourself be killed again? You would not play a video game like that, so why would you do it when it really counts. It's an absurd form of asceticism that will inevitably be exploited by others. The best that can be said of the *Tuatha'an* is that their religion is not a cult since they all "leave the wagons" when they are twenty years old and do not need to return should they so choose.[23]

The Wheel causes the *Tuatha'an* to do no harm (and not much good), but it also fuels the evil in Lanfear and Ishamael. Rather than seeing it as a blessing, Lanfear and Ishamael see time as the source of much pain, especially to them, since even death is not a release. "All I want is just to close my eyes one day and never have to open them again," Ishamael laments.[24] He has become too weary of the world. Eternal life, like clairvoyance, might not always be a great gift. For him, it's the primary source of his resentment toward others and the force behind the damage that he does. This is nihilism (literally, "the belief in nothing") at its worst. At its best, it makes life intolerable. At its worst, it can lay waste to greatness and ruin a civilization, which is what Nietzsche tried to remedy.

Conversely, the eternal return is a will to *everything*, or as Nietzsche's Zarathustra describes it, a self-overcoming. Instead of ruining ourselves and bogging down others, we should see pain as a gift and perhaps the greatest of teachers. It's the rationale behind Nietzsche's best-known aphorism: "What does not destroy me, makes me stronger."[25] It's only through willing the past, present, and future as it is and will be—that is, willing the Wheel in its entirety—that we can transcend the limitations of time and truly live according to nature, both in this life and whatever might come next.

*The Wheel of Time* is very much a Nietzschean tale, insofar as it takes strength of will as its central theme. And each of the characters takes time seriously, even though some of them act in ways that Nietzsche would call weak and unseemly. Even so, he would be pleased that the heroes and heroines of the series meet the moment such that their actions will live on long past their days.

# Notes


1. Friedrich Nietzsche, *The Gay Science*, trans. Walter Kaufmann (New York: Vintage, 1974), 273, emphasis removed.
2. Bernd Magnus, *Nietzsche's Existential Imperative* (Indianapolis: Indiana University Press, 1978).
3. Friedrich Nietzsche, *The Will to Power*, trans. Walter Kaufmann (New York: Vintage, 1967), 330, emphasis removed.
4. Friedrich Nietzsche, *Twilight of the Idols, The Portable Nietzsche*, trans. Walter Kaufmann (New York: Penguin, 1982), 468.
5. *The Wheel of Time*, season 1, episode 2, "Shadow's Waiting."
6. Nietzsche, *The Gay Science*, 168.
7. See Friedrich Nietzsche, *On the Advantage and Disadvantage of History for Life*, trans. Peter Preuss (Indianapolis: Hackett, 1980).
8. "Shadow's Waiting."
9. Friedrich Nietzsche, *Thus Spoke Zarathustra, The Portable Nietzsche*, trans. Walter Kaufmann (New York: Penguin, 1982).
10. "Shadow's Waiting."
11. Nietzsche, *Thus Spoke Zarathustra*, 214–217.
12. *The Wheel of Time*, season 2, episode 8, "What Was Meant to Be."
13. Friedrich Nietzsche, *Ecce Homo*, trans. Walter Kaufmann (New York: Vintage, 1979), 254.
14. *The Wheel of Time*, season 1, episode 7, "The Dark Along the Ways."
15. *The Wheel of Time*, season 1, episode 6, "The Flame of Tar Valon."
16. See for example, Friedrich Nietzsche, *Beyond Good and Evil*, trans. Walter Kaufmann (New York: Vintage, 1966), 226.
17. Friedrich Nietzsche, *On the Genealogy of Morals*, trans. Walter Kaufmann and R.J. Hollingdale (New York: Vintage, 1989), 107.
18. *The Wheel of Time*, season 2, episode 2, "Strangers and Friends."
19. Nietzsche, *Thus Spoke Zarathustra*, 170–172.
20. *The Wheel of Time*, season 1, episode 8, "The Eye of the World."
21. "What Was Meant to Be."
22. *The Wheel of Time*, season 1, episode 4, "The Dragon Reborn."
23. "Dragon Reborn."
24. *The Wheel of Time*, season 2, episode 5, "Damane."
25. Nietzsche, *Twilight of the Idols*, 467.

**6**

# A World Without Shai'tan: The Significance of Free Will in *The Wheel of Time*

## Kenneth Silver

What does the *Wheel of Time* (*WoT*) say about free will? Do our characters have it, and does it matter? At times, free will seems to be what the characters most want—Rand does not destroy the Dark One in order to preserve it. But, at other times, there is an open acknowledgment of the inescapability of fate and of the weight of duty. If freedom is so valuable, why don't our main characters seem to have it? Can the *Wheel of Time* reconcile these positions, and does it intend to?

It's not hard to make the case that freedom is a big theme in the series. Characters are constantly being bonded, enslaved, freed, manipulated, and so on. (There are literal leashes, for goodness' sake.) And that's just what they do to each other. In the world of *WoT*, the Pattern appears to leave little room for human freedom. Nevertheless, I think it is important to the message of the story that the characters of *WoT* are free, and an important part of their growth is in how they come to realize it.

## Free from Evil

The heroes of *WoT* are in an epic struggle to defeat the Shadow. And the job given to Rand is clear—he is to undo the mistakes of the Aes Sedai in the Age of Legends and find a way to reseal the Bore. But this isn't really what he *wants* to do, is it? No, for a long time, he wants to *rid* the world of Shai'tan. The Wheel of Time turns, and he knows that humanity will forget what it has learned. People in a new age will free Shai'tan once more, and the Dragon will have to reemerge and reseal the Bore all over again. He's already done this innumerable times, and he knows he will have to do it over and over again. Exhausting.

We will return to the significance of the wheel below. For now, though, it is enough to dwell on this desire to defeat Shai'tan once and for all. What

*The Wheel of Time and Philosophy*, First Edition. Edited by Jacob M. Held.
© 2025 John Wiley & Sons, Inc. Published 2025 by John Wiley & Sons, Inc.

is Rand after? As far as he understands it throughout most of the books, Shai'tan is simply evil incarnate. It is a conscious, malevolent force. As such, Rand wants to destroy it, to rid the world of evil. So far, this is a classically heroic attitude, but it doesn't seem related to any concern about freedom. He wants to be free of evil, but that's about it. However, there are a few dimensions of freedom at play.

Rand would in some ways be personally free if he were to destroy the Dark One, ending the ceaseless struggle against Shai'tan throughout the ages. But I think Rand views the complete defeat of the Dark One as in some ways inevitably liberating for the world. In the Final Battle, Rand weaves threads of possibility to show a world without Shai'tan. And what he sees is a world in which, "Doors did not bear locks. Coinage was a nearly forgotten eccentricity. Channelers helped create food for everyone."[1] The destruction of evil leads to a world of abundance, economic freedom, and general liberty. What could be freer than a world without locks?

Unfortunately, as I suspect many readers anticipated, it was not to be. It becomes clear as Rand explores this possibility that he absolutely *must not* destroy Shai'tan. Why not? Well, it's hard to say. This epiphany, that something is deeply wrong in this possibility, is all of two pages in the book. Still, it is not hard to read those pages as indicating that a world without Shai'tan would lack freedom in some powerful sense.

In interacting with a version of Elayne in this possible world, it strikes Rand that she is somehow different. He ultimately thinks that she has lost the "ability to *be* herself," instead appearing in some sense no different than someone who had been turned to the Dark One.[2] Insofar as Elayne has lost some kind of ability in this world, she seems less free, and this ability is somehow deeply tied to who she is as a person (an ability to live authentically or as an individual). Rand realizes that without Shai'tan all people will be this way, and he is horrified.

Understanding the scene at this level, the message seems clear: People would not be freer without the presence of evil. Freedom *requires* evil in some sense, or the possibility of *choosing* evil. As you can read about elsewhere in this volume, *WoT* is thus engaging with the problem of evil, and it seems to be suggesting a response to that problem in terms of the value of free will. There are different views about *what it is* about freedom that is so valuable and how realizing that value requires evil. What is distinctive about *WoT*, though, is that it presents a new view of the value of freedom in terms of *individuality*. A world without Shai'tan is bad because it robs individuals of their ability *to be individuals*. That is, it robs us of our ability to authentically determine ourselves, developing our unique perspective.

Ask yourself, what really *is* evil in the novels? The nature of Shai'tan is often left mysterious. Of course, there are many interpretations. Apart from elements of the Shadow being gross, mean, and harmful, Shai'tan is very controlling—and we are told by Verin that selfishness is the defining shared characteristic of the Forsaken. Perhaps connected to this last point, consider what the world would *actually* look like if Shai'tan were to win.

When Shai'tan shows Rand what it would make the world into using the threads of possibility, if it is to be believed, we are left with a world pretty similar to our own. Characters in that world are cold and without conscience, hyper-individualistic. This resonates with how Shai'tan operates, but I don't think it's essential. After all, when Rand mentions how people in this possibility lack a conscience, Shai'tan says that having a conscience isn't *relevant*: "COMPASSION ISN'T NEEDED."[3] Instead, what is essential for Shai'tan is that the world is *all Shai'tan*. (It says, "THERE IS ONLY ME."[4]) The people are entirely oppressed and live according to the laws of Shai'tan, and they don't even realize it. What we see, I take it, is a world only from Shai'tan's *perspective* and none other.[5]

This fits with *why* Rand's world without Shai'tan is *equally bad*. It may be "free from evil" in some nominal sense, but really it's just another world where characters cannot live authentically, where they are bent to live how someone else interprets how they ought to live. Shai'tan says, "IF YOU DO THIS [DESTROY ME] WE ARE ONE."[6] If the essence of evil in the novels is some kind of selfish, narcissistic lack of concern for the perspective or individuality of others, then a world where one person chooses to abolish Shai'tan is the same as a world *run* by Shai'tan.[7]

So, the *WoT* can be read as providing a new spin on an old problem. Rand and the reader learn some important lessons about freedom. Freedom is valuable to us in that it involves our expressing ourselves authentically as individuals. And freedom requires evil in the sense that we cannot act authentically if someone else is paternalistically narrowing the field of our options. We need individuality and a diversity of opinion, even where this leads us to many things that we might consider to be evil.[8] Still, this presupposes that characters in the novels are free, and this is in tension with the ways in which the characters are, and often feel, fated.

## Free from Fate

The significance of fate is a constant theme of *WoT*. Many times, characters find themselves in a fated situation they have tried to avoid. Min directly sees fates (or what could be fate) visually tied to characters. Mat seems to *feel* fate, experiencing it as rolling dice, something unsettled and yet to be determined. At later times in the novels, the characters despair and acquiesce to fate, as something resented and yet not to be outrun. But is fate a real force in *WoT*? And does it actually undermine the freedom of our favorite characters?

In our own world, many of us don't take events in our lives to be genuinely *fated* or *meant to be*. We could be wrong, but it seems a bit odd or bigheaded to take what we do or what happens to us to be of genuine *cosmic significance.* In line with this, philosophers writing about free will these days don't often consider fate. There are robust historical and theological traditions concerning the related position of "fatalism," but most philosophers today are more concerned with whether determinism about the laws of nature would undermine our freedom, rather than fate.[9]

Still, there are resources from the philosophical debate about free will that *would* help to secure free will if we *were* fated. And that's good, because fate in *WoT* is given to us as a metaphysical fact. Min really does *see* what will happen to people, and Mat really does *feel* some kind of pull. There are many prophecies given and fulfilled in *WoT*. Moreover, Rand, Perrin, and Mat are known to be *ta'veren*, which characters like Siuan Sanche can directly perceive.

We are constantly told how the Pattern weaves the characters together, and those that are *ta'veren* are portrayed as in some way central to the weaving of the Pattern and how the Pattern corrects itself. Being *ta'veren* involves being important to achieving certain things in the Pattern, and it is remarked many times how the wills and intentions of characters can be warped just by being around *ta'veren*. So, at least the main characters do seem to be genuinely fated.

First, it's worth taking a moment to appreciate how interesting the metaphysical set-up is. It's not clear that *everyone* is fated, just those that are *ta'veren*. And even though they *must* do something, it's also clear throughout that the characters have a lot of discretion. The Wheel doesn't determine everything, only certain things. It's not like their lives are set in stone—how we might normally think of fate—it's more like the characters are pushed around or nudged from time to time.

Still, the characters experience their lives as problematically and overbearingly fated. And this sense is shared across the continent of *WoT*. As Moiraine says, "The Wheel weaves as the Wheel wills, and we are only the thread of the Pattern."[10] The characters constantly feel at the whims of fate, bidden to do this or that against their own inclination. Our question is: Does fate *actually* undermine the free will of the characters, and does the narrative involve how they understand this? This is one case where I think the characters answer the question one way, but the series answers it another.

In the climax of *The Gathering Storm*, Rand wrestles at length with fate. He knows that he must fight the Dark One in Tarmon Gai'don, and Min has earlier prophesized three women standing over a funeral bier with him on it.[11] To understate things, he's upset. In a conversation with his father, he says, "My life isn't my own. I'm a puppet for the Pattern and the prophecies, made to dance for the world before having my strings cut." Pretty dark. He goes on, "my choices are made for me by the Pattern itself."[12]

How does Rand come to terms with fate, and does it make sense philosophically? Well, in that conversation with his father, Tam says, "The choice isn't always about *what* you do, son, but why you do it." He goes on a paragraph later, "You may not be able to choose the duties you're given. But you *can* choose why you fulfill them."[13] Rand shirks this off at the time, and soon rages at his father and flees, ending at Dragonmount to contemplate all of these feelings about his fate. Eventually, though, he remembers this advice, and it is exactly this point that he takes solace in, as he finds a reason to fight Shai'tan in the Final Battle.

So, Rand is satisfied by this response to fate, but should we be? Is this kind of response philosophically respectable? In the world of *WoT*, Rand might be free to determine why he does what he must do. After all, fate in *WoT* only seems concerned with certain particular events, those needed to keep the Wheel turning. Standardly, though, this is not a great answer. If you take yourself to be fated or determined, you don't want to say that you at least determine why you do what you do. If *everything* you do is fated, then choosing to act for this or that reason is *also* fated. You cannot retreat inwards to find some kind of freedom in the mind. If fate robs us of the ability to do otherwise, it does so in the mind as well.

Nevertheless, Rand is close to a popular cluster of positions on free will and moral responsibility. Rather than finding freedom in the ability to do otherwise, some have taken free will to involve our psychological relationship to what we do. The question isn't could you have done otherwise, but did your action express your values? Did it further something you care about? Is it an action you would endorse? These positions, sometimes called "real self" or "deep self" views, emphasize the significance of *standing behind* your actions, taking your actions to disclose something about you.[14]

Rand believes he cannot control what he is fated to do. Still, he believes he can make sure that he performs those actions for *his* reasons, so those actions will express what he stands for, what he is fighting for. And, in this way, Rand takes solace in having a kind of freedom.

This is a perfectly pleasant line of thought, and a perfectly respectable (and popularly held) view of freedom/responsibility. Nevertheless, when reading the account of Rand's "epiphany" on Dragonmount, it struck me as enormously (almost comically) bad faith. The idea that Rand's fate is *set* and his destiny is *out of his control* is absolutely ludicrous. He is, at that very moment, holding more of the One Power through the access key to Choedan Kal than has ever been held. "Great enough to unravel the Pattern itself …"[15] And we are supposed to believe that he has no agency, that he can't control what happens in his life?

Rand does come to an epiphany on Dragonmount, one we'll end with in the next section, but I think this point about fate is a false epiphany. Notice that what Rand is really bothered by, not just there but throughout the books, is the idea of being *controlled*. He is continually worried about others trying to control and manipulate him. (For good reason.) The last straw, which brings him to this precipice on Dragonmount, is when he realizes that Cadsuane has used *his own father* to manipulate him. And it's not just other people trying to control him. Rand is relentlessly engaged in a project of *self*-control, ever striving to make himself hard, unaffected by emotional attachments.

The version of the world shown to Rand if Shai'tan wins is a world entirely under the control of Shai'tan (though no one realizes it). But even if Shai'tan is destroyed, the world without it is still controlled by Rand's decision, and Rand recognizes this as horrible. Thus, while Rand acknowledges from the beginning that a certain kind of control is bad, it takes the whole series for him to really internalize this lesson and give up this inclination to fix things by controlling them even within himself.

Given this picture, it's worth asking: Is fate in *WoT* really *controlling* in the way that Rand perceives it to be? Mat may feel the occasional mental tug, but fate does not have any instruments through which to actually *coerce* the characters to do this or that. I think it goes against this broader theme of the dangers of control to see fate as genuinely controlling the characters.[16] The characters may be fated, but they are fated to make their own choices and control their own destinies. In fact, I think this gives us a new way of thinking about what it means to be *ta'veren*.

The characters may not choose to be *ta'veren*; they may even resent it; nevertheless, those that are *ta'veren* do not seem less free. On the contrary, *ta'veren* seem *freer* than most people. It's not just that those that are *ta'veren* get to do many interesting things that regular people in largely agricultural and pre-industrial societies would not get to do. *ta'veren* often warp the fates and wills of people in their vicinity, and their choices reverberate throughout the Pattern. If anything, *ta'veren* is a state that is *freedom-affirming*. It makes one's free choices more significant, more consequential. Rand, Mat, and Perrin are not men destined to do this or that; they are men of destiny!

## The Wheel

We have seen how the existence of evil and fate concern the characters of *WoT* as potentially undermining their freedom. One element of narrative growth in the novels is in how the characters come to grips with their own freedom in these circumstances. However, there is a final kind of concern that I haven't acknowledged.

It's not just that the characters in *WoT* are fated to go on their adventures and save the world, it's that they are fated to do it *over and over again forever*. We might worry, then, that this element somehow robs the characters of freedom. It's not just that they are fated to do as they do, but they must do it, and over and over again, for the Wheel to keep spinning.

In *WoT*, time is a wheel, and the ages recur eternally. Here, it is impossible not to be drawn into thinking about the "eternal recurrence" as a kind of construct from Friedrich Nietzsche (1844–1900). Nietzsche asks us to imagine that the universe will run its course, but then it is to begin again exactly as before, and it will do this forever. You will again, live your life exactly as you did. How should we react to this if it turned out to be true? How should we live knowing it, and how would it lead us to judge what makes for a good life? It's hard to say.[17]

One way of reading the eternal recurrence as a thought experiment, though, is as a kind of Nietzschean response to Christianity's emphasis on the afterlife. Nietzsche saw Christianity as an extremely dominating institution with an intense focus on the afterlife as opposed to the quality of the actual life we live now. Nietzsche thought this was all wrong, and the eternal recurrence as a thought experiment helps Nietzsche say why. On his picture, there is no Christian afterlife, but there is a life after this one … it's just *exactly the same one* that you're living right now. So, instead of living a life deferred in some sense, what we should really be doing is fully living the life we have.

Of course, a natural reaction to learning this might be something like despair. Mat would be *doomed* to lose an eye over and over again for eternity. But this isn't the attitude that Nietzsche thought we should have. Instead, he thought we should really lean into this, developing an attitude that is *life-affirming*. He characterized this as *amor fati*—love of one's fate. Again, there are big interpretative challenges here. Is Nietzsche saying that we should find our lives beautiful, whether or not they are? Is he saying that we should love the life we in fact live, or that we should strive to live a life that we would love? Again, it is hard to say.[18] But what is critical is Nietzsche's overwhelmingly positive attitude toward life itself, that you could love your life as yours even if you knew you would repeat it.

Returning to *WoT*, we can ask: How do the characters confront the fact of eternal recurrence in their own world, and do they take on the Nietzschean response?

In confronting this question of eternal recurrence, Rand is struck by the apparent meaninglessness of lives that turn to dust and then must be relived again. (He bellows directly, "NONE OF THIS MATTERS" interestingly in the same all-caps as the words of Shai'tan.[19]) As the tempest around him reaches a crescendo, though, Rand thinks, "each time we live, we get to love again" and then we are told "That was the answer."[20] So, rather than dwelling on all of the negative parts of life, it may seem that Rand is drawn back to all of the wonderful things that make life worth living and fighting for. This seems to suggest that the attitude he lands on is ultimately life-affirming, a matter of *amor fati*, loving his fate.

To conclude, though, I want to suggest an alternative interpretation that actually speaks to an objection sometimes raised to Nietzsche. Theodor Adorno (1903–1969) famously challenged the Nietzschean attitude of *amor fati* saying, "Love of stone walls and barred windows is the last resort of someone who sees and has nothing else to love."[21] Critically, Adorno charges Nietzsche with a failure of *hope*. An attitude of *amor fati*,

Adorno contends, involves a failure to hope for and work toward anything better. But this is *precisely* the attitude that Rand has in the climactic scene on Dragonmount.

Notice, Rand is not simply satisfied with the love he feels and will get to feel in the future, and he is definitely not ready to affirm all of the awful elements of life. Instead, Rand finds peace in the fact that in the future he *may do better*. In response to Lews Therin's question, "Why do we live again?" Lews Therin eventually also responds, "Maybe it's so that we can have a second chance." And Rand himself contributes, "I fight because last time, I failed. I fight because I want to fix what I did wrong. I want to do it right this time."[22]

Rand's attitude is not to accept his fate (joyously or not); instead, Rand has *hope*. Despite the inevitability of the turning of the Wheel, and really the inevitability of continued suffering and mistakes made all over again, Rand ends on an attitude of hope anyway. Taking a step back, though, there is something ludicrous to this line. If we take eternal recurrence seriously, then *there is no fixing things*; things are already fixed. So, there's a bit of absurdity to the thought, "I'll do better next time!"[23]

The first time I read this climax to *The Gathering Storm*, I was a bit dismayed. Was Rand just making a mistake, failing to understand the reality of eternal *recurrence*? Or was I reading too much into the text—maybe this is not *really* the eternal recurrence as philosophers think about it, since the world does not recur each time *exactly* as it did before? I'm not sure if Rand's reaction to the eternal recurrence is the *right* one, the one that we should have as readers. But it does feel like the right reaction for Rand. And, if nothing else, for such an incredible character taken through such trials and tribulations over so many books, as an attitude to have, it is undeniably heroic.

## Notes

1.  Robert Jordan and Brandon Sanderson, *A Memory of Light* (London: Orbit, 2014), 828.
2.  Jordan and Sanderson, *A Memory of Light*, 831, emphasis original.
3.  Jordan and Sanderson, *A Memory of Light*, 794.
4.  Jordan and Sanderson, *A Memory of Light*, 794.
5.  For contrast, notice that while Evil is directly personified in Shai'tan and plays an active role in the series, the Creator never makes an appearance. We are told that there is a Creator, but it is not embodied, and does not have its own perspective. So, the real contrast between good and evil in the novels is between a pluralistic society of many perspectives versus an authoritarian society of a *single* perspective.
6.  Jordan and Sanderson, *A Memory of Light*, 831.
7.  This interpretation fits with how we might understand what it is to be turned to the Shadow in *WoT*. When someone is turned, it involves an elaborate ritual that in some way puts pressure on one's will. Once broken, the person seems

entirely themselves, with all of their memories and apparent personality, but they are noticeably different to other characters. Interestingly, the series draws a difference between being turned versus merely being controlled by compulsion, and the series also leaves unsaid how to understand what *happens* when someone turns. For his part, Androl is convinced that people do not survive being turned. He says, "I can't accept that someone can be *made* to serve the Dark One" (Jordan and Sanderson, *A Memory of Light*, 134). He goes on, "the choice to serve the Dark One or the Light … surely that one choice could not be taken from a person. … The man he'd known was gone, killed, and something else—something evil—had been put into his body." I want to say that being turned changes one's perception of the available options, so that one "freely" chooses as Shai'tan would and in line with Shai'tan's perspective. And so Androl is right in the sense that being turned destroys your unique perspective, what makes you authentically you as an individual, as you instead take on the perspective of the Shadow. In this sense, in Rand's weaving of the threads of possibility, Elayne appears *as if turned* because her perspective has been destroyed, made to conform to Rand's.

8. This is the best interpretation I can offer, and it does in certain ways innovate on this question about the value of freedom. However, whether it's a good lesson to take away may ultimately depend on the significance of authenticity, which is controversial within philosophy. See Theodor Adorno, *The Jargon of Authenticity* (New York: Routledge, 1964). Alternatively, it may depend on the value of individuality. On this, see), Guy Kahane, "Individuality as Difference," *Philosophy & Public Affairs* 52 (2024), 362–396.

9. For an overview of fatalism, see Hugh Rice, "Fatalism," in *The Stanford Encyclopedia of Philosophy* at https://plato.stanford.edu/archives/sum2024/entries/fatalism. Perhaps the most studied version involves God's foreknowledge—whether part of God's omniscience would involve God's knowing everything we will do, and whether God's knowing this on its own threatens our freedom.

10. Robert Jordan, *The Shadow Rising* (London: Orbit, 2014), 573.

11. Robert Jordan, *The Eye of the World* (London: Orbit, 2014), 218.

12. Robert Jordan and Brandon Sanderson, *The Gathering Storm* (London: Orbit, 2014), 777.

13. Jordan and Sanderson, *The Gathering Storm*, 778.

14. See Harry Frankfurt, "Freedom of the Will and the Concept of a Person," *Journal of Philosophy* 68 (1971), 5–20, Gary Watson, "Free Agency," *Journal of Philosophy* 72 (1975), 205–220; Chandra Sripada, "Self-Expression: A Deep Self Theory of Moral Responsibility," *Philosophical Studies* 173 (2016), 1203–1232; August Gorman, "The Minimal Approval Account of Attributability," in David Shoemaker ed., *The Oxford Studies in Agency and Responsibility*, vol. 6 (Oxford: Oxford University Press, 2019), 140–164.

15. Jordan and Sanderson, *The Gathering Storm*, 798.

16. The characters may tell themselves that "The Wheel weaves as the Wheel wills," but the Wheel itself doesn't literally will anything. It's taken for granted that the Creator is distinct from the Wheel, and the Creator is interpreted as generally not intervening in the Pattern. In contrast to Shai'tan, then, the Creator is depicted as maximally un-controlling.

17. Though central to his thinking, Nietzsche is characteristically cryptic about how to interpret the eternal recurrence thought experiment, or whether it's even a thought experiment at all (as opposed to being meant as literally true). See Arnold Zuboff, "Nietzsche and Eternal Recurrence," in Robert C. Solomon, *Nietzsche: A Collection of Critical Essays* (Notre Dame: Anchor Press, 1973), 343–357, Paul S. Loeb, *The Death of Nietzsche's Zarathustra* (Cambridge: Cambridge University Press, 2010); Tom Stern, "Back to the Future: Eternal Recurrence and the Death of Socrates," *Journal of Nietzsche Studies* 41 (2011), 73–82; William A.B. Parkhurst, "Nietzsche and Eternal Recurrence: Methods, Archives, History, and Genesis" (PhD diss., University of South Florida, 2021).

18. It's important to clarify that Nietzsche's line here is not necessarily the same line as that of the Stoics or of Albert Camus (in *The Myth of Sisyphus*). Nietzsche is not counseling us to develop an attitude of acquiescence or acceptance of fate, as some Stoics might, nor an attitude of humor and defiance of fate, as Camus might. It's more positive than this; he wants us to joyously embrace our fate. For further discussion of *amor fati* for Nietzsche, see Brian Domino, "Nietzsche's Use of *Amor Fati* in *Ecce Homo*," *Journal of Nietzsche Studies* 43 (2012), 283–303, 145–162, Guy Elgat, "*Amor Fati* as Practice: How to Love Fate," *Southern Journal of Philosophy* 54 (2016), 174–188; Hedwig Gaasterland, "Nietzsche's Rejection of Stoicism: A Reinterpretation of Amor Fati" (PhD diss., Leiden University, 2017); Sven Gellens, "How 'Amor Fati' Became Nietzsche's Formula for Learning to Love Necessity and Human Thriving," *Filozofia* 76 (2021), 465–479.

19. Jordan and Sanderson, *The Gathering Storm*, 797.

20. Jordan and Sanderson, *The Gathering Storm*, 799.

21. Theodor Adorno, *Minima Moralia* (London: Verso, 1951/2020), sec. 61. For more skepticism of *amor fati* as a successful response to fate, see), Tom Stern, "Nietzsche, 'Amor Fati' and 'The Gay Science,'" *Proceedings of the Aristotelian Society* 113 (2013), 145–162.

22. Jordan and Sanderson, *The Gathering Storm*, 799–800.

23. This hope is even more radical than hope for Adorno. Adorno thought that the world is so bad that it corrupts our very imagination. So, a better world may be possible, and we can/should hope for it, but we might not be able to imagine it. In contrast, Rand can imagine things working out better in the future. But notice that if the world is genuinely fated to recur, then it's actually impossible that it will turn out better. So, Rand is hopeful for something imaginable yet impossible. That is radical indeed. For Adorno's conception of hope, see Timo Jütten, "Adorno on Hope," *Philosophy and Social Criticism* 45 (2019), 284–306.

# 7

# Revelations from Rhuidean: Messianism and Philosophy of History in *The Wheel of Time*

*Andrew D. Thrasher*

One way of writing fantasy is to create an "inner consistency to reality" that includes history, mythology, and religion in the creation of fantastic worlds.[1] *The Wheel of Time* certainly fits this mold. Each book begins with a formula for the world's religion, mythology, and history: "The Wheel of Time turns, and Ages come and pass, leaving memories that become legend. Legend fades to myth, and even myth is long forgotten when the Age that gave it birth comes again. In one Age, called the Third Age by some, an Age yet to come, an Age long past, a wind rose ..."[2] Implicit in this world building is a philosophy of history in which the meaning and pattern of history about the "breaking" of the world and its restoration occur through a messianic figure who will usher in a Messianic Age. This history starts with a utopia, the opening of the world to evil and the fight against it, the breaking of the world, and thousands of years where history is forgotten and legend becomes myth—until the Dragon is reborn and leads the armies of Light against the Dark One and breaks the world once more.

*The Wheel of Time* offers a philosophy of history that echoes the notions of the meaning of history, messianism, and the Messianic Age as they are found in both Jewish and Christian traditions, notably in the works of Karl Löwith (1897–1973), Reinhold Niebuhr (1892–1971), and Paul Ricoeur (1913–2005). All three of these philosophers offer helpful articulations of philosophy of history that envision a future marked by peace and flourishing, pointing us to the promise of the redemption of history and the role a messianic figure may play in bringing about a Messianic Age.

# The "Pattern" and Meaning of History in *The Wheel of Time*

Löwith spoke of the "meaning of history" as a distinctly theological enterprise that tries to systematically interpret a "universal history in accordance with a principle by which historical events and successions are unified and directed toward an ultimate meaning."[3] This ultimate meaning of history is theological in the sense that it deals with "history as a history of fulfillment and salvation."[4] Löwith claims that the meaning of history is marked by both a *finis* and a *telos*, which means it has both a limit and "a definite goal."[5] There is an aim of history that validates historical processes while also pointing toward completion.

In *The Wheel of Time*, this meaning of history is revealed by the concept of "the Pattern," the way in which lives throughout time are reincarnated. The Creator weaves the threads of people's lives together in time and across lifetimes like a tapestry that governs and determines the direction of what they are supposed to do throughout their lives. The Pattern transcends particular lives and orders them to a determined goal. In this sense, the Pattern is impersonal, even though it orders and determines the personal lives of those who are reborn according to it. Notably, the *ta'veren* play a determined role in bringing about the ends of history, and yet *ta'veren* also have a sense of free will. This raises an important question about the tension between free will and determinism. The Pattern weaves *ta'veren* into the Wheel of Time to achieve the ends of history, but *ta'veren* become the agents of the Pattern to achieve those ends. And yet, the Pattern is set by the Creator; it is cyclical and leads to the restoration of goodness. Indeed, goodness and flourishing are supposed to be the hallmarks of creation. We see this in the glimpses of the past through the lives of the People of the Dragon (i.e. the Aiel). The world before the Bore and the influence of the Dark One is a world of peace and flourishing. But when the Bore is opened and the Dark One released, violence, evil, madness, and war destroy the world.

In *The Wheel of Time*, history is a pattern determined by the Creator in two ways. Not only does the Creator create the pattern of history, but the Creator puts a messianic figure, the Dragon Reborn, into history as its agent to bring about the Messianic Age. For Christianity, the Messianic Age is understood in terms of the Kingdom of Heaven. The Kingdom of Heaven is already here in part through Jesus's first coming, and it will be fully here when Jesus returns. In *The Wheel of Time*, a new world of peace in the Fourth Age is already inaugurated in the birth, life, and death of the Dragon Reborn, and yet its consummation is not the end of history. Its consummation is the beginning of a new age restored to peace. If the Christian end of history is when time is transformed into eternity at the end of time, then the end of history in *The Wheel of Time* is not an end of history. Instead, it is a transformation and restoration of the world as marked by peace *in time*. Time does not dissolve into eternity; it continues into a new age of restoration and peace.

*The Wheel of Time*'s philosophy of history is marked by a pattern where the past is to be redeemed, but this pattern of redemption is not necessarily marked by theological beliefs, even though it is guided by prophecies that reveal the future and its possibilities. Throughout *The Wheel of Time*, the dialogues between the followers of the Dark One and the friends of the Dragon Reborn reveal that the Dark One has repeatedly warred against each incarnation of the Dragon. We get glimpses of at least two of these incarnations in the Dragon, Lews Therin Telamon, the Kinslayer, and Rand al'Thor. This cosmic pattern centers around a messianic figure (the Dragon) who will fight against the Dark One until he is finally defeated. Time is cyclical in *The Wheel of Time*, and yet the ends (*telos*) and limits (*finis*) of time are marked by a pattern of repetition and redemption.

## Messianic Analogies in *The Wheel of Time*

In Judaism and Christianity, the Messiah plays an important role in addressing and conquering evil. Reinhold Niebuhr (1892–1971) emphasizes that "messianism" is the key to the eschatological overcoming of the problem of history, namely, corruption. Messianism means that there is someone anointed by the Creator who will usher in a Messianic Age of peace, restoration, and flourishing after conquering evil. In a biblical context, Niebuhr argues that messianism has three levels: the egoistic-nationalistic level, which sees the messianic hope in the triumph and redemption of the nation;[6] the ethical-universalistic level, which sees not only the triumph of our people over enemies, but also of the triumph of good over the forces of evil through the righteous messianic King who combines power with goodness;[7] and the prophetic level, which calls a people to righteousness and casts divine judgment on a chosen people for failing to be righteous.[8]

We see these messianic themes throughout *The Wheel of Time*. The egoistic-nationalistic messianism is notably found in Aiel as the people of the Dragon, an important tool to be used in the fight against the Dark One. The redemption of the Aiel is indicated in their origins as a people of peace, who follow the Way of the Leaf. This redemption is found in the *toh*, or obligation, to come to terms with the reality that they have betrayed the Way of the Leaf in wielding spears used for killing. But what redeems the *nations* in *The Wheel of Time* is Rand's Peace Accords: he seeks to break the nations of their inclinations toward war and thus break the world with peace.

The second ethical-universalistic messianic level is accomplished in Rand's fight with the Dark One and Moridin at Shayol Ghul and with Mat Cauthon's leadership over the Armies of the Light in the Last Battle. In the

Last Battle, we see examples of how good triumphs over the forces of evil. We see this in the fights against evil in Gawyn, Galad, and al'Lan Mandrogoran's fight against Demandred. In each of these cases, we see messianic figures fighting against and overcoming the forces of evil on individual, moral, and collective levels. On an individual and moral level, Rand fights against the Dark One in Shayol Ghul through the weaving of alternate realities that reveal important lessons about good and evil. On a collective level, the fight and overcoming of evil is seen in the battle on the Field of Merrilor.

The third messianic, prophetic witness calls people to righteousness and can be seen, ironically, in Rand's intention to leave the Aiel out of his Peace Accords. Aviendha's visions of the future of her descendants reveal how Rand's intention to do so would lead to the destruction of the Aiel generations later. She calls Rand to use the Aiel as a means to enforce peace because, as Perrin notes, they are like a tool to be used, and when the tool loses its use, it falls into decay. This prophetic witness calls Rand to create a use for the Aiel in his Peace Accords so that they will not be destroyed in the generations to come.

## Analogies of a Messianic Age in *The Wheel of Time*

At the heart of the promise of a Messianic Age is the agency of a Messiah who will usher in an age of peace, wholeness, and flourishing. In the Second Temple Jewish context, the expectation of a Messiah revolved around several things. First, they expected a Messiah who would liberate Israel from foreign oppression. Second, they expected the Messiah to come from the line of David. Third, they expected the Messiah to usher in the Kingdom of God on earth. But the Kingdom of God in the Second Temple Jewish context was not universal. Different sectarian traditions of Judaism viewed it differently. Notably, the Pharisaical view of the Kingdom of God viewed the Messiah as someone who would first reconcile Israel, then nations, and finally creation with God.[9] Furthermore, this restoration of relationship with God meant that the righteousness of God would reign.

The Kingdom of God in the Christian context followed the messianic expectation noted above insofar as Jesus was a descendant of David, was believed to be the Messiah whose ministry was first to Israel, and that Jesus was the righteousness of God incarnate. And yet, while the Jewish people were expecting a militaristic, liberating Messiah, the early Christians believed Jesus to be a Messiah who inaugurated the Kingdom of God on earth as a spiritual kingdom. Christians believe that when Jesus returns, the consummation of the kingdom will occur, characterized by righteousness, wholeness, peace, and flourishing. God will reign over a redeemed and restored creation.

In *The Wheel of Time*, Rand al'Thor can be understood as a messianic figure in several senses that are analogous to the Second Temple Jewish and early Christian contexts. First, analogous to the Jewish expectation that the Messiah will liberate Israel from foreign oppression, Rand liberated nations from oppressive leaders, the Forsaken, who directed various nations across the world. Be'lal in Tear, Sammael in Illian, Graendal in Arad Doman, and Rahvin in Andor, each of these Forsaken abused power and took control of these nations until Rand liberated the nations. Second, analogous to the idea that the Messiah comes from the line of David as one of God's chosen people, Rand plays the role as having come from a chosen people, the Aiel, or People of the Dragon.[10]

Third, analogous to the messianic expectations that the Messiah would usher in a new age in which the Kingdom of God would reign over the world in righteousness, peace, and justice, Rand ushered in a new age marked by peace. Tied to this, and the Christian belief that the Messiah would conquer Satan, Rand sought to kill the Dark One. But to obtain his peace, Rand must break the world and renew the very structures of this world with systems of peace. It's not only that the nations must adhere to the Peace Accords, but also that someone must administer justice toward those who transgress the peace. This is the role of the Aiel, as noted, where they reflect an enduring role in the Messianic Age.

The pattern and promise of a Messianic Age are well illustrated in the Karaethon Cycle, "the Prophecies of the Dragon." According to Moiraine in *A Memory of Light*, the prophecies reveal how the Dragon will break the world and establish peace:

And it shall come to pass that what men made shall be shattered.... The Shadow shall lie across the Pattern of the Age, and the Dark One shall once more lay his hand upon the world of man. Women shall weep and men quail as the nations of the earth are rent like rotting cloth. Neither shall anything stand nor abide.... Yet one shall be born to face the Shadow.... Born once more as he was born before and shall be born again, time without end! The Dragon shall be reborn, and there shall be wailing and gnashing of teeth at his rebirth. In sackcloth and ashes shall he clothe the people, and he shall break the world again by his coming, tearing apart all ties that bind.... Like the unfettered dawn shall he blind us, and burn us, yet shall the Dragon Reborn confront the Shadow at the Last Battle, and his blood shall give us the Light. Let tears flow, O ye people of the World. Weep for your salvation! ... He shall slay his people with the sword of peace ... and destroy them with the leaf. ... The unstained tower breaks and bends knee to the forgotten sign. ... There can be no health in us, nor any good thing grow ... for the land is one with the Dragon Reborn, and he one with the land. Soul of fire, heart of stone. ... In pride he conquers, forcing the proud to yield. ... He calls upon the mountains to kneel. ... And the seas to give way. ... And the very skies to bow.... Pray that the heart of stone remembers tears ... and the soul of fire, love.[11]

Moiraine's recitation refers to peoples, rulers, and what the Dragon Reborn is supposed to do. Specifically, the Dragon Reborn is to fight the Dark One, lead the armies of Light against the Armies of the Dark One in the Last Battle, break the world again, break all former bonds, and bind people together in ways that transcend national and ethnic boundaries. At the heart of Rand's attempt to break the world is the attempt to break the powers and structures of violence and war with a new way of peace: the Dragon Reborn breaks the world, sundering old alliances and even slaying "his people"—the Aiel—with peace.

Here the meaning of history in *The Wheel of Time* comes to the fore: the Dragon Reborn will establish a Messianic Age wherein peace reigns. This is analogous to Christian views according to which Christ will usher in the Kingdom of God on Earth, and this kingdom will be ruled by justice, wholeness, and peace. The Dragon Reborn will usher in the Fourth (Messianic) Age, which radically renews the political systems of the world to be marked by peace and flourishing, rather than war and destruction.

## Philosophy of History in *The Wheel of Time*

Paul Ricoeur (1913–2005) can help us understand how the meaning of history in *The Wheel of Time* rescripts a Messianic Age as a philosophy of history. In *The Wheel of Time*, the messianic promises of a renewed creation and of a savior who will establish it reveals the centrality of three elements of a philosophy of history: progress, ambiguity, and hope.

Ricoeur's notion of progress holds in tension the idea that history is fated for goodness and that history will overcome corruption. This implies that a Christian meaning of history must grapple with the value of history in ways that fulfill the destiny of someone who works to break the corruption of nature and make his own history in ways that seek the flourishing of this world.[12] This is illustrated in the Dragon Reborn's mission to break the pattern of violence. The Peace Accords were Rand's attempt to break the world of its pattern of war and violence, and to initiate a world of peace, prosperity, education, and flourishing.

Ricoeur also contributes to an understanding of overcoming the ambiguity of history. This ambiguity is characterized by the tension between the promise of goodness and the role of human agency in bringing it about. To overcome the ambiguity of history Ricoeur argues that humans must have a purpose—one that is marked by a justifiable optimism that is effectuated through the very instruments of progress toward the good of this world.[13] Ricoeur's point is illustrated in *The Wheel of Time* through the use of the Aiel as the hammer and tool ready to maintain peace when the nations transgress Rand's Peace Accords. The question of the Aiel's purpose is overlooked by Rand because of his guilt over using the Aiel to achieve his power. Because of this guilt Rand sought to leave the Aiel out of his Peace

Accords, not wanting to use them any further. Yet, as Perrin and Aviendha note, the Aiel are a tool to be used, and if they are not used, they will waste away. The Aiel must be used as an instrument in Rand's Messianic Age— otherwise they have no purpose.

Lastly, Ricoeur situates hope between both meaning and mystery. He claims that meaning is the unifying source for "the courage to live in history" and that its mystery is that it is hidden and one must take a risk on it.[14] Ricoeur argues that the meaning of history is to read and perceive it as sacred history. This sacred history "is eschatological, meaning thereby that … life unfolds in the time of progress and ambiguity without … seeing this higher meaning, without … being able to discern the relation between the two histories, the secular and the sacred."[15] Though Rand al'Thor may not see history as sacred, he certainly struggled to make decisions throughout the series. He sought to shape the world into an image he saw as good, but he struggled to make it happen because the inclinations of those around him were geared toward undermining him and his purpose to break all bonds and the world. Rand took a risk. He was not sure whether his peace would last beyond his death, and yet his Peace Accords were designed to maintain this peace among the nations in such a way that even without his messianic presence, a Messianic Age of peace would be maintained.

## A Fantastic Spin

The link between the promised Messiah and the Messianic Age is revealed in *The Wheel of Time* as the promise of history. As it turns out, history is patterned toward an end, ushering in an age of peace through the efforts of a messianic figure. Robert Jordan's fantastic spin on messianism and the Messianic Age offers helpful reflections on the meaning of history. The author not only presents a philosophy of history that draws on Christian and Jewish notions of messianism, but does so in ways that reflect on the ends of history as oriented toward the overcoming of evil.

## Notes

1. J.R.R Tolkien in Verlyn Flieger and Douglas A. Anderson eds., *Tolkien on Fairy-Stories* (London: HarperCollins, 2008), 49.
2. Throughout the series, this phrase is invoked at the beginning of the first chapter of each volume.
3. Karl Löwith, *Meaning in History* (Chicago: The University of Chicago Press, 1949), 1.
4. Löwith, *Meaning in History*, 1.

5. Löwith, *Meaning in History*, 18.
6. Reinhold Niebuhr, *The Nature and Destiny of Man, Volume 2: Human Destiny* (New York: Charles Scribner's Sons, 1949), 18.
7. Niebuhr, *The Nature and Destiny of Man*, 19.
8. Niebuhr, *The Nature and Destiny of Man*, 24–25.
9. N.T. Wright, *The New Testament and the People of God* (Minneapolis: Fortress Press, 1996), 251–252.
10. This is referenced throughout the series, but finds its first major confirmation by the Green Man at the end of *The Eye of the World*. Robert Jordan, *The Eye of the World* (New York: TOR Books, 1990), chap. 53.
11. Robert Jordan and Brandon Sanderson, *A Memory of Light* (New York: TOR Books, 2012), 176–177.
12. Paul Ricoeur, *History and Truth*, trans. Charles A. Kelbley (Evanston: Northwestern University Press, 2007), 85.
13. Ricoeur, *History and Truth*, 92.
14. Ricoeur, *History and Truth*, 93.
15. Ricoeur, *History and Truth*, 94.

# THE WEB CAN BE WOVEN MANY WAYS

**8**

# The (Re)Birth of Sovereignty in Robert Jordan's *The Wheel of Time*

*Jeremy Christensen and Eric Holmes*

Robert Jordan's Wheel of Time (*WoT*) is set in an age of uncertain sovereignty that raises questions: What happens when there is no government (at least no stable government)? How should people govern and be governed? What are the different ways in which governments secure power? Given the fifteen volumes that span over 10,000 pages (not including companion pieces, the contribution of the Amazon series, as well as the voluminous observations and vibrant discussions on *A WoT Wiki*), these questions are not easily answered and remain contentious. Nonetheless *WoT* offers insight on how sovereignty functions.

*WoT*, much like Thomas Hobbes's (1588–1979) *Leviathan*, prompts us to consider a chaotic world as opposed to one ruled by a functioning government. Hobbes described the chaos as the state of nature in which people live in "continual fear, and danger of violent death; and the life of man, solitary, poor, nasty, brutish and short."[1] This world, Hobbes argues, emerges from a near total absence of commerce, innovation, growth, and technology, a world without government. Likewise, *The Eye of the World*, the first book in Jordan's series, is set in a postlapsarian age in which such sovereignty has been shattered, leaving behind fragmented villages, scourges of villains, many petty fiefdoms, and cults seeking to manage the One Power—a force that comes from the True Source and drives the Wheel of Time, a cyclical pattern of birth and death and rebirth in the universe that governs all outcomes. It is, in fact, the quest to channel the One Power, to create a perfect government, one free from the Dark One's evil, one that reflects only the good from the Creator, that led to the total collapse of a sovereign government. In the prologue to *The Eye of the World*, Lews Therin Telamon, who is referred to as the Dragon (the archetype of a monarchial-like sovereign), is depicted wandering his burnt and blasted palace reflecting upon his error that "in his pride he had believed that men could match the Creator, could mend what the Creator had made and they had broken, in his pride he believed."[2] This hubris, in attempting a moment of purified sovereignty, led to the destruction of government and the Leviathan they had built. One epigraph, after the prologue to *The Eye of the World*, a passage from the *Aleth nin Taerin alta Camora*, a found manuscript from the Age of Legends which recounts what led to the demise of the old world, echoes Hobbes's warning about the collapse of nations and the demise of sovereignty: "And the Shadow fell upon the Land, and the World was riven stone from stone. The oceans fled, and the mountains were swallowed up, and the nations were scattered to the eight corners of the World. The moon was as blood, and the sun was as ashes. The seas boiled, and the living envied the dead. All was shattered, and all but memory lost …"[3] These are the ragged conditions in which series is set, and it is from those tatters that the characters work to rebuild some semblance of a sovereign.

## The State of the Third Age

This chaotic time, this state of nature in which the series is set, referred to as the Third Age, comes after the Age of Legends, which, based upon the remaining artifacts of that period that survived the breaking of the world, was marked by a clear and stable sense of sovereignty. It is the presence of a stable government and the resulting prosperity that made this period one for which the characters yearn (at least many of those who follow the Light and Creator). *The World of Robert Jordan's The Wheel of Time*, a companion work to the novels, explains the world that existed before the Dragon's pride shattered it. This world was a "society [that] was supported by a stable worldwide economy" had an "overall harmonious balance within society," and featured a government that was "both strong and responsive" with a "worldwide parliament … of democratically elected officials."[4] This previous world was utopic (or at least it appears so from the position of the present age in which the novels are set) precisely because there was a strong sovereign to inspire awe in the masses.

Central to all conflict in the series is the question of how power ought to be wielded and who should wield it. The Wheel of Time inevitably moves, Ages come and go, and there is always a return. The Third Age represents the period in which characters are waiting for the return of the Dragon who will secure power and bring peace. The Dragon that returns, however, is neither inherently good nor evil, but instead, his behavior and the way he manages the One Power is the measure of his effectiveness. This practice is called channeling—a person's ability to manage the five threads that make up the Pattern of the universe and focus those to affect change in the world—and although the One Power is everywhere (think *Star Wars*' The Force) only a few people—"about three percent"—can control it and direct its force to heal, make war, advance knowledge, and generally bend the laws of physics.[5] The Dragon, who must meet certain conditions (being male, born in a certain place, able to arrive at a particular location in the final battle), must also be the best channeler, the one most capable of bending forces to affect change. Channeling, however, is a morally neutral ability, as both those who follow the Creator and those who chose the Dark One have this capacity.

Thus, channeling serves as the vehicle through which *WoT* engages in the discussion of sovereignty. There is no power lurking in government, even if, somehow, it exists somewhere out there. It only becomes power once it is put into practice. It is those practices, however, that are controlled by the morality, intentionality, and the logic of the one doing the channeling. As Moiraine explains to Egwene in the Amazon series: "The Power inside you is the smallest part of your strength. It's your mind, and how you use it, that will mean much more in the battles to come."[6] In this way, *WoT* depicts sovereignty as something far more than raw power or force; instead, it takes a unique shape depending upon the rules, practices, and habits used to bring it into being.

Sovereignty, however, is not something one can purchase in a tavern or pick up from raiding a Trolloc encampment. Sovereignty results from how people engage with each other, what people think is acceptable or unacceptable, and ultimately, the process by which law and the state have the authority to take away everything that is a person's, even their life, by having the power to determine what is right or wrong—even if the sovereign itself has no moral compass. In his book *Homo Sacer: Sovereign Power and the Bare Life*, the contemporary philosopher Giorgio Agamben explains that such sovereignty is the result of people accepting a fundamental contradiction when they agree to be governed: the very greed, envy, and violence that Hobbes says exists inherently among persons in the state of nature remains in whoever and whatever governs people. Nonetheless, people accept that it is better to have only one thing with the authority to preserve and exercise power of war—death, life, taking of property, giving property, and so on—over each person.[7] This authority to wield power over humans is constructed through penalties and punishments (including, in particular, capital punishment), as well as, perhaps most importantly for the consideration of Jordan's work, in practices or behaviors of individuals that enforce the prohibitions and those against whom the laws are enforced.

Significantly, the Third Age is the working out of how to institute practices that make the return of authority effective and restore the peace and harmony that existed in the Age of Legends. Though this chapter could not begin to address the numerous options presented in the forms of various city states, kingdoms, and struggles between the Children of Light and others, one group does emerge as offering a template for how power is channeled and sovereignty formed: the Aes Sedai.

## Sovereign Sedai

The Aes Sedai serve both to preserve the rituals of sovereignty, training women in the ways of channeling the One Power, and to ensure that those who channel the One Power do not do so irresponsibly. Their lives are the emblems of structure. Each Aes Sedai belongs to an order, an order they can only become a part of once they have been properly trained in the art of channeling, and after they swear oaths to both their order and to the outside world, and conform to a rigid set of rules that govern their conduct. These practices emerged after the breaking of the world, as the Aes Sedai began to cement their power, but the establishment of these practices, along with the establishment of their seven Ajah (orders) were designed to create some sense of order and control.[8] No matter how corrupt their system may have become, centuries after the Dragon broke the world, what they present is still a model for restoring order in the world.

Almost as though Jordan were referencing Hobbes's commentary on the lack of knowledge, commerce, arts, and civility in a world without a sovereign, the Aes Sedai's order mirrors what needs to be preserved. The seven Ajah (Red, Blue, Brown, Green, Yellow, Grey, and White) represent those conditions Hobbes claimed could not exist without a sovereign to hold people in awe: justice, collected knowledge, collective preparation, helping others, and diplomacy.[9]

Notably, each order represents some part necessary for worldly prosperity and the positive effects of sovereignty. They do so, quite literally, through order. It is the rules, procedures, and even structures of their living that form government, and it is that government that works its way into the world. These orders, however, do little unless they are applied and put into the practice of governing, which is, most often, not through the military-like force of the Reds, but rather through the way in which their power is physically structured and maintained.

Hobbes's notion that a sovereign must keep its subjects in *awe* can be construed to mean malevolence and outright force. However, fealty requires the subject to meet the sovereign somewhere between free will and outright slavery. Without some sense of ownership over behavior, subjects run the risk of becoming hopeless or revolutionary, neither of which works to promote a docile subjectivity. Enter the oath.

Sovereign authority is confirmed and perpetuated through what is said in the form of an oath or promise, which is often juxtaposed with the idea of a curse, both ideas that are central to *WoT*. These concepts of oath and curse are not pure fantasy. Anyone who has caught an episode of *Law and Order*, watched the president of the United States be sworn in, pledged allegiance to the American flag, or has taken the oath of enlistment for US military service is familiar with the idea that to participate in national endeavors requires saying words to show that a person means loyalty and honesty toward the sovereign. Often people view such practices as quaint or a holdover from an older system during which religion and myth governed people, rather than laws and science. From this perspective, that oaths are relics, a person could view those motifs in *WoT* as a device to create a sense of distance, to affect the vaguely medieval feeling that permeates the books and television series. The prominence of oaths and curses, thus, can be seen as something that applied to sovereignty of kingdoms and is quite distant from the sovereignty of democracies or democratic republics in nation-states of the twenty-first century.

## Of Oaths and Promises

Oaths are more than relics of the past; they are, in fact, constitutive of a sovereign's power to keep people in awe. As Agamben contends in *The Sacrament of Language: An Archeology of the Oath,* most scholarship concerning the oath, from Plutarch to the present, says that the oath and its counterpart, the curse, are infused within the laws of nation-states, expressing, in effect, the authority of the sovereign. Agamben explains that practices of swearing oaths of fealty, oaths before members of courts, and corresponding punishments for perjury are intertwined with Western (Greco-Roman-Judeo-Christian) expressions of religion and law, which he sees as inseparable institutional practices. In Agamben's view, oaths are more than simply additive elements of law and by extension sovereignty; they are the foundation of Western government and sovereignty. He contends that central to the idea of government and authority is the idea of the *logos*—the sense of order and reasoning through language that unifies and binds meaning (a concept quite similar, as we will later note, to the idea of the One Power in Jordan's work). Oaths, of which curses and even blasphemy are a part, Agamben submits, are "sacraments of power." Religion and law—the twin authorities of sovereignty, as Hobbes pointed out in *The Leviathan*—"were invented to guarantee the truth and trustworthiness of the logos through a series of apparatuses, among which is the technicalization of the oath into a specific 'sacrament.'"[10] It is the oath itself and the rituals associated with the oath that build the awesomeness of sovereignty.

This intersection between religion, politics, and the awesomeness of sovereignty—the "power over life and death," as Agamben refers to it[11]—establishes the foundation for the Aes Sedai's authority and serves as a reminder throughout the texts of what it takes for power to succeed or fail. The Aes Sedai were not always organized and as such the result was a chaotic state.

During the Age of Legends, the Aes Sedai were a "loose sort of organization" that was "not the entire government and did not necessarily dominate it."[12] In fact, they were part of a larger guild during the Age of Legends, though their purpose remains unclear, aside from "serving all," which is what Aes Sedai translates to. After the breaking, they were able to extend their authority "nearly three thousand leagues" away to Seanchan. There, on that continent, there was no order and no sense of law. Nations came and went, constantly shifting and collapsing, in large part because there was no fidelity between action and word: "Those few who were faithful to their word were considered fools."[13] Luthair Paendrag emerged amidst this broken system, leading the conquest to tame and finally control the Aes Sedai, binding their power to channel first with bracelets and later still with oaths. These initial promises evolved into the Three Oaths, which formed the foundation of the Aes Sedai's doxa. They began as quite simply a mode of maintaining trust in what a person says.

In fact, their group was part of a much larger guild which oversaw the Hall of Servants in Paaran Disen before the calamity. In the wake of the Dragon's reckoning and the end of the Age of Legends, when the Wheel turned and the "Age of Prophecy" began with its disjunction, regress, and failure, the Aes Sedai emerged as a transnational authority, a holdover from a global government that is quite distinct from the city state structure that emerged in the Second Age, in which each kingdom or town has its own power structure, governed by its emphasis on its own abilities. It is, in fact, these oaths that afford the Aes Sedai the ability to function transnationally and serve as a symbol (albeit an imperfect and contentious one) for the unification of governance in the world through their oaths, from which flow the politico-religious life.

*New Spring: The Novel*, a prequel to the *Wheel of Time* series, traces Moiraine Damodred's journey to becoming Aes Sedai. The beginning of the book features her experiences with the One Power before being called to join the Aes Sedai, her engagement with and subsequent friendship with other novices. It culminates in her admission to the Aes Sedai and her Ajah and following commissions of duty. Central to that process, she, like all Aes Sedai, regardless of which Ajah they are part of, must take the Three Oaths and, after which, wear the shawl all members of the magi wear, a garment that confirms they are now officially part of the magi and their given order. As Moiraine explains, "The Three Oaths made her Aes Sedai, yet she had not felt Aes Sedai until the shawl was put around her shoulders."[14] It is the combination of the statements and the rituals that integrate, unify, and give authority to the Aes Sedai to exercise their respective commissions according to their respective Ajah.

The Three Oaths serve as a primer on the way sovereignty is supposed to be expressed. As Agamben explains, an oath is "the conjunction of three elements: an affirmation, the invocation of the gods as witnesses, and a curse directed at perjury."[15] The oath, from this perspective, serves to affirm the sovereign's authority and confirm the sovereign's right to regulate and control behavior. The first of the Three Oaths establishes each of those conditions and, importantly, is a reminder, itself, of the purpose of an oath: "Under the Light and by my hope of salvation and rebirth, I vow that

I will speak no word that is not true."[16] The "Light" is a reference to the One Power and the Creator which invokes God as a witness. The second part, however, confirms the importance of truth telling as the foundation of the sovereign's right, which comes from the accuracy of language itself: no word that is not true. This prohibition against perjury confirms that truthfulness is not just important in a court of law, a place where the sovereign's judgment over life and death is most evident, but also in every act, word, and deed of the sovereign's representatives. As Moiraine tells the budding acolyte Egwene, it is the "exact verbiage" of the oaths that matters because "Words are important and how we use them is important."[17] The value then is not only in the promise of the oath—they won't lie, so people can trust what they say—but also the words of the oath, and all words, carry with them a force that confirms authority.

This control, and thus their sovereignty, rests upon the power of language itself, and not only as expressed in the Three Oaths. The Three Oaths, by their very announcement, affect sovereignty's restrictions on the Aes Sedai. Moiraine demonstrates this effect when, upon taking the first oath in her confirmation, she notices that "The pressure grew abruptly; it felt as though she had been sewn into an invisible garment, much too tight, that molded her from the crown of her head to the soles of her feet."[18] The ability to channel the One Power is inborn; however, the Aes Sedai create limits on both who is permitted to use this ability, and the conditions under which it may be used. These conditions both control individuals through this sovereign authority and provide a guarantee for the foundation of law: language. "Speaking no word that is not true," for instance, reflects the invaluable function of language in securing sovereign power. This first oath is affirmatory, proclaiming that language is binding, that it can be trusted, and that such a trust is inherent to a social compact.

From the position that language itself must be true, then, the Aes Sedai can promise their words can be trusted, and it is that impression of trust (even if not truth of words in fact) that gives them authority. The other two oaths are promissory, the first restrictive and the second protective. Here, then, with these three oaths, is the fundamental framework of a Western-Judeo discursive framework for sovereignty: words must be meaningful, there must be restraints on sovereign authority, and the sovereign has both the authority and obligation to defend those within their sphere of power.

Furthermore, not only are oaths a matter of confirming that an account is true, but they are also employed to bind a person's future obligation and behavior. As Hobbes writes in *De Cive*: "an Oath may as well sometimes be affirmatory, as promissory; for he that confirms his affirmation with an Oath, promiseth that he speaks truth."[19] The affirmatory oath, the one a person provides in court when sworn in, presents the first kind, and the oath a person swears in *fidelis* to a compact is promissory. Both types of oaths confirm and establish the authority and role of the sovereign.

The roles of the second and third oath are more promissory than affirmatory, demonstrating that the sovereign control is really about the truth in the language itself and the obligation to perpetuate that truth in action. The second is: "Under the Light and by my hope of salvation and rebirth, I vow that I will make no weapon for one man to kill another." The third is: "Under the Light and by my hope of salvation and rebirth, I vow that I will never use the One Power as a weapon except against Darkfriends or Shadowspawn, or in the last extreme of defending my life or that of my Warder or another sister."[20] Both statements promise future action, both in the sense there is a restraint in the use of force, conditions under which violence can be used, and in the sense that there are those against whom violence can be rightfully directed. It is in that sense, the emergence of a ban against the behaviors of Darkfriends and Shadowspawn, those who are, as Agamben might frame it, outside the law, and by that extension are subject to it.

However, the other side of the coin of the oath is the curse, in which failure to keep a promise, to affirm truthful statements, results in punishment. The opening words in the Three Oaths imply the threat of a curse. The refrain of "by my hope of salvation and rebirth," suggests that the consequences for breaking an oath are dire. The direness is illustrated when Moiraine swears an oath to leave the White Tower "and never return 'til she calls me home, or may the Creator's face turn from me and the darkness consume my soul."[21] The exercise of power is thus constrained by a threat, so that even those, maybe especially those, in service to the state, are held in jeopardy.

There are religious resonances such that the breaking of an oath violates some transcendent order. But ultimately, even the Creator and the Dark One—the two figures of this duality—are subject to a Wheel of Time that moves along without care or compassion. This kind of fatalism problematizes traditional notions of oath keeping as loyalty to God, as the universe is made up of an agent without agency. The One Power has no will, no morality, no inherent good or bad, and by extension the violation of its law is like the violation of the law of gravity. The forces that pull a suddenly released teacup to the ground and cause it to shatter are not punishing the cup (or the person who let it go for that matter). Rather, the forces are always there, a constant, and their deployment is not a matter of intention.

Herein lies the conundrum of sovereignty: If there is no divine right, then how would an oath make sense or, for that matter, why would anyone be cursed? To that extent, there is no morally "right" sovereignty or "wrong" sovereignty, only practices that obey the nature of the universe or those that misalign with it. In that context, then, the Creator and the Dark One are both equally good, insofar as they are equally effective. Like gravity, the sovereign simply *is*, and attempting to violate how it works has consequences.

Like the philosophy of Thomas Hobbes, Jordan's *WoT* recognizes the need for a sovereign amidst the chaos of the universe. Hopefully, that sovereign has benevolent designs or, as former president of the United States Ronald Reagan once didn't say, "I'm from the government, and I'm here to prepare for the return of the Dark One."

# Notes

1. Thomas Hobbes, *Leviathan* (Chicago: Encyclopedia Britannica, 2005), 85.
2. Robert Jordan, *The Eye of the World* (New York: Tom Doherty Associates, 1990), 37.
3. Jordan, *The Eye of the World*, 39.
4. Robert Jordan and Teresa Patterson, *The World of Robert Jordan's The Wheel of Time* (New York: TOR Books, 1997), 37.
5. Jordan and Patterson, *The World of Robert Jordan's The Wheel of Time*, 18.
6. *The Wheel of Time*, season 1, episode 2, "Shadows Waiting."
7. Giorgio Agamben, *Homo Sacer: Sovereign Power and Bare Life*, trans. Daniel Heller-Roazen (Stanford: Stanford University Press, 1998), 35–36.
8. Jordan and Patterson, *The World of Robert Jordan's The Wheel of Time*, 91–92.
9. Jordan and Patterson, *The World of Robert Jordan's The Wheel of Time*, 219–220.
10. Giorgio Agamben, *The Sacrament of Language: An Archeology of the Oath*, trans. A. Kotsko (Stanford: Stanford University Press, 2011), 59.
11. Agamben, *Homo Sacer: Sovereign Power and Bare Life*, 159.
12. Jordan and Patterson, *The World of Robert Jordan's The Wheel of Time*, 31.
13. Jordan and Patterson, *The World of Robert Jordan's The Wheel of Time*, 156–157.
14. Robert Jordan, *New Spring: A Novel* (New York: TOR Books, 2004), 145.
15. Agamben, *The Sacrament of Language: An Archeology of the Oath*, 31.
16. Jordan, *New Spring*, 142.
17. "Shadows Waiting."
18. Jordan, *New Spring*, 142.
19. Thomas Hobbes, *De Cive* (1651), at http://www.public-library.uk/ebooks/27/57.pdf, 16.
20. Jordan, *New Spring*, 142.
21. *The Wheel of Time*, season 1, episode 6, "The Flame of Tar Valon."

**9**

# Eyes Without Pity "... To Have Grown Up Thinking You Were a Person ..."

*Tim Jones*

In "Eyes Without Pity," episode 6 of season 2 in Amazon's *The Wheel of Time* adaptation, the Seanchan *sul'dam* Renna makes a coldly devastating claim about Egwene's identity, telling her "how hard" it must be "to have grown up thinking you were a person, only to realize you are a *damane* instead." Renna's claim suggests that Egwene's own sense of self has been incorrect and any statement she might've made about her identity—to herself, or to friends like Rand, or colleagues like Moiraine—mistaken. Egwene is not simply *becoming* a *damane* through being broken into one by Renna's torture across the course of this particularly intense episode; a *damane* is what she's always been, whether she knew it yet, or not.

This dynamic between Renna and Egwene in the second half of season 2 has a lot to tell us about the relationship between power and identity. In her novel *Nights at the Circus*, feminist author Angela Carter has one of her female characters ask, in the face of a male assault upon her own claims to self-hood, a question very relevant to Egwene's situation: "Am I what I know I am? Or am I what he thinks I am?"[1] There's a suggestion here that the seemingly obvious contrast between "know" and "thinks" is actually quite fragile, as Carter insinuates that power imbalances can render any discrepancy between the two verbs untenable, or even switch around the objective certainty of the first word and the insinuated incorrectness of the second word. Deep-rooted *knowledge* about the self becomes irrelevant under the force of claims by other people in positions that give them power to over-write that knowledge with their own assumptions about who a subordinated person like Egwene really is.

Egwene's *knowledge* that she was in fact a person, fueled by memories of growing up in Emond's Field with friends and family who loved her, of a burgeoning destiny as an Aes Sedai training to take a position of worldly power and influence, is threatened with transformation by Renna into mere faulty *thinking* that hid from Egwene's conscious awareness her true destiny as chattel. The implication is that Renna's thinking that Egwene is a mere *damane* ultimately has the power to become the knowledge that determines Egwene's destiny, through shaping every future interaction between the two of them and every possibility of Egwene's dramatically reduced world.

## All of the Westland's a Stage

What exactly makes up the substance of a person, and *how* exactly does that substance come to be formed? Erving Goffman (1922–1982) and contemporary philosopher Judith Butler both advance slightly different versions of the argument that our self is not innate, but constructed via a social performance. For Goffman specifically, we perform, in front of our audience, in a manner designed to convince that audience that we possess the characteristics or attributes that we wish that audience to *believe* that we possess.[2] Your self, he says, is "a dramatic effect."[3] When Egwene is training in the White Tower in front of her Aes Sedai instructors, she'll perform in a manner that's designed to convince them she's an able student, wielding the One Power with maturity and skill. The reality of her identity as an able student then derives *from* her successfully giving such a performance, rather than being the source of that performance; the reality of her identity as a terrible student would derive instead from her seeking to give such a performance but failing to do so convincingly.

Butler draws on the general point from Goffman that identity is constructed through performance, but focuses specifically on what this means for sex and gender, both of which, she argues, are performative, rather than intrinsic to our bodies. Think of a traveling play that Rand and his friends might have watched in the Winespring Inn back in Emond's Field, maybe a farce mocking the presumptuous arrogance of the Aes Sedai or perhaps a history play respectfully chronicling for the townsfolk one of the women's previous battles against a false Dragon. One actor would hope to be playing the Amyrlin Seat convincingly enough so that the audience could, while watching, suspend their disbelief and buy into the reality of that performance, so that as long as the performance lasts, the audience would not think of themselves as watching the actor, but the character that the actor wishes to be taken as. And how would that actor ensure this effect? Through props like jewelry or costumes that convincingly present a picture of what the *real* Amyrlin Seat at Tar Valon would look like—and through movement and voice, too, taking on the appropriate body language and gestures, as well as the tone, that present to the audience a believable image of the Aes Sedai leader. For Butler, every man and woman is continually doing the same, because "man" and "woman" themselves do not exist other than as scripted roles that we play. Genders are distinguished by differentiated clothing choices that say "man" or "woman."

Even in a fantasy world like in *The Wheel of Time* the men generally wear trousers as part of their own theatrical costumes, while the women wear skirts or dresses—or they have differentiated ways of moving and speaking that are recognizably "masculine" or "feminine," along with differentiated ways of grooming, such as women wearing their hair long, like the braids that Nynaeve spends much of her life tugging. Any society will contain sets of gender norms—how to dress, how to move, how to wear your hair— that play pretty much the same role for the members of that society as the script learned by my hypothetical traveling actors before performing at the tavern would play for them. Rand, Mat, and Lan are recognizably men because they have learned how to say the words and use the props detailed in the script for "man"; through saying these words and using these props, they become men. Egwene, Nynaeve, and Moiraine are recognizably women because they have learned a different script of their own.

The most interesting gender performances for Butler are those that skew gender scripts in unique directions, rather than following their words and instructions to the letter. This is what she praises as "gender trouble."[4] A good example of this might be Min wearing her hair short, with trousers and heels, mixing elements from the "man" script with elements from the "woman" script in her own combination.

The performativity of identity as envisaged by Goffman and Butler might arguably suggest that there's nothing more to identity than a form of free play. We imagine what we want to be and perform as such. But this is not quite what either thinker is suggesting. And if Egwene ever thought this herself, then her experiences in Falme might rapidly teach her otherwise.

## Harsh Direction

Goffman makes it clear that the successful performance of an identity is not just down to an individual looking to play whatever role they want; it's equally dependent on the *reception* of that performance by an audience. An identity is not constructed solely through the performance itself, but through the audience judging that the performer has successfully suggested the qualities they wish to be seen as possessing and then conferring the corresponding identity onto the performer.

From Goffman's perspective, it's Egwene's Aes Sedai instructors who ultimately decide whether or not her identity is that of an able student or a fool. In the world of *The Wheel of Time* there may be a concrete reality to Egwene's ability to channel *saidar* safely and competently, without stilling herself, meaning that her identity has a core basis beyond the social interactions she experiences between herself and the Aes Sedai. But for Goffman, an identity can only ever *be* social. He'd argue that you are genuinely not what you think you are if no one else agrees that's what you are; an identity is a property that opens or closes doors, that generates or shuts down life paths, all of which comes from the people around you recognizing the qualities you are attempting to press on them and acting toward you in accordance with this recognition. And while that particular audience would hopefully be impartial enough to be won over by an identity performance that genuinely does a great job of suggesting the desired characteristics, other audiences may not be. Egwene in "Eyes Without Pity" is forced to learn that there's no performance of her desired identity that Renna would find remotely credible. Goffman suggests that in the Western world, audiences generally *want* performances to be received in the manner desired by the performer. We'd be able to tell that Egwene wants to be taken as a confident, autonomous woman and we'd cough politely to let her know if her performance as one was slipping, giving her the opportunity to collect herself and get back on track. But no such luck in front of her singular audience in her cell in Falme.

Butler similarly stresses the gulf between performance and free play, which is suggested by the roots of the performance metaphor itself.[5] An actor might be performing a role, but she or he is channeled in a certain direction by the words on the script given by the producer, with a director waiting just out of eyesight ready to shout directions or even cut the scene if those words aren't being followed. It's not just that audiences can watch a performance and then refuse to confer onto the performer his or her desired identity, performances are actively policed as they happen, to ensure the script is stuck to, and pushed back on track when the identity suggested departs from the identity insisted on by the script. Imagine any potential abuse shouted at Min for not dressing as a woman should— abuse that would make it hard for any but the strongest woman not to comply with regulatory gendered dress codes next time she goes out into the world.

Renna's tool in this process is the pain inflicted through the *a'dam*, used not to help Egwene give her own desired performance like the polite cough suggested by Goffman, but to help Egwene better give the performance desired by Renna. This is supported further by the code she explains to Egwene in the season 2 finale, by which a woman who steps out of the role of *damane* on the battlefield first loses her tongue, then her hands. When it comes down to it, Renna's directing notes work. Egwene hesitates a moment when ordered to channel at the invading Whitecloaks, but quickly complies. The interactions between Renna and Egwene have successfully transformed the latter into the former's image of her.

## Identity and Power

Power is a key part of the interaction between Renna and Egwene. According to Robert A. Dahl (1915–2014), "A has power over B to the extent that he can get B to do something that B would not otherwise do."[6]

Without power getting involved, the performativity of identity could remain the safe, maybe even joyful free play that misreadings of Butler's first book suggest she's depicting it as.

In any society, fictional or otherwise, power appears inevitable, because societies are socially divided into groups of people that hold greater economic, political, cultural, and social resources than other groups, all of which can be used by the groups with *more* to determine, via the grip they have on key institutions, the life chances and life courses of those with *less*. In our world, these groups often form around social variables such as class, gender, and race. Of these, we see class, at least, operating in the world of *The Wheel of Time* pretty clearly, with aristocratic families like the Damodred household in Cairhien enjoying privilege and luxury in food, clothes, and an access to the royal family that's a far cry from the average character we meet elsewhere in their world. Consider also the extremely strict structure of Seanchan society, divided into the Blood, freemen, and then the *da'covale*, or "those who are property," whose numbers include the *damane*. Gender and race are a little less evident as variables leading to social division, if only, in the former case, because women who can channel enjoy a route to high status and influence via the White Tower (men not so much). The average woman living in a backwater like Emond's Field may benefit from this possibility very little, while for the Seanchan, being born as a female channeler looks like a fate worse than death by balefire.

And if power allows you to get someone to do something that they otherwise would not, it can allow you to force someone to perform a self or identity that they'd otherwise reject. Renna's as *sul'dam* is the power to have Egwene perform the role of *damane* when she would otherwise play the role of Aes Sedai. Steven Lukes argues that the deepest level of power involves having someone act according to *your* interests while fully believing that they are acting according to their own.[7] You do not then need to keep threatening someone to act in the way you want them to act, or take on the self that's useful to your purpose, because they'll get on with doing that autonomously, freeing up your attention for more important matters. I do not think this would apply to Egwene at any point during her ordeal in season 2, since she would not have existed under the Seanchan long enough to have been indoctrinated into thinking that taking on the identity of *damane* is genuinely in her interests, beyond that of immediate survival. When channeling from Falme's tower, she's submissive to Renna but clearly uncomfortable.

We might see this level of power operating in some of the *damane* extras, many of whom look, in the final two episodes of season 2, proud of their skill as living weapons, maybe even feeling that it's a genuine fulfillment of their destiny and potential as channelers. The *damane*'s own interests as a group would best be served by retaining a sense of their humanity and finding whatever way they could to resist the identity compelled onto them by the Seanchan. Instead, they are acting according to the Seanchan's interests, while seeming to take pride in a level of submission that has reduced them to chattel. I guess we do not know the level of overt, explicit power it took to get them to that point.

A key ingredient of power, institutionalized via social structures like the Seanchan class system, is the power both to *label* others and to shrug off the labels that they might want to give you in return. Labels in this sense work as scripts, determining the range of performance possibilities open to those labeled. *Damane* is a label, generated by the powerful and privileged of Seanchan society, to construct the identity of channelers in a particular way that leaves the only identity performance open to them that of slave.

Another incredibly powerful label in Seanchan society is *marath'damane*, constructing all free women who can channel as "those who must be leashed." But when labeling theorist Howard Becker (1928–2023) stresses that the label needs to be "*successfully* applied" (my emphasis), he points to the possibility that some labels people attempt to write onto others might instead fail.[8] The importance of the power dynamic between labeler and those the labeler attempts to label becomes clear when we consider that the women referred to by the Seanchan's labels might well consider themselves just "women" or "people," or the Seanchan labelers as "tyrants" or "monsters." You might also wonder what words pass through Egwene's head to label Renna when she's alone in her cell. Without the institutional power of the Seanchan state and society behind them, though, neither the *marath'damane* nor Egwene have the power to make any alternative labels last and can only exist instead with their identities under threat from the majority society's own. Any attempt a *damane* might make to escape the identity written onto them by such a label will be punished in the codified ways suggested earlier, with the full backing of Seanchan law. The first signs of a wider-scale rebellion, if such a movement could even get off the ground given the circumstances the *damane* live within, would be brutally put down by their Ever Victorious Army. Call the *sul'dam* brutalizing you a "monster" and there'd be absolutely nothing behind you to support that label, which would, therefore, have no bearing whatsoever on her identity or her future.

Anyone can create a label they'd like to use to twist the identity of anyone else; only the institutionally powerful can make them stick. Only the institutionally powerful can ensure that their labels have a lasting impact on the performed identities of those labeled.

## What's Left

What options might be left for people in situations like Egwene's in Falme, whose performed identities are so strongly corralled by the labels applied to them by people with power? In any socially divided world where people exist hierarchically positioned over or under others, are the identities of those with less power always open to manipulation by those with more? What levels of control over identity, if any, remain to those trapped, like Egwene and her fellow *damane*, within structures that aim at a complete dehumanization?

Anthony Giddens's concept of "structuration" offers a possible, if bleak, way forward.[9] The term suggests a middle ground in a long-standing debate between the two opposing concepts of "structure" and "agency." In terms of identity, the structure side of the debate suggests that our lives are shaped beyond our control by forces much bigger than us, pushing down on us from levels of the social structure far above, molding us in their own direction. The impact of the Seanchan state on the lives and identities of channelers living within their territories looks like it supports this position. The agency side suggests we always maintain much more individual control over our identities. Its most extreme supporters would argue that the large social forces pointed to by the structure side do not press down onto and shape people from above, but are themselves the sum product of the actions of the people on the ground. The Seanchan laws pressing down onto Egwene did not appear from nowhere, but are the result of individual Seanchan using their own agency to create the very social structures that produce and enforce the labels that shape the identities of the *damane*. And if large-scale social structures and social forces are created by the actions of individuals, they can be *reshaped*, in turn, by others.

I'm not sure what, if any, agency is left to the average *damane*, especially those living on the Seanchan Empire's mainland itself. But my point here is that the concept of structuration suggests a middle ground between structure or agency positions, suggesting that even when structural circumstances might present Egwene with an extremely narrow list of options, individuality still persists through the determination of which of those options is ultimately chosen. We can turn to Min as depicted in the books for a softer example of structuration in action. Once dating Rand, she begins to dress in a more feminine manner because she knows that's what he likes. This is her choice and an exercise of her own individual agency, not just in the fact that she does it, but in her continuing avoidance of skirts and dresses, meaning she does so on her own terms. Nonetheless the concept of "feminine" that she's working with is still a structurally authored force that she had no say in writing, as is the trend itself of women dressing to please male partners. Her response is a blend of structural forces and the choices she makes in navigating them.

For Egwene, the structural forces appear intensely more oppressive and ever-present and the choices available much more restrictive. But this is not necessarily to say that there are no choices at all. Graham Scambler explores some pretty bleak cases in our world where the structural forces pressing down on particular groups, like people trafficked for sex, are brutally dehumanizing, arguing, perhaps very contentiously, if accurately, there is always at least one choice left open to people in this position.[10]

This might include an extreme option potentially open to *damane* too. The choice would be for a *damane* to use whatever agency remains to end her life, taking final control of her identity to the extent that it is rescued from total erasure beneath another's dehumanizing label.

However, the power of the Seanchan over the lives and identities of the *damane* might ultimately be more intense than theories of structuration could imagine. Remember Egwene's attempt in "Eyes Without Pity" to attack Renna with the water pitcher left on the floor in front of her. She's unable even to pick it up without pain coursing through her body via the *a'dam*, Renna reminding her that "a *damane* cannot touch any object she believes to be a weapon." This means that the *damane* cannot simply pretend to be subjugated by the Seanchan labels; they cannot perform the role at a mental distance from what they regard as a true or ultimate identity lying preserved beneath the performance, hoping one day that they might find a means of striking back. The performance has to become the very reality of their identity. This takes the arguments by Goffman and Butler to their fullest extent; performance is not a consequence of an identity existing prior to that performance because identity is only ever constituted *through* performance. For the *damane*, understanding and internalizing the consequences of this is a matter of survival. A free woman performing the role of *damane* out of strategic necessity will experience pain every time she picks up a solid object; the pain will only stop once the performance has subsumed the whole of the person's identity and left no thoughts outside or beyond it.

What, then, about self-directed violence? It's still violence. So, if Egwene were to pick up a knife with the intent of using it as a weapon against herself, would the pain still kick in and debilitate her? If she tried to bang her head repeatedly against a wall, would the *a'dam* understand her as viewing the stonework as a weapon and prevent her interacting with it? The "Falme" chapter of *The Great Hunt* potentially answers these queries, confirming that a *damane* is unable to interact with any object she even thinks of as a weapon, including those she'd wish to use on herself. In the book, Egwene is unable to take a knife offered to her by Min without her arm cramping up and immobilizing her.[11] Egwene then tells Min that a *damane* is never left alone "where she might jump from a height" and that the window of her cell is nailed shut.[12] This implies that the *a'dam* itself would not prevent suicide by jumping through deeming Egwene as viewing the ground outside her cell as a self-directed weapon (else there'd be no need for the Seanchan to tailor the *damane*'s surroundings in this way). But there's still no option left of escape by suicide as long as she remains in an environment totally controlled by her captors. We can see in "Eyes Without Pity" that the window in Egwene's cell is barred, suggesting, if not confirming, that the same mechanics apply in the show (meaning both show and book *a'dam* take a reductively literal view of what constitutes a weapon that should probably be patched out on the Seanchan's next update). Either way, whether through the *a'dam* itself or through other means devised by the Seanchan, suicide as a means of escaping life as a *damane* appears all but impossible. My point here is that the structural constraints imposed by the Seanchan over the performed identities of the *damane* appear so intense that they seem to offer the purest example of a case study where suicide would be the only use of agency left. And yet the structural constraints may, from the logic we are presented with on screen, challenge arguments about structures always leaving an element of agency in their wake by presenting a social context where even this final level of agency over structural constraints on selfhood is completely denied.

Perform the role of *damane*. Understand that that's what you always were; acknowledge that you were never a person. Or …

The power of the Seanchan is evident in there not really being any conceivable way of completing that sentence.

# Notes

1. Angela Carter, *Nights at the Circus* (London: Vintage Classics, 1994), 344.
2. Irving Goffman, *The Presentation of Self in Everyday Life* (London: Penguin, 1990).
3. Goffman, *The Presentation of Self in Everyday Life*, 245.
4. Judith Butler, *Gender Trouble: Feminism and the Subversion of Identity* (London: Routledge, 2006), 201.
5. Judith Butler, *Bodies That Matter: On the Discursive Limits of Sex* (London: Routledge, 2011).
6. Robert A. Dahl, "The Concept of Power," *Behavioral Science* 2 (1957), 202–203.
7. Steven Lukes, *Power: A Radical View* (London: Red Globe Press, 2021).
8. Howard Becker, *Outsiders: Studies in the Sociology of Deviance* (London: Free Press, 2018), 1–19.
9. Anthony Giddens, *The Constitution of Society: Outline of the Theory of Structuration* (Cambridge: Polity Press, 1984).
10. Graham Scambler, *A Sociology of Blame and Shame: Insiders Versus Outsiders* (London: Palgrave, 2019), 3.
11. Robert Jordan, *The Great Hunt* (London: Orbit, 2023), chap. 42.
12. Jordan, *The Great Hunt*, chap. 42.

# Glimpsing the Pattern and Salvaging a Semblance of Choice

## *Dean A. Kowalski*

In "Dark Along the Ways," Moiraine Sedai assembles her Emond's Field charges on the eve of her desperate plan to battle the Dark One. She abruptly announces, "We leave tomorrow at sunrise." But the group is wary, and tensions are running high. Rand inquires, "Who was she? That bartender." Moiraine answers, "She sees glimpses of the Pattern, the future, and I hoped she'd tell me which of you is the Dragon, so I could save the rest." Moiraine further discloses, "I do not want you to die, any of you, but whichever of you goes to the Eye of the World and is not the Dragon … you will die there. Ground to dust between two forces of nature." She continues, "And so tomorrow I will take all of you to the Eye, knowing that three of you will not return. … I did not choose this path for myself any more than you did, but I will follow it because I must." Nynaeve remains suspicious of the Aes Sedai: "You've made your choice. But we'll make our own." To which Moiraine gravely replies, "Running, hiding … will not save you from the weaving of the Pattern. Make your decisions tonight, then. We leave at dawn."

While Min Farshaw—the bartender in question—does not divulge to Moiraine which of her charges is the Dragon Reborn, she does inform the Aes Sedai—albeit somewhat vaguely—that Perrin will become a Wolfbrother, that Egwene and Nynaeve will begin Aes Sedai training, and that the Amyrlin Seat will be Moiraine's downfall—each of which occurs, in varying degrees, in season 2. (Min also foresees Rand holding a baby, which occurs in the season 1 finale, while Ishamael retains Rand in a *Matrix*-like dream-state at the Eye of the World.)

What's more, Min subsequently informs Egwene, Perrin, and Nynaeve, "All I know is that everything I've ever seen, the best things and the worst. … They've all come true eventually" (and then has a vision of Nynaeve's skin burning from the inside out, which later happens during the defense of Fal Dara when Trollocs overrun Tarwin's Gap). But if Min can

*The Wheel of Time and Philosophy*, First Edition. Edited by Jacob M. Held.
© 2025 John Wiley & Sons, Inc. Published 2025 by John Wiley & Sons, Inc.

foresee future events and has true beliefs about those events before they happen, then presumably she already knows the outcomes. So, how could things be any different than Min had foreseen? Are the Emond's Field four (or five, if you include Mat) actually able to "make their own choices?" Are they, including Moiraine, *ever* able to choose their own destiny?

In this chapter, we will use Min as a touchstone to explore a particularly vexing philosophical question: Can foreknowledge of human events be reconciled with our acting freely in them? Philosophers are divided about how to answer this question. As we'll see, *The Wheel of Time* does not help us come any closer to an answer, but it does remind us of why the question is both important and inescapable.

## Clear and Strong Visions to Illuminate the Problem

During Moiraine's "quite invasive" interrogation-like meeting with Min at the Fal Dara tavern (in "The Dark Along the Ways"), Min intuits the struggle between the Light and the Dark over who grooms the Two Rivers troupe. She informs Moiraine, "They're all linked, all four of them. … I see sparks of light trying to fill the shadows, and the shadows trying to swallow the sparks." This metaphor, of course, becomes a dominant theme of season 2. Min continues, "For what it's worth, they are all very clear visions. Usually, the more important someone is to the Pattern, the clearer the vision."[1] In the hopes of discerning who among them is the Dragon Reborn, Moiraine asks, "Is any vision stronger than the others?" Unfortunately, Min answers, "Hmm … Not particularly."

Later that evening, Rand returns to the tavern alone, stating, "I think we got off on the wrong foot. I'm sorry, I did not even introduce myself." Min quickly replies, "I know who you are. Look me in the eye and tell me that you want to know what I've got to say. Because once you do, there's no turning back." They sit, as well they should, because she is about to recount her clearest vision, and Rand is about to discover his origins. Obviously, Min pours them a stiff drink.

Min begins by telling Rand that she was a young girl living in Tar Valon near the end of the Aiel War. One day, a soldier carrying a heron-marked blade passed her in a damp alleyway. In her words, "And when I looked at him … I saw snow and blood. I saw a baby born on the slopes of Dragonmount. The man raised him in a wooden house beside fields of sheep, in a sleepy village surrounded by two rivers. And that baby … that baby was something impossible." It remains unclear how Rand or his birth was impossible, but some things are clear, including that young Min had foreseen Rand's birth. It's also clear that Tam al'Thor is the soldier who helps the Aiel Warrior birth Rand. And Min's vision included the many choices Tam made upon assisting with the birth: raising Rand as his own child with his wife, leaving the military, becoming a sheepherder, and making a homestead near Two Rivers. Rand's importance to the Pattern as the Dragon Reborn is emphasized by the clarity of the flashbacks, leading us to believe this vision was (among) Min's clearest.[2] They are not in any way hazy, as are Min's other visions, but displayed to the viewer in hi-def!

The idea that foreknowledge of future events seems inconsistent with persons acting freely in them goes back at least as far as St. Augustine of Hippo (354–430), but early articulations of the problem can be found in Cicero (106–43 BCE) and Aristotle (384–322 BCE). In any case, unpacking the reasoning driving the intuition takes some doing. (Are you sitting down? If only Min would pour us a drink!)

The worry begins with what's required for (factual) knowledge. On standard accounts, for someone to possess knowledge, that person must have a belief, that belief must be true, and there must be justification properly supporting the true belief in question (even if philosophers disagree about the finer details of the third condition). So, if Min knows that Tam al'Thor becomes a sheepherder and raises Rand near Two Rivers when young Tam al'Thor the soldier passes her in the Tar Valon alleyway—that is, prior to any of the "Tam al'Thor-at-Two Rivers" events happening—then it was true at the time of young Min's vision that these events will, indeed, obtain. Otherwise, she could not know them at the time of her vision—that is *foreknow* them before they happen.

That insight leads to the next important step in the argument: If it is *now* true that future events obtain as Min foresees, then it seems that they *must* come to pass in accordance with Min's foreknowledge of them. If it were possible to be otherwise than the way Min has foreseen, then it could be true that Tam (aged 45) is a sheepherder and raising Rand near Two Rivers, just as Min foresees when Tam the soldier passes her in the alleyway, *and* false that Tam (aged 45) is a sheepherder and raising Rand near Two Rivers, on the supposition that events do not come to pass exactly as Min foresees—perhaps because Tam subsequently decides, contrary to young Min's vision, to stay in the military or he and his wife decide to give up the red-haired babe for adoption. But contradictory statements cannot be true together; it cannot be both that Tam at age forty-five is and is not a sheepherder raising Rand near Two Rivers.[3]

What's more, if events must come to pass as foreseen, then it is impossible for anyone to do anything different than what was foreknown about them. If it's impossible for someone to act differently than how, in fact, that person does, then that person does not act freely; free action requires the ability to do otherwise. Thus, foreknowledge of what people do in the future renders the corresponding choices unfree, which, in turn, would explain why everything Min sees—the good and the bad—eventually comes true. It *must* come true.

# Hazy and Incomplete Visions Darken the Way Forward

Yet if Min were completely honest, she would have to admit that not everything comes true *exactly* as she foresees. Imagine that Mat walks into an unfamiliar tavern soon after the events in Falme only to see Min behind the bar. After buying Min a drink, he might remind her of their last meeting, in the rented room, with Min being quite drunk. Mat would probably further remind Min that she (slurring her words) claimed, "You kill him. You kill Rand. Yeah, with that dagger—the ruby on the golden hilt. In Falme" ("Eyes without Pity"). At that point, Mat would happily report that Rand did not die, even though it was true that Mat unintentionally mortally wounded his mate. But it wasn't his fault!

Mat might explain how, prior to his being on the Falme tower, he securely attached the ruby-hilted dagger to a pole to make a spear. That way he would not touch it, and so keep himself separate from the darkness within it. Spear in hand, he intended to kill the Forsaken Ishamael. Rand was "shielded"—or something like that—by a strange channeling-woman standing in a boat off-shore, and Ishamael was about to do something nasty. So, Mat threw the spear at Ishamael to *save* Rand, but it was a trick, an illusion. Ishamael magically projected his image to make it look like he was standing in front of Rand. The spear sailed right through the fake-Ishamael and grievously pierced Rand's side. But Elayne healed him! He did not die!

After some further reminiscing, and probably a few more drinks, Min might confide in Mat that she foresaw Rand's ruby-hilted dagger-wound differently. From the first time Min and Mat met in Tar Valon—and at that point she probably would apologize again for playing her part in Liandrin Sedai's evil plot—Min saw Mat *stab* Rand with the ruby-hilted dagger; Mat was clearly holding the dagger in his hand as he thrust it into Rand's torso. Knife still in hand, Mat gently assisted Rand to the ground. What's more, in her vision, at the fatal moment, Mat and Rand were close together, almost in an embrace. Mat did *not* wound Rand by throwing a spear while standing many paces away. So, not only did Rand not die, but he was not wounded as Min had foreseen—leaving us to wonder whether everything Min has foreseen indeed comes true eventually.[4]

It's tempting to argue that because Min's visions are not always completely accurate, what she foresees does not necessarily come true; thus, her "glimpsing the pattern" does not prevent the *Wheel of Time* characters from freely choosing and deciding their own destinies. But making this move does not get to the heart of the philosophical problem. It does not address whether Min's accurate previsions of future human events render unfree any choices made in them. After all, sometimes Min's precognitions are extremely accurate. Nynaeve was indeed burned alive and mortally wounded attempting to channel the One Power while defending Fal Dara from rampaging Trollocs. Was Nynaeve able to do otherwise at Fal Dara than what Min's foreknowledge revealed? What's more, if Min did *foreknow* that Nynaeve chooses to channel dangerously at Fal Dara, then we are not any closer to determining whether Nynaeve's choice to risk her life was freely or unfreely undertaken. And note that Min's partial or incomplete visions always contain elements of truth. Once foreseen, must *those* truths come to pass? Was it within Mat's power to not pierce Rand's torso with the ruby-hilted dagger given Min's foretelling of that event?

So, even if there is something philosophically interesting about Min's visions being occasionally inaccurate, that fact alone is insufficient to dispel the worry that foreknowledge of future events is inconsistent with persons acting freely within them. More careful approaches to the problem are prudent. Only then can we get clearer about whether the Emond's Field five are in control of their own destinies.

## Glory to the Early Freedom and Foreknowledge Philosophy-Ogiers

Not surprisingly, questions about foreknowledge and human freedom often presuppose God's existence. Philosophers who believe in an all-knowing creator God are called monotheists. Monotheists are particularly motivated to reconcile divine foreknowledge with human freedom. If these cannot be reconciled, then monotheists must either curtail God's knowledge of the future to preserve moral responsibility for the choices humans make or somehow explain how God justly punishes the sins human beings commit even though we could not have done otherwise than God has foreseen. Neither task seems all that inviting.

One of the more popular reconciliation projects from the history of philosophy relies on the idea that God is an eternal and thus a timeless being. Monotheistic philosophers Boethius (477–524) and St. Thomas Aquinas (1225–1274) are notable proponents of this project. On Aquinas's formulation, God has "no before and after in Him ... nor can any succession be found in his being ... God, therefore, is without beginning and end, having his whole being at once."[5] As such, God's existence consists of no succession of activities or events. An eternal being does not begin as an infant and then mature into adulthood, because this would mean there was a time at which the being was immature and then becomes mature at a later time. Rather, eternal life is akin to one permanent and unchanging "now" completely without beginning, end, or any intermediary temporal parts or aspects.

Yet Aquinas believed that God has access to what happens in time, similar to how the center of a circle, while remaining motionless and independent, can be connected to any point on its circumference. God is the center of the circle; what happens in time are the points on its circumference. According to Aquinas, "Whatever is found in any part of time co-exists with what is eternal as being present to it, although with respect to some other time it be past or future."[6] God's eternal "gaze" is "co-present" with each point in time, regardless of whether they are past, present, or future to us. As such, an all-knowing and eternal God can access—know—*all* earthly events "all-at-once," even if from our perspective some events have slipped into the past and are no more, but others are yet to be.

So, monotheists like Aquinas argue that, technically, God does not *fore-know* anything. The alleged problem with human freedom, then, never truly arises because eternal knowledge is akin to knowledge of the present and *presently* seeing or knowing something *as it happens* does not mean that it could not have been otherwise. Understood as happening in one eternal moment, God's vision does not "lock-in" our future because God's timeless knowledge does not predate the events known. God's eternal vision infallibly encompasses our past, present, and future, but we remain responsible for the choices we freely make.

While there are references to the Creator in *The Wheel of Time*, relying on what an eternal being knows to preserve free choice in future events is not much help. The reason is simple: Min is not a timeless being. She was a young girl in Tar Valon when she had her clearest vision and is older than Rand when she shares its details with him. If Min is not a timeless being, then her foreknowledge of events obviously predates their existence. If those future events include what humans (will) choose to do, it remains unclear whether persons act freely in them.

An alternative reconciliation project attempts to clarify the order of explanation between the choices we make and what is known—including foreknown—about them. This project began with Augustine, who explored the problem with his dialogue partner Evodius. Evodius, also a mono-theist, fears that the problem is unsolvable: God's perfect knowledge of the future is inconsistent with God's moral perfection, because it is unjust to punish those God has foreknown will sin; the sinners could not have done otherwise than God has infallibly foreseen.

Augustine attempts to put Evodius's mind at ease. He begins by asking whether human freedom is in conflict with foreknowledge of our choices or with God's foreknowledge of them. When Evodius answers God's fore-knowledge creates the conflict, Augustine subsequently inquires, "Well then, if *you* foreknew someone was going to sin, would it not be necessary that he sin?"[7] Evodius admits that if he, although not divine, foreknew someone was going to sin, then that person must sin when the time comes. The two agree, then, that foreknowledge (itself) causes the problem.

Augustine invites Evodius to continue rethinking his position by pointing out to his friend: "Unless I am mistaken, you would not force someone to sin as a result of foreknowing that he is going to sin. Nor would your foreknowledge force him to sin, despite the fact that he undoubtedly *is* going to sin, since otherwise you would not *foreknow* that it is going to be so."[8] Augustine contends that knowing something to be true does not entail that the knower causes that truth to obtain. If anything, the order of explanation runs in the opposite direction: the truths that do obtain, one way or another, cause someone to have knowledge. Augustine utilizes the example of memory to substantiate this point. The fact that you remember something did not cause that thing to happen; rather, because it happened, you (are able to) remember it. Likewise, what someone foreknows is explained by what will happen, not vice versa. Because one's choices are prior in the order of explanation, foreknowledge does not determine the future; rather future events determine one's foreknowledge of them. And with that insight, the alleged problem with foreknowledge disappears.

Augustine's reconciliation project pertains to any supposed knower: Evodius, you, God—and, importantly, Min. And it does not require the knower to be a timeless being. All it requires is that the supposed knower— the person possessing foreknowledge—be properly situated to facts about the future. Min's ability to glimpse the pattern is singular and almost certainly mystical, but there is some sort of unnamed mechanism that allows her to peer into the future. Consequently, what Min foreknows is explained by how people choose to act in the future, not vice versa, providing a glimmer of philosophical hope that the Emond's Field five (and Moiraine) are able to shape their own destinies.[9]

Yet even the most skillful philosophical Ogier-like construction, regardless of all due admiration and respect for the builder, has its detractors. Some skeptics object to Augustine's project because it seemingly requires an odd sort of cause-and-effect relationship. For example, Augustine would have us believe that Tam's future choice of adopting Rand and raising him near Two Rivers causes Min to know these things about Tam and Rand when Tam-the-soldier passes her in the Tar Valon alleyway; otherwise, she could not *fore*know them. This means that effects occur chronologically prior to their causes. What's more, it means that things that do not yet exist have causal powers. Both implications are implausible. If they cannot be explained away, they are damaging to Augustine's project.

Other skeptics argue that Augustine's project entails human beings, when making free choices, have the ability to change the past. The idea is that if Tam's choices to leave the military, adopt Rand, and raise sheep near Two Rivers are freely made when he makes them, then up to the times of those decisions, it remains within Tam's power to stay in the military, give Rand away for adoption, and reside in Tar Valon. If he were to exercise his free will and opt for any of those alternatives, then his doing so results in either falsifying Min's true belief about what Tam aged forty-five will do or altering Min's foreknowledge about what Tam aged forty-five will do.

Yet Min's true belief and foreknowledge of what Tam aged forty-five will do have been in place for decades—since Tam-the-soldier passed young Min in the Tar Valon alleyway. That young Min believed this about Tam, and that her belief is true are historical facts. So, Tam's exercising his free will would result in altering facts about the past—making a previously held true belief false, or somehow altering the content of one's foreknowledge. Because it is within no one's power to change the past—what's done is done—then human beings cannot do otherwise than has been foreknown about them, despite Augustine's best efforts to reconcile freedom and foreknowledge. Unless this counterintuitive result can be explained away, other reconciliation projects must be sought.[10]

## *The Wheel of Time*'s Thematic Spins Cloud Its Message

*The Wheel of Time* television series complicates typical philosophical discussions of freedom and foreknowledge. Things begin well enough with Min's claim that everything she sees comes true eventually, which sets the familiar stage. Plus, the Aes Sedai are secretive about Min's abilities, bolstering the idea that her mystical powers are both impressive and reliable; Moiraine visits her at Fal Dara because she believes Min can foresee who the Dragon is even if currently this is undetermined. But the complications thereafter multiply, beginning with the obvious thematic fact that Min is a human being and, thus, not timeless. What's more, Min's foreknowledge seems limited in scope, evidently consisting of seeing only the futures of people who come into direct physical contact with her. And, perhaps most problematic of all, Min's alleged foreknowledge seems fallible in that future events do not always turn out exactly as she has foreseen, despite her autobiographical assertion that everything she sees eventually comes true.

These complications come to the foreground with Min's vision that Mat kills Rand with the ruby-handled dagger. She clearly believes her vision is true, but she is mistaken. Rand is not stabbed, but pierced with a spear, and survives the wound. What to make of this? Is the series suggesting that Mat, perhaps counterintuitively, has some mystical ability to change the past? (Doubtful, but he is able to magically rematerialize the Heroes of the Horn, which is a pretty neat trick.) Let us note that if Min's foreknowledge were infallible, as God's is traditionally believed to be, then it would be impossible for Mat to do anything that would result in Min having a false belief, thereby upholding a venerable (and thorny) aspect of the freedom and foreknowledge problem. Maybe the point is simply to remind us that Min is human and thus fallible. But this leaves us with no way to discern the difference between when Min actually foreknows something and when she does not, which makes one wonder why Moiraine desperately seeks her out to identify the Dragon Reborn (to say nothing of Min's claim that everything she sees eventually comes true).

It might be, though, that Min's foreknowledge is a microcosm of *The Wheel of Time's* ambiguous message about fate, freedom, and human destiny. If there is a tagline for the series, surely it is: the Wheel weaves as the Wheel wills. (In the novels, the tagline is more ominous: the Wheel weaves as the Wheel wills and we are only a thread of the Pattern.) If all that exists, metaphysically speaking, is "the Wheel," which is turning from one moment into the next in perpetuity, then each of us is woven into its Pattern, regardless of the design that thereby results. Weaves do not spin the Wheel; they are woven by its spinning. Putting aside the question of what it means for the Wheel to will anything—a topic worthy of its own chapter—if the futures of the Wheel characters are part of the woven design, then this jeopardizes their ability to make their own choices and thus shape their own destinies.

Yet, for the sake of building dramatic tension—to draw us into its characters—*The Wheel of Time* filmmakers also spin yarns that counteract a straightforward fatalistic interpretation of the show. They create characters who struggle mightily against fate and other impersonal forces that shape their destinies. These characters act to shape their own destinies, regardless of what the Wheel "wills to weave"—including whatever Min "glimpses" about its future designs.

The two opposing dramatic themes of the series are emphasized by two exchanges involving the Amyrlin Seat. The first has Siuan chiding Nynaeve and Egwene for their reluctance to take part in the Last Battle: "The Wheel … does not care if you are young or afraid, petty or weak. It certainly does not care what you want. The Wheel calls you to this. Whether you can bear it or not" ("The Flame of Tar Valon"). The Amyrlin Seat clearly calls Nynaeve and Egwene to struggle against the forces working against them; she implores them to do their part to shape the future, because "all that matters is what you do." The second has Siuan schooling Rand about his role in the pending Last Battle as the Dragon Reborn. Rand exclaims, "What kind of a choice is that? Dying or going mad and killing everyone I love? What if I'm tired of being a spoke in the Wheel?" To which Siuan gruffly replies, "You're not a spoke, boy. You are the water that turns the Wheel itself or dashes it to pieces" ("Daes Dae-mar"). Here, Siuan is clear: Rand is not merely someone who is turned by the Wheel, some spoke or weave subjected to its spinning Pattern—but someone who can exert agency to determine how it spins, including whether it keeps spinning at all.[11] Nevertheless, Min is somehow able to "glimpse" Nynaeve, Egwene, and Rand as weaves of the emerging Pattern and mystically foresee the future design for each—just not always perfectly so, which, of course, draws us further into our favorite characters.

As *The Wheel of Time* continues to spin, so do its efforts to make us see its rich characters as both free and fated—their actions are their own, but also mystically foreseen and, perhaps, fated. This might make for good storytelling, but at the expense of always conveying a clear and consistent philosophical message. Maybe that's okay. It is a story first and foremost, albeit one that raises lots of interesting philosophical questions, putting its own spin on how to think through them.

## The End as the Beginning

Perhaps there is a deeper message about the alure of *The Wheel of Time*. After Moiraine divulges her desperate plan to the Emond's Field four on the eve of battling the Dark One at the Eye of the World, she retires wearily to her room. She seems crestfallen, but Lan is there to comfort and reassure her, "You've given them a semblance of choice. That's all they need."

This insightful consolation is not merely limited to Moiraine's charges. It pertains to the viewer and, indeed, speaks to the human condition. We recoil at threats to our freedom—be they political, psychological, genetic, or as they are expressed here, metaphysical. *The Wheel of Time* thus reminds us of how important it is for us to feel as if we are making our own decisions—our choices shape our destinies, not vice versa. This psychological need is undeniable and part and parcel of what makes life meaningful. As such, we would do well to remember Lan's sage advice. Seek avenues and strategies—including philosophical—that will secure one's sense of free will. In this, we do what we can to keep the wheel turning. Even partial success is welcome. We will settle for a semblance of choice if need be—without it, the challenges life presents us may be too much to bear.

## Notes

1. In the book series, Perrin, Mat, and Rand being *ta'veren* is emphasized regularly. Being *ta'veren*, one around whom the pattern is woven, can alter events, and in many ways determine one's future as if it were fated.
2. Although not a foretelling, recall that the blind Gitara Sedai (in "Daes Dae'mar") has a mystical experience of Rand's birth on Dragonmount, further emphasizing the importance of the Dragon Reborn. For some reason, Min does not explicitly state Rand is the Dragon Reborn, but the context makes it safe to assume she knows this to be true.
3. There is nothing special about Tam being forty-five years old, but it is easier to understand how the alleged problem forms if some specific age is chosen.
4. Pop culture aficionados of a certain age might wonder whether Rand died for an instant, reminiscent of how The Master technically fulfilled Slayer prophecy by momentarily killing Buffy (in season 1 of *Buffy the Vampire Slayer*), only for Xander to quickly resuscitate her; however, at no point was Rand unconscious as Elayne healed his wound.
5. Saint T. Aquinas, *Summa Contra Gentiles Book I*, trans. Anton Pegis (Notre Dame: University Press of Notre Dame, 1975), 98.

6. Aquinas, *Summa Contra Gentiles*, 219.

7. Saint Augustine, *On Free Choice of the Will, On Grace and Free Choice, and Other Writings*, trans. Peter King (Cambridge: Cambridge University Press, 2010), 80, emphasis original.

8. Augustine, *On Free Choice of the Will*, 80, emphasis original.

9. Augustine provides only the rudiments of this sort of reconciliation project. English philosopher William of Ockham (1287–1347) and Spanish Jesuit Luis de Molina (1535–1600) offer more robust and (arguably) defensible accounts.

10. For an accessible contemporary discussion of this objection, see William Hasker, *The Openness of God* (Downers Grove: Intervarsity Press, 1994), 126–154. Those sympathetic to Augustine-influenced reconciliation projects sometimes counter by appealing to Ockham's distinction between facts completely about the past ("hard" facts) and those that include references to the future ("soft" facts).

11. The paradoxical nature of what is woven that also does the weaving is intriguingly conveyed in season 2 in another way. It seems that Rand acts autonomously throughout season 2 as he makes his way to Falme, but Moiraine represents the ancient prophecy of how the Dragon Reborn will announce himself. As Rand makes his decisions, Moiraine, and by extension, the ancient prophecy, seems to be guiding him toward its fulfillment, including the incredible fire-show of a dragon wrapping itself around the Falme tower in the season 2 finale. Is there any genuine sense in which Rand and Moiraine brought about this climatic end when all of it was prophesied long ago?

**11**

# Their Choice to Make: Rand's Vision of Free Will and Evil

## *Jacob M. Held*

The denouement of fifteen books and more than four million words is the Last Battle, waged near the end of *A Memory of Light*. At Shayol Ghul, Rand confronts the Dark One. Since the first book, the reader has been anticipating this, the coming of *Tarmon Gai'don*, the confrontation between the dark and the light, the Dark One and the Dragon Reborn. The reader has been offered plenty of material, and time, to ruminate on the breaking of the world and the possible breaking of the Wheel itself. However, this final confrontation is marked not by an epic sword fight or other sword and sorcery spectacle, but by a struggle of competing visions of what might be. And Rand's victory does not come by destroying the Dark One. Rand does not eliminate evil. In a brilliant recapitulation of the classic freewill defense in response to the theological and philosophical problem of evil, Rand recognizes that the light needs the dark and that good needs evil, or at least the possibility of evil.

## Something to Make Your Soul Weep

There is evil in the world. At least, there are circumstances that no reasonable human being could call anything other than tragic, unfortunate, undesirable, painful. ... Any village wisdom could recount numerous examples: children dying of break bone fever, drought and famine, wolf attacks, and so on. How does one reconcile such seemingly undeserved and random suffering with a perfect creator.[1] Shouldn't we be safe if we walk in the Light? To simply say "The Wheel weaves as the Wheel wills," is as hollow an assurance as "God works in mysterious ways."

David Hume (1711–1776) notes in his *Dialogues Concerning Natural Religion* that "Epicurus's old questions are yet unanswered. Is [God] willing to prevent evil, but not able? then is he impotent. Is he able, but not willing? then is he malevolent. Is he both able and willing? whence then is evil?"[2]

*The Wheel of Time and Philosophy*, First Edition. Edited by Jacob M. Held.
© 2025 John Wiley & Sons, Inc. Published 2025 by John Wiley & Sons, Inc.

In a more modern accounting, Albert Camus (1913–1960), in *The Plague*, approaches the issue from the perspective of a Catholic priest administering to a plague-stricken city, including a young child who suffers greatly and dies. The priest claims that God is beyond comprehension and deserves our love even in the face of this evil. One of the men assisting the priest retorts: "Until my dying day I shall refuse to love a scheme of things in which children are put to torture."[3] Nynaeve surely has myriad similar accounts, and her response would be no less acerbic. The fact of evil, or at least what we, reasonably, perceive as evil, is evidence against the explanatory hypothesis that the world is the construct of a benevolent, all-powerful creator. Those convinced by such evidence deduce: evil persists, so God is either incompetent or non-benevolent. Yet it's not so cut and dry.

Throughout the history of ideas there have been many attempts to resolve the problem of evil. St. Thomas Aquinas (1225–1274) offers the argument that what one perceives as evil is redeemed through God's perfect plan.[4] St. Augustine (354–430), reiterating the lesson of the book of Job, notes that the problem of evil is generated by one's perspective. Augustine reminds his reader that she cannot see the whole. It is a human being's limited perspective that leads her to believe that what is truly good in God's grand scheme is evil. Sounding like Moiraine discussing the impenetrability of the Pattern or the inscrutability of an ancient prophecy, Augustine points to our ignorance as argument against a hasty judgment regarding the nature of reality. Suffering, as "evil" in this regard, is more indicative of human ignorance than a flaw in creation, and God does not owe us an account of creation and its goodness.[5] The real question is "am I glad that I am alive? Or is my existence, on the whole, something which I regret."[6] From this point of view, the problem of evil could be articulated as an expression of resentment. Humans resent being mortal. We resent being finite and limited. We despair of our inability to be anything we want or everything we desire, and so lament our finitude and resent creation. But Augustine reminds us, we are ineluctably human. We cannot change the fundamental reality of our condition. We are finite, we are temporal, and we are embodied. As one scholar expresses the sentiment: "The idea of a world without evil, is the idea of a world without differentiation and finiteness. It is, in short, a self-contradiction and an absurdity, and to create an absurdity is not the mark of omniscience, nor is it a limitation of power to be unable to produce a self-contradiction."[7]

Simply put, when it comes to someone claiming to know how evil plays a role in the world, "we must ask him why he thinks he is in a position to know things of this sort. We might remind him of the counsel of epistemic humility that was spoken to Job out of the whirlwind: ... Knowest thou the ordinances of heaven? Canst thou set the dominion thereof in the earth?"[8] Can you see the weaves in the Pattern? Yet, even if we cede this point,[9] we can still look at the evil people do. We can wonder why God would make humans such that they are able to choose to do wicked things.

Why allow people to be Darkfriends, to destroy cities, nations, worlds? Even if suffering is a part of human life, could not the creator have made people such that they do not want to be or do what is wicked, brutal, callous, and mean?

## The Path of Righteousness: The Freewill Defense

To begin, we should state some basics. The existence of free will presumes that human beings have choice, that is, we decide and have the ability to act on intentions without coercion or compulsion. In so doing, we choose to sin, or not. We choose to commit heinous, immoral acts, or not. The existence of this capacity carries with it culpability. Insofar as we are the authors of our actions, we are deserving of praise or blame. In addition, since we are responsible for our actions, we have an obligation to act rightly, that is, both to behave as free individuals in a way consistent with our nature as free and to treat others as free beings worthy of respect.

The freewill defense to the problem of evil responds to evil by claiming that humans abuse their freedom and in so doing choose to do evil things. The Forsaken were once Aes Sedai and chose to serve the Dark One. "People make evil choices, and God is not at fault for this."[10] It boils done to a simple notion: "About free choice we know the essentials: I can choose evil for no other reason or motive than that I choose evil. Some apparently do."[11] If God were to remove the capacity for choice from human beings, God would be removing culpability from human beings. Humans would cease to be moral agents, and would instead become mere automatons. Thus, the freewill defense maintains that the existence of free will is itself a good, regardless of consequence. As Alvin Plantinga notes, "A world containing creatures who are significantly free … is more valuable … than a world containing no free creatures at all. … God can create free creatures, but He cannot *cause* or *determine* them to do only what is right. For if He does so, then they aren't significantly free after all."[12] If we value agency, we value choice. Thus, the freewill defense rests, ultimately, on a value claim: that human freedom is better to have than not. As a value claim, it requires justification. One must be prepared to account for the value of freedom, especially if the cost of freedom is suffering and evil.

If we begin from a theistic perspective, as does *The Wheel of Time* and most traditions responding to the problem of evil, then we readily find an answer. We may begin, with Augustine, by simply recognizing that human beings have been endowed with freedom of the will, and then speculate as to the value or reason for why they were so endowed. Augustine notes that freedom allows humankind to be amenable to rule by rational command, that is, we can abide by laws insofar as they appeal to our rationality and we have the wherewithal to obey.[13] Free will allows us to choose to do what is right, but it also makes us susceptible to defect. Although we are created with free will so that we can obey the law, we are not "supremely" and "immutably" good. As created beings we are corruptible. As Augustine notes, "When … a thing is corrupted, its corruption is evil because it is, by just so much, a privation of the good."[14] One may recall Loial's disgust at the Blight as he travels to see the Green Man. What he reviles is not the presence of evil, but the destruction, the corruption, of the good.

In human beings, this corruption is expressed through the will, through our freely choosing sin as opposed to righteousness. Sin is committed in assenting to what is wrong, and we may fall into sin for various reasons, such as weakness or ignorance.[15] For a philosopher and theologian like Augustine, God's grace affords us the ability to avoid sin, but we are culpable for evil insofar as we consent to it. This consent may be intending to so act or even failing to suppress the desire for what we know to be wrong.[16] One can see freedom in this sense in *The Eye of the World*. As Rand finds himself struggling against an evil force he identifies as Ba'alzamon, Moiraine provides this guidance: "There are limits to the Dark One's power inside you. Yield even for an instant and he will have a string tied to your heart, a string you may never be able to cut. Surrender, and you will be his. Deny him, and his power fails."[17] As Rand struggles through this conflict he asserts, "I deny you, you have no power over me, and I will not kneel to you, alive or dead."[18] Here we see, "[t]he possibility of the evil is bound up with the possibility of the good, and the one cannot exist without the other."[19] Rand could not be righteous were it not possible for him to give in to the Dark One. Freedom is the precondition for the existence of good as well as evil. Yet, this approach is an explicitly religious account of freedom and its value, one tied up with a contentious metaphysics. If one is sympathetic to religious accounts, one can explain the value of free will with reference to God and those "spiritual struggles that lead to spiritual strengthening,"[20] a form of soul-making theodicy articulated by John Hick.[21] This is reminiscent of the Tinkers who "accept and endure" the "suffering sent to test" them.[22] One could speculate alongside Augustine, Aquinas, and other theologians that perhaps it is all for the good in God's most perfect plan. But another way to understand the value of freedom is to contemplate the alternative: domination and compulsion.

## They Still Fought

Freedom seems like an absolute value. But if having free will means that we will sometimes choose poorly and thereby harm ourselves or others, would not it be better to remove choice and ensure a positive outcome? Let us presume, like good Aes Sedai, that we know what the proper outcome is, so we do not have any epistemic qualms about asserting our will, merely an ethical quandary. So phrased, the problem of evil and the freewill defense come down to a matter of the value of choice. Appreciating the value of choice is more easily done in juxtaposition to the alternatives: domination, subjugation, and compulsion.

The world of *The Wheel of Time* is full of cases of domination. The reader sees numerous examples of challenges to freedom, both meta-physical and political. We see Whitecloaks and their fundamentalist pseudo-theocracy. We are faced with the forced gentling of male chan-nelers by the authoritarian and (ironically) paternalistic Aes Sedai. Compulsion is a reviled abuse of the One Power because it dehumanizes those against whom it's used, and indicates the misanthropic, vile character of the user, of whom the most notable is Graendal. The Seanchan's use of the *a'dam* is unambiguously wicked, a form of domination denying the humanity of those enslaved, not to mention their invasion and attempted conquest of the mainland. In addition, characters such as Mat routinely lament fate and recalcitrantly attempt to assert their wills against the weaving of the Pattern. In all these cases, the reader feels for the character being so manipulated. It's an infringement of their autonomy, their agency, and thus a degradation of their personhood. We see what human life looks like when free people are denied their autonomy. We are repulsed when one's fundamental humanity is denied by one's will being manipulated and distorted, as in the case of Egwene being forced to wear the *a'dam*. Something is fundamentally amiss when one's ability to choose is itself removed, if one is denied choice in the metaphysical sense, that is, if one loses one's free will. To better illustrate this point, we can look to Rand and the Dark One's competing visions during their confrontation in the Last Battle. It is through these visions that both Rand and the reader learn about the value of free will.

The competing visions begin near the end of *A Memory of Light* and continue over several hundred pages. We will not recapitulate all the details here, but the major themes will be illustrative. The Dark One begins by showing Rand what will be once the dark is victorious, using shadowed threads of the Pattern to weave one possibility. In this world, Rand sees misery and blight, but one striking observation is that when he interacts with people in this vision he notices, "The eyes were all wrong."[23] In this world the Wheel was broken and rewoven so that all would believe the Dark One had always ruled. Manipulated thusly, all, even his friends, have turned to the Shadow. The corruption is total and Rand notices there is something inhuman about them after they have been so manipulated. Rand responds, weaving his vision of "paradise." It's a vision of victory, but the Dark One taunts him, pointing out that it is a weak vision, and that people will still suffer, they will still die. As Rand notes, it is better, but the Dark One strikes again.

The second vision of the Dark One recapitulates themes from the first. The Dark One, manipulating the Pattern, allows everyone to think they won the Last Battle, even though the Dark One was truly victorious. In this vision, Rand sees utter lack of compassion and common humanity as he witnesses a child shot to death for stealing a peach. The Dark One explains that this is a world with no good or evil, but rather only the Dark One. Convincing them that they had won removes their will for rebellion, and so he can rule as a tyrant, unopposed and without resistance. Rand sees this vision for what it is, a further perversion of humanity. Something is lacking, or diminished, in human beings manipulated thusly. Rand lashes out with a vision of his own, one of a world without the Dark One.

Rand's final vision is the true denouement of the struggle; it's an epiphany for Rand and the reader regarding the nature of evil. When Rand first begins to weave this possibility the threads "resist." He's not sure what that means. It may be not that this is a difficult or unlikely possibility, but rather one so far outside the strictures of creation that it violates fundamental natural laws. Perhaps in trying to weave a world without shadow Rand is trying to re-create creation itself in a pattern beyond the divine plans of the Creator. Regardless, Rand weaves a possibility of a world without shadow. He envisions a paradise, where all have what they need, there are no weapons, there is no war, there's no currency or money, and no borders. It's truly an idyllic, and naive, vision of reality. The threads resist, and Rand discerns why. Not only is reality recalcitrant to flights of fancy, but there's something missing in a world without the dark. When he sees Elayne in this vision she is "simpering" and "vapid." Aviendha, the fierce, independent Aiel warrior, spends her days playing games with children. Behind their eyes Rand sees a shadow, as if they had been turned to the dark. They behave like those compelled. Rand deduces the nature of the problem quickly. He has removed the Shadow and so he has removed choice. He has removed the possibility of people deciding to be good, of them building character amid challenges and temptations. When Rand removes the Shadow from the Pattern, he alters what it means to be a human being, he diminishes the capacity for goodness, righteousness, and greatness. The Dark One removed the light in his visions and it altered people to be less than human, to be callous monsters. Rand removed the Shadow, and it equally diminished them. They might not be callous monsters, but only because they have no option of being so.

The people of this vision do not choose kindness. They do not choose decency. The world simply is structured in such a way that decency is the only option. Every need is met, and every whim indulged. All is easy and freely given. These people twitter away their days going through the motions. It's a pain-free life, but it's seemingly meaningless. These are not "good" people. We have no reason to believe they are "good," for they have never had an opportunity to choose between options. These are not moral agents; these are complacent automatons. These are not Rand's friends and our heroes. There must be another way. The Dark One does offer a final vision of oblivion, but Rand quickly dismisses it.[24]

In the end, Rand comes to an important realization: freedom is essential to the human condition. Free will is necessary for the possibility of humans to be good, and is a precondition for love and worthwhile relationships. A perfect illustration of this occurs at the end of season 1 of the Amazon Prime series. As Rand struggles against Ishamael at the Eye of the World he is tempted with a vision of a potential future life back in Emond's Field. In this vision, Rand and Egwene are married and carry on a pastoral life in an idyllic paradise. But Rand sees through the vision. It may be what he wants, but he knows it is not what Egwene wants. She wants to go the White Tower; she wants to be Aes Sedai. His vision is not one of paradise, or true love, because it is predicated on denying Egwene the future of her choosing. Since this life would be based on manipulation, it would not be real love, for love is only valuable when freely and reciprocally given, and this demands free will.

## We Would Not Be Human If There Wasn't a Balance

We are corruptible beings. That is our nature. As such, when we call a person evil and attribute blame, it is because we recognize that the evil done by human beings is a result of choice; the evil person decides to choose evil.[25] One cannot abrogate one's responsibility. The Dark One does not make you do it. No one becomes a Darkfriend accidentally. We choose. If a creator had wanted us to only choose the good and had thus created us such that the good was our only possibility, as we see in Rand's vision without the Dark One, then it would be the creator who "chooses" for us. Choice presumes the ability to veer from the good. Rand sees this clearly. He could, perhaps, slay the Dark One. He could remove the Shadow from the Pattern, but in so doing he would remove the capacity for his friends, for all people, to choose to be good. He would remove their capability to develop a moral character, even if this means accepting that some will use this capacity for evil. In the final struggle, Rand hears Tam's voice: "Let go. … Let them sacrifice. … It is their choice to make." Rand resists, but hears Egwene, "Let us die for what we believe, and do not try to steal that from us."[26] So he will let them be heroes, he will let them choose and in so choosing live their lives their way.

In this struggle, Rand learns a valuable lesson. The Dark One is a force, a force of corruption. It is the darkness between lights.[27] Recapitulating Augustine, we see that evil is a privation, an absence of the good. Evil is also necessary, as there cannot be light without dark. The evil that people do is a choice to deviate from the good. Our nature is corruptible, but we have the choice to open ourselves up to grace, to strive for the light and to choose the good. The decision to be moral, to do the virtuous thing, is of no value if the alternatives, wickedness and cowardice, aren't also options. As Augustine notes, "This, then, is true liberty: the joy that comes in doing what is right."[28] This is our lot, and so long as it is, there will be heroes and cowards, there will be saints and sinners, there will be good and evil.

To wish otherwise is to wish humanity to be other than it is, to give in to misanthropy; to hate humanity for the failing of some by myopically focusing on depravity and ignoring heroism and decency. Can Egwene be a hero if Rand removes her choice, her ability to sacrifice herself? Can we be better people the next time we are spit out by the Wheel if we lack the ability to choose to be worse?

We may wonder, getting back to the crux of the freewill defense to the problem of evil, why the creator would make the world this way at all? Why make the world a fallen place where humans must struggle? We could speculate as some have, "For God judges it better to bring good out of evil than to not permit any evil to exist."[29] For those disposed to accept religious responses or speculative metaphysical conjectures this may be enough. For others, it will not be. But for those not open to religious or metaphysical accounts what could justify the existence of human life? Why is it better to exist rather than not? If we were Ishamael, if we were anti-natalists or nihilists, we might prefer the void. But maybe, alongside Albert Camus, we recognize that "whether life is or is not worth living amounts to answering the fundamental question of philosophy."[30] And, in the end, "[t]he struggle itself toward the heights is enough to fill a man's heart."[31] We struggle onward because that is our lot, and insofar as we are going to struggle we ought to do so for the good. Perhaps all this philosophizing is just after-the-fact rationalization to appease our need for an answer to the problem of ineluctable human suffering, an attempt to avoid despair. One can travel down the rabbit hole of existentialist quandaries if one so desires. As far as philosophical theories go, the freewill defense may provide a meaningful way to engage an inescapable fact of human existence: there is good and evil, light and dark, and we cannot, nor should we desire to, escape the responsibility of choice. There would not be, nor could there be, good without the possibility of evil or heroes without the possibility of cowards. Choice is essential to human greatness, even if it opens up the possibility of wickedness. As far as why the Creator chose to make the world this way instead of some alternative, Moiraine, as usual, has a response: No one knows the Great Pattern the Wheel weaves.

# Notes

1. In the *Wheel of Time* universe, it is unclear whether the Creator should have attributed to it the same properties normally affiliated with the Judeo-Christian God, namely, omniscience, omnipotence, and moral perfection. For the sake of this chapter, we can presume they are similar. I do not believe anything in the following discussion is dependent on a particular concept of divinity.
2. David Hume, "Dialogues Concerning Natural Religion," in J.C.A. Gaskin ed., *Principal Writings on Religion Including Dialogues Concerning*

*Natural Religion and the Natural History of Religion* (Oxford: Oxford University Press, 1993), 100.

3. Albert Camus, from *The Plague*, anthologized as, "Physical Suffering and the Justice of God," in Michael L. Peterson ed., *The Problem of Evil: Selected Readings* (Notre Dame: University of Notre Dame Press, 1992), 78.

4. See Jacques Maritain, *St. Thomas and the Problem of Evil: The Aquinas Lecture* (Milwaukee: Marquette University Press, 1942).

5. See William E Mann, "Augustine on Evil and Original Sin," in Eleonore Stump and Norman Kretzmann eds., *The Cambridge Companion to Augustine* (Cambridge: Cambridge University Press, 2001), 45.

6. William Hasker, "On Regretting the Evils of This World," in Michael L. Peterson ed., *The Problem of Evil: Selected Readings* (Notre Dame: University of Notre Dame Press, 1992), 154.

7. Errol E. Harris, *The Problem of Evil: The Aquinas Lecture 1977* (Milwaukee: Marquette University Publications, 1977), 42.

8. Peter van Inwagen, "The Problem of Evil, the Problem of Air, and the Problem of Silence," in William L. Rowe ed., *God and the Problem of Evil* (Oxford: Wiley Blackwell, 2001), 218.

9. In the literature, there is a distinction to be made between evil resulting from human choice and natural evil, such as hurricanes, earthquakes, disease, famine. … What follows looks at the issue from the perspective of free will and does not delve deeply into the issue of natural evil. I have addressed this aspect of the debate elsewhere. See C. Taylor Sutton and Jacob M. Held, "There Is No God in Desperation: Tak and the Problem of Evil," in Jacob M Held ed., *Stephen King and Philosophy* (Lanham: Rowman & Littlefield, 2016), 13–34. For additional readings see: *The Problem of Evil*, ed. Michael L. Peterson (Notre Dame: University of Notre Dame Press, 1992); *God and the Problem of Evil*, ed. William L. Rowe (Malden: Blackwell, 2001); *The Problem of Evil*, ed. Marilyn McCord Adams and Robert Merrihew Adams (Oxford: Oxford University Press, 1990).

10. James S. Spiegel, "On Free Will and Soul Making: Contemporary Approaches to the Problem of Evil," *Philosophia Christi* 13 (2011), 406.

11. Malachi Martin, *Hostage to the Devil: The Possession and Exorcism of Five Contemporary Americans* (New York: HarperCollins, 1976), 26.

12. From Alvin Plantinga, *God, Freedom, and Evil* (Grand Rapids: Eerdmans, 1974), 30, Cited in Spiegel, "On Free Will and Soul Making.

13. See Saint Augustine, *Enchiridion on Faith, Hope, and Love*, trans. and ed. Albert C. Outler (Grand Rapids: Christian Classics Ethereal Library, 1999), chap. VIII.

14. Augustine, *Enchiridion on Faith, Hope, and Love*, chap. IV.

15. Augustine, *Enchiridion on Faith, Hope, and Love*, chap. XXII.

16. Mann, "Augustine on Evil and Original Sin," 45.

17. Robert Jordan, *The Eye of the World* (New York: Tom Doherty Associates, 1990), 675.

18. Jordan, *The Eye of the World*, 793.

19. Dom M. Pontifex, *Providence and Freedom* (London: Hawthorn Books, 1960), 58.

20. Adam Blai, *The Exorcism Files: True Stories of Demonic Possession* (Manchester: Sophia Institute Press, 2022), 7.

21. See Spiegel, "On Free Will and Soul Making."

22. Robert Jordan, *The Shadow Rising*, Vol. 420 (New York: Tom Doherty Associates, 1993), 415, respectively.
23. Robert Jordan, *A Memory of Light* (New York: Tom Doherty Associates, 2012), 817.
24. In this vision there is nothing but the void. Rand notes that the end of existence is not peace. He values existence, so he is not tempted by the "anti-natalism" of the Dark One.
25. Immanuel Kant, *Religion Within the Limits of Reason Alone*, trans. Theodore M. Greene and Hoyt H. Hudson (New York: Harper Torch Books, 1960), 16.
26. Jordan, *A Memory of Light*, 1018–1019.
27. Jordan, *A Memory of Light*, 1021.
28. Augustine, *Enchiridion on Faith, Hope, and Love*, chap. IX.
29. Augustine, *Enchiridion on Faith, Hope, and Love*, chap. VIII.
30. Albert Camus, "The Myth of Sisyphus," in Gordon Marion ed., *Basic Writings of Existentialism* (New York: The Modern Library, 2004), 441.
31. Camus, *Basic Writings of Existentialism*, 492.

# ONE RULE, ABOVE ALL OTHERS ...

**12**

# Kantian Commentary on the Three Oaths: "It Just May Not Be the Truth You Think You'll Hear"

*Dean A. Kowalski*

Rand Al'Thor confides in his new innkeeper acquaintance Dana, "I just always done what I thought was right, then moved on to the next thing and tried to do right again. But now … I do not know. I do not know what's right. I do not know what to do" ("A Place of Safety"). It's understandable that Rand is feeling unsure of himself. He's witnessed a devastating attack on his hometown, and the attackers—fearsome Trollocs led by mysterious Fades—doggedly continue pursuing him and his Two Rivers friends. But you do not need your world turned upside down by eight-foottall snarling monsters or hooded eyeless ghouls to wonder whether you are doing the right thing. In fact, philosophers have been pondering the nature of right and wrong for a long time.

In this chapter, we'll explore the German philosopher Immanuel Kant's (1724–1804) ideas about distinguishing right from wrong, including when people are properly praised or blamed for their choices. We'll apply Kant's ideas to the ways in which the Aes Sedai uphold the Three Oaths, paying particular attention to their truth-telling strategies. As we'll see, although Kant agrees that we always ought to tell the truth, he would undoubtedly disapprove of how the Aes Sedai "speak no word that is not true." Whether Kant speaks the whole truth about such things remains to be seen.

## Upholding the Three Oaths and Moral Agency

Upon fleeing their Trolloc attackers and with the group camping for the night, Moiraine Sedai (in "Shadow's Waiting") separates Egwene from her sleeping Two Rivers friends, only to abruptly inquire, "What do you know of the Three Oaths?" Egwene replies, "Uh … they are the promises made by the Aes Sedai to end Artur Hawkwing's siege of the White Tower." Moiraine concurs, but presses her further, requiring "exact verbiage" because "words are important, and how we use them is important." When Egwene admits—rolling her eyes—that she does not know them *exactly*, Moiraine recites: "One, to speak no word that is not true. Two, to make no weapon with which one person may kill another. Three, never to use the One Power as a weapon, except in the last extreme defense of her life or the life of her Warder or another Aes Sedai."

These three promises convey sound ethical advice for anyone. After all, we tend to blame those who purposely hide the truth from us. Dana seems blameworthy for concealing her Darkfriend-plan to gain Rand's confidence, only to deliver him and his friends to the Dark One. And do not forget the Dark One is called the Father of Lies—itself testament to how "walking in the Light" requires truth-telling. Further, those who regularly act in morally upright ways are to be commended. When Karene Sedai (in "The Dragon Reborn") asserts, "The White Tower and the women within it have stood for 3000 years, not because we do what is expedient but because we do what is right," her words seem profound. Those who regularly do the right thing even within one lifetime, to say nothing of 3000 years, are moral exemplars. Thus, it seems that the Aes Sedai are praiseworthy for their staunch commitment to doing the right thing.

Yet sometimes things are not exactly as they seem. Women who become Aes Sedai are indeed thereby bound by the Three Oaths. However, their being so results in the inability to break them, as Moiraine explains to Egwene, "These oaths are bound by the One Power itself. It's not that we do not break them, it's that we cannot break them" ("Shadow's Waiting"). Moiraine never clarifies how Aes Sedai are literally unable to lie, craft deadly weapons, or harm others except in self-defense or in defense of those close to them. Perhaps it is similar to how (in "The Flame of Tar Valon") Moiraine is bound by the Amyrlin Seat's decree that she be exiled from the White Tower. When Moiraine grasps the Oath Rod and repeats the judgment leveled against her, we see weaves of the One Power mystically work through the Oath Rod and enter Moiraine's body. Presumably, this results in Moiraine being physically unable to re-enter the White Tower (at least until the Amyrlin Seat "calls her home again"). Henceforth, it is not that Moiraine will not re-enter the White Tower in that she could return but chooses not to; she *cannot* enter it. Likewise, when a woman becomes an Aes Sedai, we can imagine her repeating the Three Oaths while grasping the Oath Rod. The One Power works through the Oath Rod, mystically entering the newly minted Aes Sedai's body and thereby rendering her incapable of breaking any of the oaths. This would explain why Aes Sedai simply *cannot* break the Three Oaths.[1]

One of Kant's foundational axioms regarding moral judgments is "ought implies can." In his words, "The action to which the 'ought' applies must indeed be possible under natural conditions."[2] Kant's point is that moral agency requires genuine choice, which conforms to common-sense, as it seems clear that you are improperly blamed for things over which you had no control. What's more, if you are properly blamed for doing something you ought not have, then given the circumstances, it must have been within your power to do something else, presumably something that was not wrong (or not as wrong). Kant's point also applies to being morally praiseworthy for doing the right thing. If, given the conditions, it was impossible for you to not do the right thing, then, technically, it's not a moral choice; in fact, it really wasn't a choice at all. If it's not a genuine choice, then you are not acting as a moral agent and not morally praiseworthy for doing the right thing, even if it was good that you did it.

So, if an Aes Sedai tells the truth because the current natural conditions of the One Power compel her "to speak no word that is not true," she is improperly commended for doing the right thing. She cannot do otherwise than tell the truth. It makes no more sense to praise her for telling the truth when asked a question than it does to praise water for freezing when it reaches a certain temperature. Clearly a cup of water is not a moral agent. Likewise, an Aes Sedai is not a moral agent with respect to truth-telling (or keeping the other two promises made over the Oath Rod).

Yet we might wonder whether a woman is morally praiseworthy for choosing to become an Aes Sedai and agreeing to the Three Oaths in the first place. Even if an Aes Sedai is not morally praiseworthy for truth-telling *now*, perhaps she is commendable for expressing her moral agency *then* in agreeing to give up her ability to lie. Further, as the show repeatedly reminds us, an Aes Sedai seems to have control over *how* she keeps the Three Oaths, especially the artful—or conniving, if you are a Whitecloak Questioner—ways they "speak no word that is not true." Evidently, then, a woman does not *completely* give up her moral agency when upholding the Three Oaths. As it turns out, Kant offers interesting perspectives on both suggested clarifications—the proper motivation for making a moral decision, on the one hand, and the flexibility moral agents have when doing the right thing, on the other.

## Acting from Duty and Ending Hawkwing's Siege

When describing the motivations a person might have for acting, including for the "inner pleasure in spreading happiness around them," Kant maintains: "In such a case an action of this kind, however right and however amiable it may be, has still no genuine moral worth ... for its maxim [principle] lacks moral content, namely, the performance of such actions, not from inclination, but *from duty*."[3] So, for Kant, even if you do something out of the goodness of your heart (as my mom used to say), that action is not genuinely morally praiseworthy. Your choice is morally praiseworthy only if you do it because it's the right thing to do and you do it exactly for that reason.

For Kant, if you act in a way that duty requires—for example, telling the truth rather than lying for personal gain—but do so because it makes someone happy (including your mother), then you act *according* to duty, but not *from* duty. If personal circumstances constitute your sole motivations for telling the truth, then removing them results in you not doing the right thing. What's more, if the consequences of your telling the truth were disadvantageous to you, presumably you would then be inclined to lie. Both eventualities lead Kant to hold that acting from duty—doing the right thing because it's right—is required for being genuinely morally praiseworthy for the choices we make.

We now know how Kant would evaluate the suggestion that an Aes Sedai might be morally praiseworthy for agreeing to abide by the Three Oaths. If the Aes Sedai originally agreed to the Three Oaths to end Hawkwing's siege of the White Tower, then they were undoubtedly motivated by self-interest. As such, Kant would hold that this choice was not morally praiseworthy.

In fact, it is difficult to identify any obvious example of a woman accepting the Three Oaths that Kant would deem morally praiseworthy. Young Siuan Sanche begrudgingly left her father behind for the White Tower out of self-preservation, with her childhood home destroyed and smoldering. We are led to believe that young girls who have natural aptitudes for channeling the One Power are persecuted (including by the Whitecloaks—more on them in a bit). This is confirmed by Liandrin Sedai, as she explains to Nynaeve, "Women hold the One Power, but men still control much of this world. And they are rarely kind to little girls who show a spark of being greater than they are" ("Blood Calls Blood"). Nynaeve, for her part, does not wish to become an Aes Sedai at all, but because she is "the most powerful channeler known in 1000 years," the Amyrlin Seat (none other than Siuan Sanche now a woman grown) convinces her that she really has no choice but to begin her training. Thus, it seems that, as a rule, if a young woman is able to channel, training to become an Aes Sedai is standard fare; this is *not* because it is the right thing to do, but, practically speaking, it is the only thing to do.

Perhaps Moiraine serves as the only clear example of an Aes Sedai, who Kant would commend for making a moral choice. Recall her explanation to her Emond's Field charges, "I did not choose this path for myself any more than you did, but I will follow it because I *must*. Because I know what is right" ("The Dark Along the Ways"). Assuming that Moiraine's conviction leads her to risk her life by taking the Dragon Reborn to the Eye of the World because combatting the Dark One is the right thing to do—and for no other reason—then she is deserving of full Kantian moral esteem for that choice.

Still, Kant's view about moral praise is controversial because he seems to discount completely any other motivation for right action than simply doing one's duty. To that end, consider Ila's exchange with Perrin in "The Dragon Reborn." Speaking as the matriarch of her band of Tinkers, she explains the Way of the Leaf: "If I can change two people's minds, just two, well, then I've left the world a better place than I found. And if those two each change two more minds, well, then, eventually …" Perrin interjects, "Even if you are right, you will not live to see this peace. And neither will the rest of your people here, or their grandchildren, or their great-grandchildren's grandchildren." With that, Ila shares with Perrin that she had a daughter who was brutally slain for sport. She wished revenge upon the murderers. When Perrin notes, "That does not sound like the Way of the Leaf," Ila's rejoinder is both insightful and instructive: "What greater revenge against violence than peace? What greater revenge against death than life? I could not protect my girl in this turn of the Wheel, but one day, long after I'm gone … the Wheel will turn out my daughter's soul again. I do what I can to forge a better world for her then, where she can enjoy the life she should have had with me." Ila's motivation is to make the world a better place—yes, for her descendants, including her daughter if she is reborn—but more importantly for *everyone*. Making the world a better place involves increasing happiness and decreasing suffering, motivations grounded in consequences, something Kant's view of moral worth has difficulty incorporating. Still, the Way of the Leaf combats violence with peace so that eventually peace will reign, even if its followers never experience that world in their lifetimes. If Kant's stringent requirement for moral praise discounts this sort of noble motivation, then perhaps we have reason to reexamine Kant's view.

## The Categorical Imperative and Lying Promises

When Moiraine asserts that she *must* march into the Blight with the Dragon Reborn, the context suggests that she is able to refrain from this action; however, she will march forward because it is the right thing to do. She is upholding her moral obligation to thwart the Dark One and her use of "must" emphasizes its significance. Similarly, when Rand and Mat flee from the darkness that infests Shadar Logoth, Rand exclaims, "We cannot leave without them!" Mat reflexively replies, "I'm pretty sure we can" ("Shadow's Waiting"). Here, Mat is affirming that they are, in fact, physically capable of escaping Shadar Logoth even if it means leaving Egwene and Perrin behind. But Rand, like Moiraine in Fal Dara, wasn't claiming that they were physically unable to escape; he was asserting that it was wrong to do so—they ought not. This distinction, like the ones previously discussed about making moral choices at all and being appropriately praised for them, is preliminary to discussions about determining what, exactly, one ought or ought not to do. But how do we determine what we ought or ought not to do when faced with a situation that seems to call for a moral choice?

Kant's fundamental action-guiding ethical principle is known as the "categorical imperative." It represents the benchmark for all morally significant behavior and applies equally to all moral agents everywhere. In Kant's initial phrasing, known as the "universal law" formulation, it reads: "*Act only on that maxim* [principle] *through which you can at the same time will* [intend, accept] *that it should become a universal law*."[4] It's not immediately clear how the categorical imperative helps those like Rand figure out what he ought or ought not to do. Yet Kant believed that from it, one derives an obligation against committing suicide, making it impermissible for Warder Stepin to take his own life. Kant also believed that the categorical imperative brings an obligation to develop one's latent but natural talents. Consequently, Mat is to be disparaged for his tendencies to spend his days drinking, thieving, and gambling. And from the categorical imperative Kant believed we have a duty to offer aid to those in need; as such, Kant would commend Tam's choice to raise the red-haired newborn baby of his enemy as his own child (and perhaps commend Mat, too, insofar as he cares for his younger sisters when his parents seem incapable of doing so).[5]

To put the categorical imperative into action, Kant requires you to discern the corresponding implicit principle or rule of your pending action (and the intention from which it is made). This requires you to generalize, or better yet, universalize. In effect, from your specific situation, you are proposing a rule for anyone in that situation: whenever someone is in circumstances like mine, that person should act as I do (or am about to do). Having articulated the rule, the next step is to ask yourself: Can I rationally accept that everyone acts as I am about to do? If there would be contradictory or self-defeating results were everyone to do as you are about to, then you cannot rationally accept that your implicit rule becomes a universal law. Attempts at acting on an implicit rule that cannot be universalized require making an exception for yourself that you are not willing to grant others, even though they are exactly like you in every morally relevant way. By allowing an exception only for yourself, you put yourself ahead of or above others, morally speaking, but this fails to recognize that each of us is equally deserving of respect. Kant contends that this (logical) result provides you sufficient reason not to perform that act. If you perform it, you have thereby done something morally wrong.

The moral force of Kant's categorical imperative is perhaps most obvious in cases that involve making a lying promise and, by extension, being dishonest generally. Imagine you are contemplating asking someone for a loan, but you have no intention of repaying it. (Well, not *you*, of course, but perhaps someone like Mat after a long night of unlucky gambling.) The implicit rule would be: whenever a person wants money, one should make a lying promise to secure the desired funds. We should note that dishonesty only achieves its intended goal in cultures that presume truth-telling (and cultures that do not operate on this assumption aren't long for this world). But if everyone made lying promises whenever desiring money, then people would cease lending money—no one would be able to get a loan. Your implicit rule thus becomes self-defeating because you could not secure any funds if it were put into practice. So, if you were to proceed, you would have to make an exception for yourself that you would not be willing to allow others, which is the Kantian hallmark of acting wrongly. (Again, the point is not merely about securing a loan, but about being dishonest. So, Stepin acted impermissibly in both taking his own life and not being truthful with Nynaeve about why he really wanted the Goatstongue sedative.)

## Aes Sedai Truth-Telling and Kant's Misgivings

The Whitecloak Questioner known as "Child" Valda is probably not someone you'd invite to a backyard barbeque. If you did, he would only bring that gruesomely weird roasted bird dish that punctures your mouth when eaten. As your more squeamish guests go running for the exit, he might "explain" how "the flavor does not come only from the bird. Its bones and beak and feet cut the inside of your mouth. Not so much that it hurts. Just enough that you bleed." This dude *likes* the taste of blood?!

If any of your guests were polite enough to stay, perhaps some, noticing his strange garb, would be brave enough to ask Valda what he does for a living. He probably would smile as he proudly displayed his collection of gold serpent-shaped rings, and then begin asking your female guests if they can do something called "channeling" because the "Creator never meant for us to have access to so much power." His unrepentant life's purpose is to find "witches" who can "channel" because they "make a mockery of our very existence"; the suggestion that something called "The One Power" coming from "anywhere other than the Dark is absurd." He will "stamp it out—woman, by woman, by woman." And if any of your remaining guests become morbidly fascinated with Valda (and if so, you might wonder why you invited *them*), the conversation might turn to his penchants for severing the hands of "witches" before burning them at the stake, slicing a grid pattern on the backs of young men as a way to interrogate and psychologically torture women who may or may not be witches, and breaking the oaths of his cleric-like occupation to accomplish his life's goal. After all, "sometimes brutality is the surest path to mercy"—whatever that means. At best, Valda possesses the unwavering courage of his (misguided) convictions. But the actual truth is pretty clear: he's a murderous sociopath.

Kant, whose stodginess probably would have led him to politely decline your barbeque invitation, contends that our moral obligations hold without exception, making him a moral absolutist. So, we have an obligation to be honest—always and everywhere, including to people like Valda. The idea seems to be that just as there are no exceptions to the principle that the sum of the interior angles of a triangle is 180 degrees, there are no exceptions to the principle that being dishonest is always wrong. Both are grounded in rational or logical considerations, and principles so grounded hold without exception. Because we have a moral duty to tell the truth— the opposing implicit rule cannot be universalized, remember—it follows that there are no circumstances in which we may permissibly break our word or practice dishonesty.

So, Kant would disparage the sort of moral flexibility Aes Sedai often employ when "speaking no word that is not true." But, truth be told, Kant's rigid view about truth-telling seems strained in some circumstances, especially when interacting with people like Valda. Why are we obligated to tell the complete truth to murderous sociopaths, especially when not being completely honest would save innocent lives?[6] Moiraine Sedai, despite her inability to lie, is among those who would ask Kant this very thing.[7]

To better understand Moiraine's viewpoint, recall (in "Shadow's Waiting") the Whitecloak encounter she navigated. As the Whitecloaks approach, she instructs her young charges, "Do not speak unless spoken to. And try to answer any question as truthfully as you can. Do not mention the White Tower or Aes Sedai. I am a lady from a fallen house. You are under my care." When "Child" Bornhald asks Moiraine's group to dismount, she informs him that they are headed for Whitebridge and hope that a sister of hers will provide them lodging. Unfazed, she remains steadfast when Valda jingles his chain of Great Serpent rings; she knows that if Valda learns that Moiraine is Aes Sedai, he will swiftly utilize his "brutality as mercy" methods that will result in adding her ring to his collection. Moiraine calmly but humbly informs the two Whitecloaks that she was grievously injured by a monster with a mouth like a boar near the Mountains of Mist; further, they were traveling from Taren Ferry and many people were injured. Hopefully the Whitecloaks can provide aid to the victims.

Every word that Moiraine spoke was true. Rand, Perrin, Mat, and Egwene are under her care. Her family house has fallen on rough times (even if we do not learn this until season 2). But, of course, she was not *completely* truthful. Given the context, being completely truthful probably would include volunteering that she's an Aes Sedai. What's more, while her claim that "wars and witches do not concern us" is true, it is only true because Moiraine believes Logain is the False Dragon and she does not believe that Aes Sedai are witches. With the Whitecloaks behind them, Egwene chides Moiraine's somewhat duplicitous answers. She does not have a sister in Whitebridge! Moiraine smiles and reminds Egwene, "All Aes Sedai are my sisters," and then continues to instruct the group, "We [Aes Sedai] will always tell the truth. It just may not be the truth you think you hear. So, listen carefully."[8]

As Moiraine's words hang in the air, along with her subtle sly smile, it's undeniable that if she had been completely honest with the Whitecloaks, especially Valda, she would have been tortured to death, the lives of her innocent charges thereby jeopardized, and the final battle against the Dark One over before it begins—a battle that Moiraine is convinced that she ought to fight, even at great personal cost. Thus, it seems that Moiraine is on solid moral ground with her choice to be less than completely honest. If so, there seem to be some circumstances where it's permissible to not disclose the truth in full, for example, if one is trying to protect one's life or the innocent lives of others (or to prevent the cataclysmic rise of the Dark One, even if that one is *really* specific). And this seems to conform to common sense, even if Kant staunchly disagrees.

It's important to note that when in such circumstances, an Aes Sedai does not lie to save her life or the life of another; she carefully and creatively "speaks no word that is not true." What's more, the Aes Sedai approach does not seem to run afoul of Kant's universalization test; there do not seem to be any self-defeating or contradictory results from an Aes Sedai carefully and creatively "speaking no word that is not true." Questioners continue to inquire about and with Aes Sedai even though they know that, to paraphrase Valda, Aes Sedai are adept at "twisting the truth." So, it is not obvious that Aes Sedai cannot rationally accept that everyone acts as they do when in similar circumstances. And, so, one begins to wonder what Kant would say about all this.

Conflicting duties are problematic for any moral absolutist. Kant, for one, believes that we have a duty to be honest and a duty to protect innocent lives. If you cannot act on both of the conflicting duties, what ought you to do? Moiraine Sedai (implicitly) offers a suggestion. In this, *The Wheel of Time* offers another intriguing potential strategy for reexamining Kant's view.

## Philosophical "Weavings" and "Hearing" the Truth

Does Kant "speak no word that is not true" about such things as being morally praiseworthy for the choices we make and whether our moral obligations hold without exception? It's not that Kant intends to deceive us about such things, but are his views completely true? Might the truth about such things, at least in part, lie elsewhere, including implicitly in how the Aes Sedai "speak no word that is not true," but do not always convey the truth in all its detail? Does this pop culture source harbor the beginnings of a reply to Kant? These are difficult questions, but we ought not overlook the fascinating realization that we can begin asking them as a result of carefully watching and thinking about *The Wheel of Time*.

Kant is not the only philosopher who has offered views about moral praise, moral obligations, and moral absolutism. Many philosophers have had their say about these topics, and not all of them agree with Kant. In this, philosophers are engaged in dialogue with one another—what is sometimes called "the great conversation." As you (continue to) engage this dialogue and "converse" with the perspectives of other philosophers about topics that interest you, there is always something new to learn. As you continue to think philosophically, and engage "the great conversation," remember Moiraine's sage advice: "Words are important and how we use them is important" and do your best to "speak no word that is not true." What's more, it might be that what you "hear" is not always the truth you thought you were seeking. So, "listen" carefully.

## Notes

1. Admittedly, the exact verbiage of Moiraine's exile oath might suggest she could try to re-enter the Tower, if she were willing to endure the extreme negative consequences of the attempt. Further, it's true that Liandrin breaks the third Aes Sedai Oath by using the One Power to attack and kidnap Egwene and Nynaeve in "Damane"; however, it might be argued that her new oaths to the Dark One, thereby becoming a member of the Black Ajah, supplant her pledge to the Three Oaths.

2. Immanuel Kant, *Critique of Pure Reason*, trans. Norman Kemp Smith (New York: St. Martin's Press, 1965), 473. Another often-cited passage is Kant's *Religion Within the Boundaries of Mere Reason*, trans. Werner S. Pluhar (Indianapolis: Hackett, 2009), 6: 50.

3. Immanuel Kant, *Groundwork of the Metaphysics of Morals*, trans. H.J. Patton (New York: Harper, 1948), 66. Emphasis original, but words in brackets are added for clarity.

4. Kant, *Groundwork*, 88. Emphasis original, but words in brackets are added for clarity.

5. To be fair, Kant's three derivations are clearer on his "ends as themselves" formulation of the categorical imperative. See *Groundwork*, 95–98.

6. Kant was familiar with this sort of criticism. He attempted to answer it in his 1797 essay "On a Supposed Right to Lie from Altruistic Motives," which appears in Immanuel Kant, *Critique of Practical Reason and Other Writings in Moral Philosophy*, trans. Lewis White Beck (Chicago: University of Chicago Press, 1949). Whether Kant's rejoinder succeeds is often contested.

7. Arthur Schopenhauer critiques Kant's stringent view of lying by arguing it can be a form of self-defense. Just as it may be permissible to physically harm an aggressor to protect your life, it may be permissible to lie to someone who poses an obvious threat to your safety. See Schopenhauer, *On the Basis of Morality*, trans. E.F.J. Payne (Indianapolis: Hackett, 1999), sec. 17. I am grateful to Jake Held for this reference.

8. Moraine's advice also applies to her Aes Sedai sisters. Recall Verdin Sedai's words to Leane Sedai: "The city's burning. The Amyrlin requires your strength to protect Cairhien. I've been told to watch the boy. This is an order, Leane Sedai. I'll take his shield" ("Daes Dae'mar"). Interpreted carefully, all of Verin's

claims are true. Cairhien is burning, and the Amyrlin would benefit by additional help to defend it. She has been told by *someone* to watch Rand and because Verin is a senior Aes Sedai, it is an order. She takes the shield, but promptly releases Rand. All this leads Moiraine to comment, "You are very clever with your words, Sister." Whether Verin's careful verbiage is beyond all reproach is controversial. In addition, in the books, Verin "escapes" her oath to the Black Ajah, namely, to hold their secrets until the hour of her death, by taking poison and then revealing what she knows about the Black Ajah, thus completing her role as a spy for the tower.

# 13

# On the Supposed Right to Slay Dragons Because of Philanthropic Concerns: The Mysterious Ethics of the Aes Sedai

*Steve Bein*

Suppose you win a round-trip ticket in a time machine. You get to go back and make one change in history, then come back home and live your life. Would you make a more comfortable life for yourself, maybe by investing in the stock market with foreknowledge? Or would you make a better life for millions by assassinating Adolf Hitler? "Everyone kills Hitler on their first trip," says the sci-fi writer Desmond Warzel, in his short story "Wikihistory."[1]

Killing Hitler is a nifty little thought experiment, one you may have run across before. But Moiraine and Lan don't need a time machine to conduct this experiment. They are facing it live: three boys from the Two Rivers, one of whom is the Dragon Reborn.[2] The last time he circled around the Wheel of Time, the Dragon was worse than Hitler. He nearly broke the world. Now the fate of the world hangs in the balance again, but Moiraine and Lan could save the day. If the prophecies are correct, the Dragon Reborn can only become the Dark One's champion or the Dark One's downfall. Moiraine's preference is to identify the Dragon Reborn so she can manipulate him into fighting the darkness. But that's playing with fire, isn't it? Surely the Red Ajah's strategy is safer: still the bastard before he can do any harm. Those who survive a stilling say it's a fate worse than death, but so what? If the alternative is the entire world falling to the Dark One and his mightiest servant, the Dragon Reborn, then shouldn't Moiraine and Lan do whatever they need to do, even if that requires them to still—or even kill—three rubes from Emond's Field?

One knee-jerk response is *duh*, of course they should. But that violates the widely shared intuition that we ought not to kill innocents. However, that intuition itself contradicts another commonly held intuition: when

*The Wheel of Time and Philosophy*, First Edition. Edited by Jacob M. Held.
© 2025 John Wiley & Sons, Inc. Published 2025 by John Wiley & Sons, Inc.

grievous harm is both foreseeable and preventable, we ought to prevent it. So yes, the three boys have yet to commit any atrocities like the Dragon Reborn, and in fact two of them never will. But no one proposes going back in time to kill Hitler *after* he orchestrates mass murder. The whole point is to take him out while he's still innocent.

What would an Aes Sedai tell us do with the time machine? As it turns out, their ethics are pretty mysterious. This chapter seeks to unravel the mystery.

## Killing Innocents: Is It *Always* Wrong?

Maybe you have already thought of the most important objection to killing Rand, Mat, and Perrin: we don't *know* the Dragon Reborn will become a villain. Logain speaks as if the odds of that are fifty-fifty, and sometimes the Aes Sedai do too: the Dragon will either ally with the Dark One or become the only person capable of defeating him. It's not quite a coin flip, though, because touching *saidin* is certain to drive him insane, and a magic-powered madman is not a reliable ally. So, let us say the possible outcomes are these:

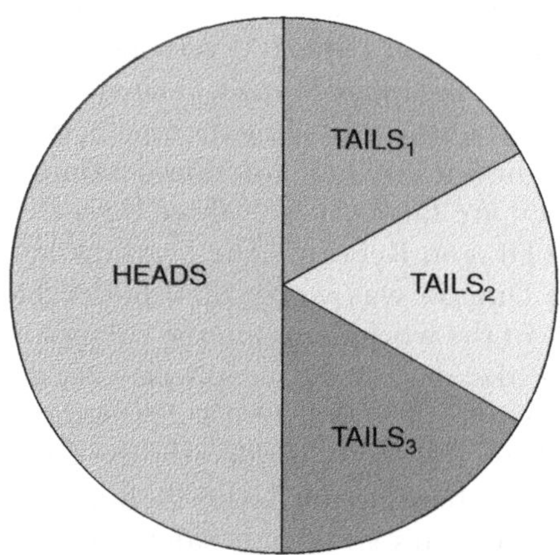


Heads: The Dragon Reborn breaks bad. He sides with the Dark One and together they break the world. Then the Dragon Reborn goes insane, unless the Dark One kills him first.

Tails$_1$: The Dragon Reborn stays good. He tries to side against the Dark One, but too quickly he goes insane, wreaking havoc and leaving a swath of death and destruction in his wake.

Tails$_2$: The Dragon Reborn stays good. He defeats the Dark One quickly enough that he doesn't go insane until *after* the world is saved. Then he starts up the whole havoc and destruction thing.

Tails$_3$: The Dragon Reborn stays good. He quickly defeats the Dark One, then willingly submits to being stilled before going insane.

So really, that supposed coin flip is more like a die roll: the only tolerable outcome is the last one, where the Dragon Reborn saves everyone and then spends the rest of his days wishing the Aes Sedai had killed him instead of having stilled him. In short, every outcome is bad for the Dragon Reborn himself, and three of the four possible outcomes are bad for everyone else too.

Earlier I mentioned the commonly held moral intuition that we ought to prevent grievous harm when we can foresee it. The next question is, how certain do we have to be that it's coming? For most people, the answer is "not very." I don't *know* that I'll live to retirement age, yet I contribute to my IRA with every paycheck. I think the odds of actually *needing* my seatbelt are something like one in a million, yet I wear it every time. In this case, if Moiraine and Lan choose to play dice, they are gambling with the fate of the world. Maybe you think their odds are better than the 16.7 percent chance I've laid out here, but whatever the odds may be, they are long. The safe bet—safer by far—is to kill the Dragon Reborn *now*, before he reaches his full potential.

But the safer bet is still a gamble, and maybe you're not willing to base your ethics on mere probability. Maybe you want to be certain. If so, you agree with an especially strict German named Immanuel Kant (1724–1804), and at least at first glance, the ethics of the Aes Sedai resemble Kant's thinking.

## "Duty Is as Heavy as a Mountain"

Kant is a strong advocate of *deontological ethics*. Deontological means "duty-based," and as Kant sees it there are no exceptions to the laws of duty. That sounds like the Three Oaths, which are inviolable because they are enforced by the One Power itself:

1.  To speak no word that is not true.
2.  To make no weapon by which one man may kill another.
3.  Never to use the One Power as a weapon except against Darkfriends or Shadowspawn, or in the last extreme defense of her life, the life of her warder, or another Aes Sedai.[3]

However, these oaths are far too loose to meet with Kant's approval. Moiraine cannot use the One Power to kill, but she *can* say, "Hey Lan, loan me your sword for a sec?" She didn't use the One Power to create that sword, so she breaks no oaths by killing with it. Similarly, Liandrin can tell her sisters to deliberately let their wards down, enabling Logain to attack them so they can retaliate. If she calls that self-defense, she's not lying but she's definitely bullshitting.

The truth is, the Three Oaths are less like an honor code and more like Star Trek's Prime Directive: terrific as a plot device, trash as a moral compass. Moiraine lies all the time, not with untrue words but with ambiguous innuendoes she knows others will interpret the wrong way. When she tells the Whitecloaks "I have a sister in Whitebridge" ("A Place of Safety"), she knows full well that reasonable people will assume she means "my female sibling lives in Whitebridge," not "there's an Aes Sedai stationed in Whitebridge, and as I'm an Aes Sedai myself, she and I refer to each other as sisters." Imagine trying to run a marriage this way, where each partner obfuscates what they mean whenever they don't want to do something:

| | |
|---|---|
| YOU: | Are you going to wash the dishes? |
| SPOUSE, SPEAKING NO WORD THAT IS UNTRUE: | Yes. |
| SPOUSE'S TRUE MEANING: | I have no intention of washing any dishes tonight, but grammatically your question refers to the indefinite future, and yes, I'm sure there will be some point before I die when I have to wash some dishes. |

Kant, on the other hand, says lying is always wrong. No exceptions, not even to save an innocent person from a murderous Fade.[4] He'd also say it's wrong to sacrifice a ferryman's livelihood—to say nothing of the ferryman himself—to prevent an army of Trollocs from crossing a river ("Shadow's Waiting"). Why? Because it's wrong to treat people solely as a means to an end. If Moiraine had got the ferryman's consent before sinking the ferry, that would have been one thing, but she didn't. She sinks the boat anyway, because it serves the greater good. Sacrificing the good of the few for the good of the many sounds more like Kant's nemeses, the consequentialists.

## "Leave Everyone Feeling They Reached the Best Possible Result"

Consequentialism is a broad school of moral theories united by their shared definition that right and wrong are measurable in positive and negative consequences. If you have ever done a cost–benefit analysis, you have practiced consequentialist reasoning. Ditto if you've ever justified doing something you usually wouldn't do because in this particular case it did more good for everyone involved.

Aes Sedai often seem to justify their behavior in consequentialist terms. Liandrin and her fellow Reds hunt down men who can touch the One Power, gentling them against their will, in the name of the greater good. Moiraine is skilled at lying by omission, but usually she does it when telling the truth plainly would bring about avoidable suffering. And yes, sometimes she deceives people merely to manipulate them like puppets. (Yet another

Kantian violation.) But even this is in service of what she perceives to be the greater good.

The Amyrlin Seat is an especially interesting case. When Liandrin, Moiraine, and Alanna give a consequentialist argument for gentling Logain instead of bringing him in to stand trial, the Amyrlin Seat rebukes them with a consequentialist counterargument. The three sisters say if they hadn't gentled him, he'd have killed everyone there and he'd still be at large—with an army at his back, no less. That's a consequence the Amyrlin Seat is willing to live with, because as she puts it, "Our laws do not exist to protect our lives. ... They exist to protect our people from us" ("The Flame of Tar Valon"). She thinks Aes Sedai should follow the rules not because them's the rules, but because following the rules promotes the greater good.

It's not unusual to see consequentialists disagree with each other. Kantians disagree with each other too. The fact is, moral philosophy is complex, and smart people disagree over how rules work, how consequences will unfold, and so on. The low-hanging fruit here is the conclusion that the Aes Sedai are consequentialists who sometimes disagree with each other. But that ignores some blatantly anti-consequentialist commitments on their part.

## "Change What You Can If It Needs Changing"

The second oath forbids the making of weapons. Cunning as they are, the Aes Sedai wriggle out of this one by disputing what's meant by "weapon." (Lightning bolts don't count, so long as you use them in self-defense.) But consequentialists would ask whether that oath really promotes the greater good. Hitler's ambitions might have been nipped in the bud if only Poland had a few Aes Sedai crafting *cuendillar* bullets to punch through armored panzers.

The same goes for the third oath, which allows lethal use of the One Power so long as it's used either offensively against Darkfriends or Shadowspawn, or defensively to protect Aes Sedai and their warders. Notably *not* defense of innocent bystanders, unless the person threatening them happens to be a servant of the Shadow. For instance, the Aes Sedai cannot channel the One Power to kill Child Valda, because evil as he is, he's not actually a Darkfriend. And that puts him in the same category as Adolf Hitler. Surely a well-placed lightning bolt could fry *der Führer* and advance the greater good, but to that the Aes Sedai can only say, "Sorry, we just can't do it."

So maybe the Aes Sedai *think* they are consequentialists but they're bad at consequentialist reasoning. Moiraine acts mostly out of act utilitarianism (except when rule utilitarianism suits her), the Amyrlin Seat acts mostly out of rule utilitarianism (but who knows how consistent she really is, given all the other Aes Sedai shenanigans), and Liandrin is neither, acting instead out of her own self-interest (which makes her not a utilitarian but an *ethical egoist*). That's a compelling conclusion, but it's not very charitable, and a good rule when doing philosophy is to give other people the benefit of the doubt. This goes double for an army of wizard women who have collected wisdom for 3000 years. So, giving credit to their wisdom, let us look at one last philosophical tradition, one that puts wisdom at the forefront of its ethics.

## The Buddha Way of the Aes Sedai

Like wizards and philosophers, Buddhists revere wisdom. The prime virtue of Buddhism is wise compassion, or compassionate wisdom, depending on which side of the coin you're looking at. (For Buddhists, when you advance far enough in either wisdom or compassion, you discover they're the same thing.) For that reason, it's easy to assume that Buddhism is basically another school of consequentialism. "Observe the situation carefully, then do what will bring the most benefit to the greatest number" is a decent summary of utilitarianism, and not too shabby as a working model of how to practice wise compassion.

The difference is subtle, but it's there. Consequentialists will say compassion is a good character trait only insofar as it advances the greater good. The Buddha says compassion—and with it, wisdom—is the key to releasing yourself from misery and delusion, therefore compassion is good regardless of whether or not it actually does anyone any good.

If that distinction is too abstract, let's look at a concrete case. Tam al'Thor meets the pregnant Tigraine Mantear after she has just butchered a boatload of his brothers in arms. (While in labor, no less! She's quite the badass.) Wisely, he does not try to kill her, so when she gives birth to her baby, Tam is still alive to name the boy Rand and raise him as his own son. Let's say Tigraine approves of this, and let's say it'll be another hour before she bleeds to death. Now Tam has a choice: he can leave, or he can sit with this warrior woman so she does not have to die alone. He cannot save her; all he can do is suffer with her, or leave her behind.

Let's set all the other variables as equal. Baby Rand won't freeze to death if Tam stays, Tigraine won't try to kill Tam, and Tam won't try to kill her either. If he sits with her, he will be cold and miserable. (Plus, he'll have to watch someone die, which cannot be pleasant.) She will be cold and miserable and then die, no matter what he does. So, there's a reasonable consequentialist argument to be made that it would be morally wrong for Tam to stay with Tigraine. Her outcomes are the same either way, Rand's are too, so the only relevant variable is whether Tam spends the next hour being needlessly sad, cold, and uncomfortable. Whatever comfort Tigraine takes in not being alone, it's faint; she's a Maiden of the Spear, after all, and not one to fear death. The longer he waits, the worse he'll feel, while her fading consciousness may not even register his presence. There's a compelling case to be made that he ought to abandon her.

*If* he's a consequentialist, that is. If he's a Buddhist, there's no question: the compassionate thing to do is tend to this dying warrior, even if it won't prolong her life. Maybe Tam can learn something from the experience, but that's not why he should stay. Some Buddhist monks meditate on cold mountaintops, but that's not why he should stay either. He should stay because freezing to death sucks, bleeding to death sucks, and having to do both all by yourself is a giant avalanche of suck. If he can take some of that weight on his shoulders, he should. Compassion is good even if it doesn't bring about any good.

What if the Aes Sedai only *seem* like bad consequentialists because they agree with the Buddhists that not all harm is bad? Asceticism—deliberately enduring pain as a means to religious insight—is a time-honored tradition among monks and nuns of many cultures throughout history, including the Buddha himself. And it usually doesn't work, at least not on the first try; ascetic hardship is a *practice*, not a one-time gig. Consequentialists have a hard time with that. They can make sense of minor unpleasantness that's known to deflect greater pain (think Novocaine shots at the dentist's office), but suffering with no promise of reward is harder to justify. However, if the Aes Sedai are wiser than the rest of us—and wizards usually are—then maybe their mysterious moral code turns a blind eye to some kinds of misery. Maybe sharing in someone's suffering as she freezes to death is just the right thing to do, regardless of the discomfort that comes with it. To this we mere mortals might reply, okay, fine, but then why don't you Aes Sedai just say that? Why don't you write down a set of oaths that are clear and specific, so the rest of us can trust you?

The Buddha can answer that question in a single word: *upāya*. Often translated as "skillful means," *upāya* is how the best teachers tailor their lessons to the student. Lan can train just about anyone how to fight with a sword, but he's not going to come at you full speed if you're just a beginner. With other warders he'll pull out his best tricks, but for noobs he's going to start with the most basic concepts: how to stand, how to hold a sword, even how to breathe.

The same goes for ethics. When you were little and you misbehaved, maybe an adult asked you, "How would you like it if someone did that to you?" Today, in a college ethics class, you can explore the same question at a more advanced level, with terms like "reciprocity," "social contract theory," and "universalized maxim." That's *upāya*, and *upāya* explains why the Amyrlin Seat can talk like a rule utilitarian while Moiraine can behave like an act utilitarian, yet both of them can see Liandrin is not a utilitarian at all, but rather an egoist pretending to be a utilitarian whenever it's in her best interest. Moiraine and the Amyrlin Seat skillfully adapt their speech and behavior as the situation requires, in order to be true "Servants of All."

(Which, of course, is the meaning of "Aes Sedai" in the Old Tongue.) But we need a little more help from Buddhist philosophy if we are to make sense of their moral code.

## "Whatever the Dark One Wants, I Oppose"

If the Aes Sedai code does in fact come closest to Buddhist ethics, that would be fitting, since the image of a Wheel of Time is clearly born of Indian philosophy. The moral ideal of a Servant of All is not so far from the Buddhist ideal of the *bodhisattva*, one who attains enlightenment and is therefore entitled to escape the cycle of reincarnation, yet chooses rebirth in order to help all beings become enlightened. As it turns out, the Aes Sedai's rather bendable rules about lying and killing—rules that look dysfunctional in consequentialist ethics—make more sense in the context of *upāya* and Buddhist ethics.

If compassion is the foundation of Buddhist ethics, the first building blocks are the first five steps of Buddhism's Eightfold Path. A teacher at the White Tower might adapt them like this:

Right views: See reality as it truly is, not as deluded or corrupted minds have taught you.
Right intent: Based on your corrected vision of reality, make it your goal to defend the world from the Dark One and his servants.
Right speech: Speak in a way that defends the world from Shadow.
Right action: Act in a way that defends the world from Shadow.
Right livelihood: Be a practicing sorceress in a way that defends the world not just from Shadow but also from the tyrants that we Aes Sedai might become if we did not follow this Five-Step Path.

Conspicuously absent from the list are the Three Oaths. This, our hypothetical teacher would explain to her students, is because the Three Oaths and the Five-Step Path are independent. They complement each other and must be observed simultaneously. While the first oath says speak no word that is not true, the third step says you *can* allow people to reach the wrong conclusion if deceiving them this way helps defend the world from darkness. The second oath guides the fifth step: the proper profession of the Aes Sedai is not an ironmonger but a servant. Thus, sisters may occasionally use the One Power to kill, but never to arm others to kill. The third oath guides the fourth step: because sisters put themselves in harm's way, specifically to defend the world from the Dark One, there will be times when violence against the forces of darkness is unavoidable. So, the Aes Sedai are less like the typical pacifist Buddhist nun and more like the Shaolin nuns whose mastery of kung fu is paradoxically intended to *reduce* violence in the world. In Shaolin temples this is mostly theoretical, while the Aes Sedai have the unenviable duty of putting it into practice.

## The Takeaway

I'm not suggesting that Robert Jordan deliberately made the Aes Sedai an order of Buddhist nuns. (If he did, he did it poorly, because they don't seem very interested in the whole enlightenment thing.) I *am* arguing that they're definitely not Kantians, and if they're utilitarians they're pretty bad at it. And, since the Aes Sedai aren't known for their incompetence—if anything, their critics say they are *too* good at what they do—I'll suggest they have not misunderstood their own moral code. Therefore, they are *not* bad utilitarians. They're closer to skillful Shaolin nuns.

I don't see an equivalent of the Eightfold Path in Jordan's novels, but borrowing the first five steps does help us make sense of why the Aes Sedai's ethics seem so weird. And drawing on Buddhism is not a random choice; clearly Jordan drew from Indian philosophy in creating the metaphysics of *The Wheel of Time*. Reincarnation, the balance (rather than opposition) of good and evil, even the Wheel itself, they are all evidence of this. So really, it should come as no surprise if the ethics follow the metaphysics.

## Notes

1. Desmond Warzel, "Wikihistory," *Abyss and Apex*, 3rd quarter 2007, at https:// www.abyssapexzine.com/wikihistory.
2. Or three boys and a girl, at the beginning of the TV series. But by season 2 we know it's one of the boys.
3. In the book series, the oaths are mentioned sporadically throughout, and can be found in the glossary of most volumes. One noticeable mention occurs in *New Spring: The Novel* in the chapter "Just Before Dawn," when Moiraine takes her oaths. In the television series these are first mentioned in season 1, episode 2, "Shadow's Waiting," with slightly altered wording.
4. He doesn't mention Fades by name, but he does say it's wrong to tell a white lie even to a would-be murderer in order to save someone's life. Immanuel Kant, "On a Supposed Right to Lie Because of Philanthropic Concerns," in James W. Ellington trans., *Grounding for the Metaphysics of Morals* (Indianapolis: Hackett, 1981), 63–65.

**14**

# Asha'man, Kill: On "Making Weapons" and the Ethics of War

*Tobias T. Gibson*

The suicide terrorist is the ultimate "smart bomb" …[1]
You could not train men to be weapons without expecting a certain amount of arrogance.[2]

It's clear from the beginning that the war between light and dark, between the Dragon Reborn and the Dark One, is a moral, just war for Rand, Perrin, Mat, and their allies to join. When Trollocs invade the Two Rivers and kill innocent villagers the die is cast for an epic good versus evil battle. This is a moral fight. However, questions remain regarding whether the actions of Rand and others are moral. Despite what the cliche says, not all is fair in love and war. With the creation and design of the Asha'man, Rand may be doing something that is morally wrong and yet he may be right to do it. He seems to face a dirty hands problem, or a "necessity [that] demands … he perform actions that are morally objectionable."[3] This is not just the stuff of fantasy novels. As we'll see, reflecting on the Asha'man can help us morally evaluate the use of emerging technologies, especially autonomous weapons whose "increasing real-world application are creating a new set of conditions for the conduct of war and the broader employment of violence in international affairs."[4]

## Dirty Hands Problem

The political theorist Michael Walzer first posited the problem of "dirty hands" in 1973.[5] Walzer says that "conventional wisdom" suggests "that politicians are a good deal worse, morally worse, than the rest of us."[6] This "presumption is especially great because the victorious politician uses violence and the threat of violence—not only against foreign nations in our defense but also against us, and again ostensibly for our greater good."[7] The

*The Wheel of Time and Philosophy*, First Edition. Edited by Jacob M. Held.
© 2025 John Wiley & Sons, Inc. Published 2025 by John Wiley & Sons, Inc.

scholar C.A.J. Coady finds an earlier version of dirty hands in Machiavelli, who "thinks that the ordinary processes of politics require that the Prince 'must learn how not to be good,' though he should maintain the appearance of virtue and indeed behave virtuously when the cost is low."[8]

Rand is not a political leader, at least not in the same way that Elayne is or Egwene becomes, but he struggles in making difficult decisions. For example, one of his biggest qualms as a military leader is putting the lives of women in danger—even those of the Aiel *Far Dareis Mai*, or Maidens of the Spear. In an exchange with Sulin, he admits "I … do not like to see a woman die. I hate it, Sulin. It curdles me up inside."[9] This does change, a bit, when Rand selects the Maidens as his honor guard. But not until Sulin insists to Rand that not allowing the Maidens to engage in battle dishonors them does he begin to allow this to happen. According to Sulin, "I am the spear. … No chief would hesitate to send me wherever the dance is hottest. If I died there, my first-sisters would mourn me, but not a fingernail more than when our first-brother fell. A Treekiller who stabbed me to the heart in my sleep would do me more honor than you do. Do you understand now?"[10] Despite this explanation, Rand continues to struggle, not only about the *Far Dareis Mai,* but about his responsibility when any woman is harmed.

Again, there is no doubt in *The Wheel of Time* series that the fight is just. Jordan makes clear throughout that the fight between Dragon Reborn and the Dark One is existential. Thus, it is important to note that Walzer believes that there may be justification for a leader to get their hands dirty without their conscience being clean. After all, a dirty hands problem is a "choice in which there will be grave moral loss either way" and "political and military leaders may sometimes find themselves in situations where they cannot avoid acting immorally."[11] Walzer posits that a "supreme emergency" may provide justification for a dirty hands decision, and a supreme emergency is one in which an aggressor clearly constitutes an existential threat.

Well after Rand learns that he is both the Dragon Reborn and the Aiel *Car'a'carn*, he devises a plan to train male channelers to fight the Dark One at Tarmon Gai'don. These male channelers are called Asha'man. Rand's dirty hands are evident in his decision to form the Black Tower— the male channelers complement the Aes Sedai's White Tower. The Black Tower is designed and intended to be a place where male channelers are trained to enhance and control their powers. Unlike the White Tower which trains Aes Sedai widely, the Black Tower trains its students in war. It is no accident that "soldier" is the first rank a male reaches.

Justified or not, Rand's hands are filthy with the creation of the Black Tower. Although, ostensibly, Rand felt that "An Asha'man was a man who defended truth and justice and right for everyone. A guardian who would not yield even when hope was gone,"[12] that does not overcome two major issues that seemingly undermine this position in Rand's mind.

The first issue is that there was fear and distrust of the Asha'man. Min, one of Rand's lovers and perhaps his most trusted advisor, "without meeting even one of the [Asha'man], [Min] was afraid of them, men who could channel, men who wanted to channel."[13] This fear is understandable, as men who could channel had in the past gone insane. Even Rand wasn't comfortable with the Asha'man. In fact, although he was the most powerful of all male channelers, Rand was "suspicious of any man in a black coat"[14] (the official uniform of the Asha'man), but "he had to lead them. The Asha'man were his making, his responsibility."[15] Distrust of the Asha'man includes Mazrim Taim and Logain, both of whom were False Dragons.[16]

The other major issue is that although Rand knew "he had to lead" the Asha'man, he left the Black Tower and its lessons to Mazrim Taim's leadership. He ignored the Black Tower because he did not like Taim.[17] As it turns out, his fears were correct. While Rand ignored the Black Tower, Taim undermined Rand's leadership and created an army loyal to him—a Dark Friend, and the newest Forsaken.[18]

In an extension of Walzer, Ben Jones and John M. Parrish argue that "dirty hands" should never be justified in a codified policy, but rather should only take place in cases of emergency.[19] The creation of the Black Tower and the training of the Asha'man were part of the regular planning for war, so neither constitute an emergency—and the training purpose and regimen were established policy. As Walzer writes in a refinement of his 1973 article, "[e]ven in wars where the stakes are very high, they may not be so high at every moment in the course of the war as to bring the supreme-emergency argument into play. Each moment is a moment-in-itself; we make judgments again and again, not once for each war."[20]

It takes Logain telling Rand about Taim to begin Rand's decision to "wash his hands" of the issues he's created. From Logain, Rand learns that "Taim does a great many things people think are at your direction." Moreover, Taim "has his own plans" and has a special group that he "keeps close and trains privately."[21] Logain goes on to warn Rand that Taim will break the Black Tower, and that most Asha'man would be loyal to Taim (as most have not met Rand).[22]

To recap, Rand created a training space for male channelers to learn how to use the One Power as a weapon of war—despite his initial misgivings. He then turned over the training program to a man he did not like or trust. Yet, Taim was entrusted, even if not trusted, to teach the men and lead them into the Last Battle. Given the existential threat of Tarmon Gai'don, it is understandable that Rand, despite his dirty hands in creating the Black Tower, felt it necessary to create every advantage possible over the Shadow. Rand's burden is a "choice in which there will be grave moral loss."[23] Given his feelings toward Taim and the importance of the Black Tower, Rand's lack of oversight is inexcusable. After all, "[t]he Asha'man were his making, his responsibility."[24]

## Asha'man as Autonomous Weapons

In the epigraph at the start of this chapter, renowned terrorism scholar Bruce Hoffman says, "The suicide terrorist is the ultimate 'smart bomb.'" This is based on current technology, but also indicates the importance of thinking of a weaponized human *as a weapon*. The connection to the Asha'man is clear. The distinction between training a person to wield weapons and being a weapon wasn't lost on Rand, who realized in a discussion with Torval—an Asha'man loyal to Taim—that "[y]ou could not train men to be weapons without expecting a certain amount of arrogance."[25] In a nod back to the dirty hands problem, Rand agreed to allow Mazrim Taim to recruit aggressively, despite his misgivings, and with Taim's express goal being to ensure "every man a weapon."[26]

Taim's training plan lacks humility, even for low-level trainees. On one visit to the Black Tower, Torval tells Rand that he does not "look so grand" and begins to suggest that he is superior to Rand. Though Taim punishes Torval quickly, Taim adds to Rand, "You cannot tell a man that he has the power to make the earth shake, then expect him to walk small."[27] Similarly, new Asha'man learn a bit of healing from Taim, because as Taim explains "[a] weapon loses its utility if it's going to be laid up with the first wound."[28] But, Rand, too, expects Asha'man to *be* weapons. In a heated discussion with Torval, Rand insists that "The Asha'man are a weapon to be aimed where I say."[29] A few pages later, Rand reflects that although the Aes Sedai have years of training, the Asha'man's training was more focused. "An Asha'man only needed to know how to kill. ... that was all they had been created for."[30]

Rather than building inanimate weapons, such as a sword or a spear, both Rand and Taim purposefully "built" intelligent, autonomous, learning weapons. Consider the similarities between these walking, talking, thinking weapons and what we currently call "lethal autonomous weapon systems." According to a 2025 Congressional Research Services document "[l]ethal autonomous weapon systems (LAWS) are a special class of weapon systems that use sensor suites and computer algorithms to independently identify a target and employ an onboard weapon system to engage and destroy the target without manual human control of the system."[31] The report further notes that the US Department of Defense defines lethal autonomous weapons as "weapon system[s] that, once activated, can select and engage targets without further intervention."[32] Surely, the Asha'man meet this standard.

Because Mazrim Taim was a Forsaken, and loyal to the Dark One, and because Rand failed to have competent oversight over the Black Tower, Taim was able to establish "a Tower of his own hidden in the Black Tower, and the men inside it are loyal to him, not [Rand]."[33] In some ways, this is akin to a poorly designed or faulty algorithm in an autonomous weapon. Ingvild Bode, writing for the International Committee of the Red Cross, says that "[w]e can think about algorithmic bias in three main ways: (1) bias in data, (2) bias in design and development, and (3) bias in use."[34]

Bias in data is an issue based on the inputs that train the autonomous weapon. Needless to say, even an advanced machine cannot have literally every piece of data in existence. There can be both direct biases, such as "stereotypical language and images" and indirect biases, inherent in the data choices used to inform the autonomous weapon, such as unintended biases of characteristics of potential targets (skin color, gender, hair styles, or something similar). Bode succinctly makes the point that "[b]ias in data therefore results from unrepresentative data leading to unrepresentative outputs."[35]

Bias in design and development illustrates that the biases in autonomous machines and weapons often "mirror" and amplify the biases of the designers of these autonomous weapons. That is, "bias may not be intentional, but nonetheless infiltrate an application through training data, or the way computer engineers design the weights assigned to factors."[36]

The third category, bias in use, is also pernicious. Bode states that by "simply … employing [these] systems … any biases that these contain will be amplified." And, once these autonomous weapons are employed, decision makers may simply rely on the accuracy of the outputs of the automated system.[37]

In some ways, Taim's training of the Asha'man ensured that all three biases existed in the men he trained. As Bode argues, bias in data, or how the data is trained, offers but a "snapshot" of the world. So, for example, because both Rand and Mazrim Taim are men—who have a strong distrust of the Aes Sedai—and because Taim is loyal to the Dark One, we can assume the data used to train these "autonomous weapons" has strong biases. Rand and Taim are primarily responsible for the design (Rand) and development (Taim) of the Asha'man—again, there is much evidence to suggest that, for example, Taim's development of a coterie loyal only to him meant there was a development bias. Bode notes that bias in use can occur in two ways: first, "any biases that these contain will be amplified. Second, people will act on the outputs that AI systems produce."[38]

The creation and use of emerging technologies, including autonomous weapons, may challenge the understanding of just war theory.[39] One of the key benefits of autonomous weapons is the speed with which they can act. In the "real world," this is evident in machine versus human—and research is especially prevalent in tools of war.[40] As the ICRC suggests, "While speed might be advantageous to militaries in some circumstances, when uncontrolled it risks escalating conflicts in an unpredictable manner and aggravating humanitarian needs. … All autonomous weapons that endanger human beings raise these ethical concerns, but they are particularly acute with weapons designed or used to target human beings directly."[41]

The lessons are applicable in *The Wheel of Time*, too. There are many advantages of speed built into the story of good versus evil. Consider that the ability to create Gateways for speedy travel, and the ability of Egwene (and others) to Dream Walk in *Tel'aran'rhiod* allows for communication across long distances. Of course, both have perils as well—including the risk of being cut via closing gateways, and the risk of death in dreams, as your death in dreams means your death in the living world as well. Most importantly for our purposes, the speed of having a trained autonomous weapon on the battlefield, as Asha'man, involves serious risk. Jordan is very clear throughout that there is a balance in the universe, between Light and Dark, good and bad, and this is evident in many places—including the One Power, which has both Saidin and Saidar.

## "I Bring Change. Not Peace, but Turmoil. What Will Be, Will Be ..."[42]

Rand al-Thor, as the Dragon Reborn, is very literally a (or perhaps *the*) force for good in *The Wheel of Time*. He is also a young man, largely untested, who lacks experience and wisdom. He is distrustful of people he does not know, even when we—as the readers—know they have the wisdom and experience to guide him. He is often overwhelmed, fighting insanity, and because the weight of the world is on his shoulders, he often abdicates his responsibilities. In other words, he's human. But he is a human who makes a decision to create a weapon that he then loses control of, and that has consequences. This is not just the stuff of fantasy worlds. As we have seen, *The Wheel of Time* can start us thinking about the ethical complexities of a serious real-world issue—the increasingly important development and potential use of autonomous weapons.

## Notes


1. Bruce Hoffman, *Inside Terrorism*, 3rd ed. (New York: Columbia University Press, 2017), 141.
2. Robert Jordan, *The Path of Daggers* (New York: TOR Fantasy, 1998), 296.
3. Linda Eggert, "Dirty Hands Defended," *Journal of Moral Philosophy* (2023), https://doi.org/10.1163/17455243-20234097.
4. Ash Rossiter and Peter Layton, *Warfare in the Robotics Age* (Boulder: Lynne Rienner, 2024), 1.
5. Michael Walzer, "Political Action: The Problem of Dirty Hands," *Philosophy & Public Affairs* 2 (1973), 160–180.
6. Walzer, "Political Action," 162.
7. Walzer, "Political Action," 163.
8. C.A.J. Coady, "The Problem of Dirty Dands," in *The Stanford Encyclopedia of Philosophy*, https://plato.stanford.edu/archives/spr2024/entries/dirty-hands.
9. Robert Jordan, *The Fires of Heaven* (New York: TOR Fantasy, 1993), 640.

10. Jordan, *The Fires of Heaven*, 640.
11. Coady, "The Problem of Dirty Dands."
12. Robert Jordan, *Lord of Chaos* (New York: TOR Fantasy, 1994), 245.
13. Jordan, *Lord of Chaos*, 538.
14. Jordan, *The Path of Daggers*, 296.
15. Jordan, *The Path of Daggers*, 296.
16. Robert Jordan, *Knife of Dreams* (New York: TOR Fantasy, 2005), 391.
17. Jordan, *Lord of Chaos*, 539.
18. Jordan, *Knife of Dreams*, 392.
19. Ben Jones and John M. Parrish, "Drones and Dirty Hands," in Kerstin Fisk and Jennifer M. Ramos eds., *Preventive Force: Drones, Targeted Killing, and the Transformation of Contemporary Warfare* (New York: New York University Press, 2016), 283–312.
20. Michael Walzer, "Emergency Ethics," in *Arguing About War* (New Haven: Yale University Press, 2004), 46.
21. Robert Jordan, *Crossroads of Twilight* (TOR Fantasy, 2003), 557.
22. Jordan, *Crossroads of Twilight*, 558.
23. Coady, "The Problem of Dirty Dands."
24. Jordan, *The Path of Daggers*, 296.
25. Jordan, *The Path of Daggers*, 296.
26. Jordan, *Lord of Chaos*, 216.
27. Jordan, *Lord of Chaos*, 540–541.
28. Jordan, *Lord of Chaos*, 541.
29. Jordan, *The Path of Daggers*, 297.
30. Jordan, *The Path of Daggers*, 299.
31. Kelley M. Sayler, "Defense Primer: US Policy on Lethal Autonomous Weapon Systems," Congressional Research Service, at https://crsreports.congress.gov/product/pdf/IF/IF11150, 1.
32. Sayler, "Defense Primer," 1.
33. Jordan, *Knife of Dreams*, 392.
34. Ingvild Bode, "Falling Under the Radar: The Problem of Algorithmic Bias and Military Applications of AI," *International Committee of the Red Cross, March* 14 (2024), https://blogs.icrc.org/law-and-policy/2024/03/14/falling-under-the-radar-the-problem-of-algorithmic-bias-and-military-applications-of-ai.
35. Bode, "Falling Under the Radar."
36. James E. Baker, Laurie N. Hobart, and Matthew G. Mittelsteadt, *AI for Judges: A Framework* (Center for Security and Emerging Technology, December,, 2021), at https://cset.georgetown.edu/publication/ai-for-judges, 30.
37. Bode, "Falling Under the Radar"; Baker, Hobart, and Mittelstadt, "AI for Judges," 28–30.
38. Bode, "Falling Under the Radar."
39. Matthew W. Hallgarth, "Just War Theory and Remote Military Technology: A Primer," in Bradley J. Strawser ed., *Killing by Remote Control: The Ethics of an Unmanned Military* (New York: Oxford University Press, 2013), 25–46.
40. Brian W. Everstine, "Artificial Intelligence Easily Beats Human Fighter Pilot in DARPA Trial," *Air & Space Forces*, August 20, (2020) at https://www.airandspaceforces.com/artificial-intelligence-easily-beats-human-fighter-pilot-in-darpa-trial; Associated Press, "US Air Force Leader Takes AI-Controlled

Fighter Jet Ride in Test vs Human Pilot," VOA, May 5, 2024, at, https://www.voanews.com/a/air-force-leader-takes-ai-controlled-fighter-jet-ride-in-test-vs-human-pilot-/7597733.html.
41. International Committee of the Red Cross, "What You Need to Know About Autonomous Weapons," ICRC, July 22, 2022, at https://www.icrc.org/en/document/what-you-need-know-about-autonomous-weapons.
42. Robert Jordan, *The Shadow Rising* (New York: TOR Fantasy, 1992), 667.

**15**

# The Way of the Leaf: Pacifism in the Third Age

## *Jacob M. Held*

The world of *The Wheel of Time* is supersaturated with violence: wars, murder, stilling, gentling, torture. You can't go long without encountering Trollocs, Darkfriends, Fades, or the Forsaken. In a world such as this, violence may appear to be inevitable, and in fact many treat it as such. Those in the borderlands live in a mindset of perpetual war. Aiel culture is built around martial virtues. If you are Rand or one of his compatriots, you know it's only a matter of time before your next life-or-death struggle. Yet not all who live in this precarious, blood-soaked world see violence as inevitable. The *Tuatha'an*, or traveling people, also known as Tinkers, choose a different way, the Way of the Leaf. Simply put, the Way of the Leaf "means that no man should harm another for any reason whatsoever. ... There is no excuse for violence. None. Not ever."[1] The Tinkers are pacifists.

In the world of *The Wheel of Time*, pacifism may seem naive. After all, when Trollocs and Fades pour out of the Blight to ransack towns in the borderland, when creatures that only desire to kill come after your children, how could you refuse to fight, allowing yourself and your family to be murdered, or worse? The Tinkers pose a counterpoint, reflecting a philosophical tradition—pacifism—that has continually challenged thinking on war and violence.

The pacifism espoused by the Tinkers can have an initial appeal. If it didn't, Elyas wouldn't be so hostile to Raen as he decries his attempts to "convert village younglings."[2] If one grew up in a violent world, a lifestyle that eschews violence would be attractive. The Tinker way of life, freewheeling travel, dancing, songs, no fighting, would be very appealing—like hippies or dropouts running away to follow the Grateful Dead, "Just looking for 'The Song,' man." But, as one scholar notes, "a pacifist response [has] an appealing moral clarity but [is] not always easy to reconcile with the harsh realities of daily life, where force might sometimes be necessary to allow the right to prevail—for example, to protect the innocent from assault."[3]

*The Wheel of Time and Philosophy*, First Edition. Edited by Jacob M. Held.
© 2025 John Wiley & Sons, Inc. Published 2025 by John Wiley & Sons, Inc.

In what follows, we'll explore the philosophical underpinnings of pacifism and consider whether the Way of the Leaf is a viable alternative to justified violence.

## The Leaf Does No Harm ....

"We harm no one. No one! There is no reason good enough to justify killing another human being. None!"[4] Although we are introduced to the Tinkers in *The Eye of the World*, their prohibition on killing goes back to their origins as Aiel, Da'shain serving Aes Sedai, before the breaking of the world—a history revealed in Rand's visions at Rhuidean. These visions indicate that the Way of the Leaf, that is, nonviolence, is a basic tenet of what it means to be Da'shain, Tinkers (or the Lost Ones), and Jenn Aiel. The Tinkers maintain there is no justification for killing, not war and not even self-defense. Although the quote above indicates that they will not kill human beings, it reflects a broader prohibition. They would not kill Nym, they do not eat meat, and even violence against Trollocs and Fades is forsworn. Importantly, this is because the prohibition does not stem from the inherent worth or value of the victim of violence, but rather from the impact that acts of violence have on the agent.

The reader first meets the traveling people when Egwene and Perrin happen upon them while traveling with Elyas Machera, a wolfbrother and former warder. As a wolfbrother, one that lives by hunting and killing, a natural apex predator, and a warder, one trained for a singular purpose, to protect Aes Sedai, Elyas is the inverse of the Tinkers. They eschew all violence whereas he lives by violence as a natural part of existence. The reader sees this tension play out in the interactions between Elyas and Raen, the leader, or Seeker, of this particular band of Tinkers. But it is Aram, the grandchild of Raen and Ila who articulates the philosophical tenets of the Tinkers. As Perrin expresses consternation at the fact that young children are playing with enormous dogs, Aram assures him, "they are trained according to the Way of the Leaf." He elaborates, "The leaf lives its appointed time, and does not struggle against the wind that carries it away. The leaf does no harm, and finally falls to nourish new leaves. So it should be with all men. And women." Perrin is intrigued, "What if somebody hits you, or tries to rob you, or kill you?" Aram patiently explains how he'd try to reason with the fellow but would never turn violent, because "violence harms the one who does it as much as the one who receives it." Perrin is doubtful, and explains how if someone hit him, he'd hit them back, for to do otherwise would incentivize the aggressor to continue to use violence. Aram condescends to Perrin noting that some people never overcome their "baser instincts." Perrin retorts, "I'll bet you get to run away a lot."[5] And so the conversation devolves into passive aggressive slights and mockery.

Although simplistic, Aram and Perrin's exchange opens up a conversation on pacifism. As with any philosophical doctrine or theory there are many variations on the theme of nonviolence. If one is opposed to violence, one may be a universal pacifist and so "morally opposed to all violence, not just killing."[6] The reasons for being so opposed might be religious, metaphysical, or rights based. If one were not opposed to all violence, one might be a private pacifist. A private pacifist "renounces violence in personal relations but condones the use of force in the political sphere."[7] Such a person may not support the idea of using violence in cases of self-defense, but would support war in the case of national defense. Philosopher and theologian Saint Augustine of Hippo (354–430) is sometimes characterized as a private pacifist. As a final possibility, one might be an anti-war pacifist. Anti-war pacifists "condone the validity of personal self-defense, but they deny that war can be justified by appeal to self-defense or any other right."[8] Although these categories cannot fully articulate the numerous and nuanced forms of principled stances against violence, they provide a useful taxonomy within which we can place the Tinkers: they are universal pacifists. They oppose violence of all kinds, self-defense and war, even to the point of being vegetarians.

In the conversation with the Tinkers noted above, we can see that the foundation for their nonviolence is metaphysical. They do not oppose violence because of scriptural edict, as do some Christian pacifists. Nor do they appeal to divine commands or revelations. In addition, they are not pacifists because they think violence generates more suffering on the whole. They are not utilitarians. They don't appear to oppose violence because it is inefficient or may generate more harm than the alternative. Their absolute prohibition does not provide an escape clause for using violence when it is deemed necessary or most likely to produce a favored outcome. Their history makes this clear.

If one recounts the origins of the Tinkers, from the Aiel of old, as witnessed by Rand in Rhuidean, one may recall his vision of Lewin. After some girls from camp, including Lewin's sisters, are abducted by raiders, Lewin and several of his friends set out to rescue them. They find them in a raider camp and in the process of trying to surreptitiously rescue them are forced to fight. In the process they kill the raiders, but one of Lewin's friends is killed as well. It is obvious from the scenario that these girls have been brutalized. Aside from physical wounds they bear the psychological marks of sexual assault. These raiders were vicious. Yet when the young men return to their camp with the rescued girls the response is hostile. Adan, the leader of the group, states, "You ... killed? Killed *men*? What of the Covenant? We harm no one. No one! There is no reason good enough to justify killing another human being." Lewin protests, noting that the raiders took young girls, their sisters. They hurt them. But he is chastised, "There is no reason!"[9] The young men are put out of camp, exiled. If killing a handful of raiders can't be justified even when they have abducted and raped young girls, even if the cost is the loss of only one volunteer, it is clear that no outcomes-based rationale could justify violence within the doctrine of the Way of the Leaf. The Tinkers are absolute, universal pacifists and not for religious or utilitarian grounds. In addition, they do not speak in terms of "rights." They never mention that people have a right to life. This wouldn't justify their position either, since if one has a right to life, as do the girls noted above, then someone might have an obligation to secure that right; at a minimum self-defense would be justified to protect one's right to life should someone try to violate it. If it's not religion, utility, or rights, on what grounds might the Tinkers justify universal pacifism?

The Tinkers seem to base their principle of nonviolence on a metaphysical understanding of the care of the self. As noted above, Aram claims that violence harms the doer as much as the recipient. In this way, they echo the teachings of Mohandas Gandhi (1869–1948). The goal for this kind of pacifism is to purify one's soul. Of course, one could equally say "one's self" if one were seeking a secular, non-metaphysically loaded account. According to such an account, violence taints, or pollutes, the soul and so should be avoided at all costs. The taking of a life may save a life, as in the case of Lewin above, but it does not save souls, and may cost the life-taker dearly. The soul of a killer is damaged or tainted through the act of killing. This belief explains why Adan shuns Lewin and his comrades. It also explains the tragedy of Aram's story arc in *The Wheel of Time*.

In *The Eye of the World*, Ila expresses concern for her grandson. That concern comes to fruition when, after a Trolloc raid on his camp, one which kills his mother, Aram abandons the Way of the Leaf to take up the sword. His life is then defined by violence and, ultimately, he is killed in battle. Although some may see his response to a Trolloc raid as justified, from the Tinker point of view he has broken the Covenant, he is lost, and as Ila notes "The Lost cannot be happy."[10] For the Tinker, as for the universal pacifist, the most important value is the care of one's soul or self. Thus, the proper response, as articulated throughout Rand's visions at Rhuidean, is to "accept and endure" the "suffering sent to test" them.[11] Importantly, the Way of the Leaf is not forced upon anybody, it couldn't be. Coercion and force are anathema to the fundamental teaching of the Way. So it must be voluntarily accepted by all those that decide to travel with the Tinkers. Those who do not wish to follow the Way may leave. The Tinkers merely present their way to the world in the hope that it will inspire by example. Perhaps, like Bertrand Russell (1872–1970), the Tinkers believe that war and violence will lose their appeal, their rhetorical force, if met with nonviolence. "War is brutal and horrible, but seems to be ennobled by the fact that the warrior risks his life. If no one resists, the heroism is gone; if the brutality survives, it can no longer command admiration ..."[12] One can appreciate the appeal of such a perspective. But Tinkers face difficult questions: Aren't lives, other peoples' souls, sometimes worth the sacrifice? As the shadow looms over the world and the forces of the Dark One devastate nations, cities, communities, and families, isn't resistance appropriate? What if Rand, the Dragon Reborn, chose to be a pacifist?

## ... And Finally Falls ...

The Tinkers are products of a long history reaching back over 3000 years to before the breaking of the world. In *The Shadow Rising*, Rand is presented nine visions walking him backwards through generations of Aiel until he is finally back at the very moment when the bore is driven into the Dark One's prison. This history indicates that the Aiel began as servants to Aes Sedai. They had a harmonious existence with the earth and all life around them, sharing in song with the Nym, and practicing nonviolence. But during the breaking, as male Aes Sedai went mad, they were given the duty by female Aes Sedai (Solinda Sedai, specifically) to carry wagon loads of *angreal*, *sa'angreal*, and *ter'angreal* to a place of safety. They were also instructed to maintain the Covenant, the Way of the Leaf. However, after the breaking, as scarcity drove many to theft, raids, and murder, they were continuously attacked, and with no protection, routinely brutalized. During one vision, his fifth, Rand sees the splitting of the Aiel in two. One group, led by Sulwin and later referred to as the Lost Ones, leaves the caravan, tired of the raids, to seek a safe place where they can focus on singing and finding "the song." This is the origin of the Tinkers. The remaining Aiel carry on, trying to uphold their duty to the Aes Sedai. In Rand's fourth vision, he sees the Aiel break again, after the incident noted above with Lewin and the kidnapped girls. The Jenn Aiel continue onward with the Aes Sedai artifacts to ultimately found Rhuidean. But the splinter group, led by Lewin, become the Aiel with whom the reader is most familiar. In Rand's third vision, the reader sees the beginning of the spear maidens when Morin takes up a spear to rescue her daughter.[13] This history helps to illuminate key components of the Tinkers' pacifism: (i) it is a steadfast, absolutist doctrine affording no exceptions, (ii) it is about the care of the pacifist's soul, or self, and (iii) it is challenged time and again by real-world circumstances.

When Aram and Perrin argue, Perrin raises the usual challenges. What if somebody attacks you? Rand's visions raise other questions: What if somebody attacks those you love or have a duty to care for? What if you have a duty to uphold, such as being stewards for Aes Sedai treasures, and meet violent resistance from others? An additional question not raised in these circumstances, but worth asking, is: Can you maintain and protect a community, a state, a civilization if you are not allowed to use force to dissuade or protect against invaders or would-be conquerors?

Perrin's questions raise issues around self-defense. Two points are worth noting. First, if we have a right to life, or a right to live as free, autonomous beings, then that right would come to nothing if we didn't also have the moral right to protect our freedom against assailants. Saint Thomas Aquinas (1225–1274) sees protecting oneself as perfectly consistent with the moral command of self-preservation.[14] Like Elyas, Aquinas would see killing to protect oneself, or one's allies, as simply a broader edict of nature. This may also apply to protecting others from attacks. As Gratian (eleventh century) notes, "The law of valor lies not in inflicting injury but in repelling it; for he who fails to ward off injury from an associate if he can do so, is quite blamable as he who inflicts it."[15] In fact, the visions Rand has, whether of Lewin rescuing his sisters, or Morin rescuing her daughter, are about protecting the innocent and the helpless from undue and unjust violence. In these cases, there is an ostensive familial obligation to protect those under one's care. To neglect that obligation, when an alternative is practicable, would seem morally dubious. In fact, in Rand's fifth vision he sees Adan as he huddles over children whose parents have just been slaughtered. He watches as raiders take his daughter. In this instance, Adan's thought process is not immediately about the Way of the Leaf. Instead, pacifism is a conclusion reached after considering that resistance would lead to his death for sure. His daughter would still be taken and the children would probably be killed as well. Pacifism is accepted reluctantly as a fatalistic conclusion. Adan will suffer and endure. His only option is to remain faithful to the Way and the Aes Sedai. If he had an option to save his daughter, even using violence, which had a high probability of success it is hard to imagine he'd watch her being carted off to be brutalized. If he'd had a viable option and still chose to do nothing, we'd be justified in viewing him as a coward, as a selfish, dishonorable man who puts his own well-being above his daughter's. But these are private matters. One issue not dealt with in Aram and Perrin's argument, or even in Rand's visions, is how this all applies to nations. Can war be justified?

A tradition in political philosophy, just war theory, lays out the morally permissible conditions under which one can go to war, *jus ad bellum*, and the moral requirements under which one must conduct war, *jus in bello*. In terms of *jus ad bellum*, various conditions must be met before the declaration of war is just. First, war must have a just cause: it must be declared for a morally permissible reason such as self-defense, defense of allies, or humanitarian intervention. Second, a military response must be proportionate. The harm caused by war has to be justified by being the most desirable outcome; it must be less harmful to go to war than not. Third, war must be declared by a competent authority. States declare war. War is not personal violence, it is a political solution to a political necessity, namely, the maintenance of political sovereignty in the face of aggression. In addition, war should be a last resort and there should be a reasonable chance of success. War is undesirable and should only be undertaken when no other option remains, and even then, if there's no chance of success, you're only compounding harms. (Note Adan's reasoning above.) Finally, a state must have the right intentions when going to war. That is, war is about national defense, which must be claimed legitimately and not as subterfuge for conquest. Under these conditions, resorting to force is argued to be a proper response that minimizes harm while protecting a nation's right to exist. In the conduct of war, similar rules apply.

*Jus in bello* dictates that during war, proportionality is crucial. One can't overkill or do more damage or harm than is necessary to achieve legitimate military objectives. Nuclear, biological, and chemical weapons are out, as is Balefire. In conducting oneself, one must also operate under a principle of discrimination, that is, one must distinguish combatant from noncombatant and never intentionally target or harm noncombatants. In modern warfare this is difficult because civilians often become combatants in terrorist organizations. Also, terrorist groups may purposefully hide among noncombatant civilians using them as human shields. This scenario is not new, however. In fact, Aquinas has a response to it with the doctrine of double effect. As he explains, "Nothing hinders a single act from having two effects, only one of which is intended. ... Now moral acts get their character in accordance [from] what is intended, but not from what is beside the intention. ... Accordingly, the act of self-defense may have a double effect: the saving of one's life ... and the slaying of the attacker. ... Since saving one's own life is what is intended, such an act is not therefore illicit ..."[16] If killing a person is the incidental result of a permissible action, self-defense, the action takes on the moral properties of the permissible act, self-defense, and is thereby rendered permissible. So it is in war. If striking a military target is necessary and proportionate, even if it has the incidental and foreseeable result of leading to the deaths of innocent people, so long as the target is legitimate and the intention pure, it is permissible. How many examples could be drawn from *The Wheel of Time* where innocents are dragged into or otherwise impacted by the myriad wars and battles fought? How many people have died as a result of Rand or the Asha'man or Aes Sedai? Would pacifism that results in the Dark One ruling be a morally desirable alternative? Herein lies the greatest challenge to the Way of Leaf: Could Rand, the Dragon Reborn, be a pacifist?

## The Strength of Their Swords Will Cut You Down ...

In *The Dragon Reborn*, Perrin meets another Tinker, Leya, and they have a brief exchange. She begins rehearsing the usual Tinker line, "Violence harms the doer. ... It is better to die than ..." Perrin cuts her off, "If you run, they will hunt you, and kill you, and eat your corpse. Or they might not wait till it *is* a corpse. Either way, you are dead, and it's evil that has won. And there are men just as cruel ... see how many of you the strength of your belief can keep alive."[17] This is prescient, as Mat himself stumbles upon a decimated Tinker caravan later in the series. The world is full of bad people with bad motives and the means to cause harm.

Augustine expresses the tension between one who morally desires pacifism but accepts the necessity of violence. He distinguishes between the
Earthly City and the City of God, and he prioritizes the latter as he prioritizes salvation. But he does not deny that this world, the earthly world,
possesses value. Insofar as political institutions, like the state, are necessary
to provide the circumstances in which people can live and pursue salvation, they are worth protecting. Augustine states, "Waging war and extend-
ing the empire by subduing peoples is therefore viewed as happiness by the
wicked, but as a necessity by the good. But because it would be worse if
wrongdoers dominated those who are more just, it is not inappropriate to
call even this necessity 'happiness.'"[18] Much like Perrin, Augustine eschews
violence as a first resort, but if it is forced upon him through unjust aggression, then violence, as necessary, may be justified, lest one allow the unjust
to dominate.

Unfortunately, these circumstances may be endemic to the human
condition. Although Rand may have seen a vision wherein, before the
breaking, conflict was minimal and violence unnecessary, the way in which
the world is presently constituted is different. Forces do walk the earth
intent on domination. Violence is a fact of life. Augustine had a similar
view of humanity. Although he begins from a theological base claiming
that humankind, as fallen, is naturally sinful and thus prone to conflict, his
conclusion is no different from those who might have secular reasons for
believing the same. "The most salient feature of political authority is just
that feature an authority would have to have in order to govern a society
of people all of whom are constitutionally prone to conflict: the authority
to coerce them."[19] As sure as peaches are poison, human beings are prone
to conflict, as most political philosophers note. Whether it's motivated by
avarice and greed under conditions of scarcity, out of diffidence, insecurity,
or fear due to our basic constitution, or from some perceived slight or
provocation, reason and persuasion are insufficient to resolve all disputes
that face humankind. When reason breaks down, force becomes necessary,
unless one wishes to acquiesce to the aggressor and sacrifice the welfare of
the innocent on one's own altar of self-righteousness. The Seanchan consider their assault on the mainland righteous, they call it "The Return."
They murder and enslave in order to accomplish their goal. No argument
about innocence, just deserts, due process, or rights will dissuade them.
They will only be repelled by force. Even one prone to pacifism in one's
personal life, like Augustine, may accept the necessity of violence. But
accepting the necessity of violence does not have to lead to the perversion
of one's soul. Aram or Leya's concern that the one who does violence is as
injured as the recipient presumes a myopic view of intentionality, and
would taint a heroic defender of innocent women the same as a murderous
villain. But intentions matter. Why one acts is an important variable in
determining the moral worth of the action. If one agrees that using minimal
violence to save an innocent young girl from sexual abuse and eventual

murder is different than cold-blooded murder for personal gain, then one has already begun to doubt the moral foundation of the Way of the Leaf.

Regarding intention, one scholar notes "When adopting 'necessary' measures against wrongdoing, even to the point of using lethal force, Christians were expected to refrain from sentiments of hatred and lust for revenge and to treat the vanquished with mercy."[20] Recall that in *jus ad bellum*, one's intention, or goal, affects the moral worth of the action. One's disposition in committing that act reflects one's character. A reluctant warrior is morally different from a willing brigand. For Augustine, as one scholar notes, "[W]hat Christ requires 'is not a disposition of the body but of the heart …' … This suggests that at least some forms of violence may be justifiable if they proceed from a heart which loves rightly."[21] The Horn of Valere gives us a perfect example of something properly attuned to motive and intention. As noted in *The Great Hunt*, with respect to the prophecy of the horn, "Let whosoever sounds me think not of glory, but only of salvation."[22] In fact, Lord Agelmar is glad to be rid of it since he is too tempted to take it himself and ride to Shayol Ghul, with glory as his clear motive. Aquinas echoes a similar point: "For if his sole intention be to repel the injury done to him, and he defend himself with due moderation, it is no sin. … But if, on the other hand, his self-defense be inspired by vengeance or hatred, it is always a sin."[23] Glory, personal glory, may be an equally problematic motive, as it is also driven by ego, considering one's own desires as primary. The Horn's limiting factor regarding who can sound it is simply a clear example of the notion that intentions matter in determining the moral value of an action.

Nonviolence, the Way of the Leaf, may be ideal, and would be preferable all things being equal. But Perrin, Mat, and Rand, the Aes Sedai and Borderlanders, do not live in a world where that is a viable option, and neither do we. A lack of fighting or cessation of violence isn't peace. Do the Tinkers know peace? Rand's visions show that the Way of the Leaf may seem like peace but in the real world it is something else entirely. "[P]eace is tranquility of order."[24] If there is no order, but only chaos, and peace, or cessation of fighting, is wrought of fear or self-concern, then what one has is not peace, it is not laudable, it is self-serving and ultimately harmful. The Way of the Leaf is not peace.

## … So Should It Be with All Men and Women? …

Justified violence and pacifism are alternative responses to real-world scenarios, and beyond the moral salience of a position, namely, its internal coherence or consistency, one must also consider if it is practicable. If your moral theory cannot answer the problems you will face, if the answers it provides are unusable, then it is not a moral theory worth considering. So we arrive back at the Tinkers. Clearly, those that remain with the caravan believe pacifism is a viable theory. But remember, the Tinkers are a small, nomadic group. They do not have to maintain and protect property or land. In addition, membership is, for the most part, voluntary. Adults who do not want to be a part of the band can leave. Thus, there is no expectation that your fellow travelers will protect you. They are a small group of nomads who are of a consensus when it comes to nonviolence. This works for them, as far as that goes. That is, it will work for them until someone decides to raid and decimate their caravan. But in the meantime, they are content to live this lifestyle. Could it be scaled up? What if more than merely Tinkers adopted universal pacifism?

Any group of individuals that is a permanent settlement, not a small, nomadic tribe, requires certain things. Private property must be established. Property is necessary insofar as freedom, or self-determination, requires that one have some control over one's material circumstances and so can distribute the resources available to oneself in a way consistent with one's view of the good life. Property is also necessary if one values stability and being able to distribute scarce resources in an orderly, predictable manner. The basic economic rule of the universe is scarcity: there is not enough to provide everybody with all they think they need to craft a life of their choosing. Thus, we have private property, which is predicated on excluding others from using that which one acquires. However, once you have property, which presumes exclusive use rights, there will be people who are jealous of others' possessions. There will, therefore, be conflict. Augustine provides an exemplary account of how to deal with this all-too-human scenario in a morally praiseworthy way. The state may be necessary. Coercion and violence may be necessary. But violence only ought to be used minimally, when necessary, and in the spirit of charity.

One event continually marks Rand's nine visions of the Aiel in Rhuidean: the failure of the Aiel to uphold the charge given by the Aes Sedai. The Aiel were charged with protecting *angreal*, *sa'angreal*, and *ter'angreal*. They failed. They were continually raided, and these irreplaceable, powerful items, were lost. Because they were pacifists, the Aiel witnessed their people slaughtered and Aes Sedai treasures stolen. Their failure to protect each other and their property allowed wickedness to prosper. In the Third Age, the Tinkers live only because others fight the Shadow, others fight the Dark One. If Mat, Rand, or Perrin, if Borderlanders, decided to be pacifists for the good of their own souls, the world would be overrun with Shadowspawn, ruled by Forsaken, Dreadlords, and ultimately Shai'tan. The Tinkers' very existence is parasitic on the good will and heroism of others. The world is livable because others do what the Tinkers, selfishly, refuse to, namely, endure the harshness and hazards of war and self-defense. Essentially, the Tinkers free ride on the sacrifice of all those that die in the Blight.

This last summation may seem a harsh assessment of a band of otherwise endearing characters. But one ought not lose sight of the reality of Rand's world, and ours. There are bad people in the world who seek to harm the innocent, and who will continuously and relentlessly do so as long as they are among us. To cede this world to them, even out of a well-meaning care of one's soul and distaste for violence is still to hand this world over to them and therein to condemn all innocent men and women to their domination. Rand, Moiraine, Lan, Thom, Egwene, … no hero of *The Wheel of Time* could be a pacifist. If the characters were pacifists, the series would have ended after 100 pages with Emond's Field awash in blood, the Dragon Reborn slaughtered, and the Dark One victorious. Violence may be necessary at times to prevent even graver evils. Violence may be necessary to protect the very preconditions of civilized life. If it is necessary, that does not mean it is desirable. One should still only use violence as a last resort in proportion to the threat, and one should always maintain pure intentions, not acting out of hatred or malice. The Tinkers pose an important challenge to those too ready to resort to violence. They also present an idyllic lifestyle many may desire. But until there is no violence, nonviolence is untenable. So long as the world remains broken, we must take life as it comes and respond with a tenable moral theory: "Run when you have to, fight when you must, rest when you can."[25]

# Notes


1. Robert Jordan, *The Eye of the World* (New York: Tom Doherty Associates, 1990), 406.
2. Jordan, *The Eye of the World*, 406.
3. David Fisher, *Morality and War: Can War Be Just in the Twenty-First Century?* (Oxford: Oxford University Press, 2012), 64.
4. Robert Jordan, *The Shadow Rising* (New York: Tom Doherty Associates, 1993), 420.
5. Jordan, *The Eye of the World*, 408.
6. Douglas P. Lackey, "Pacifism," in James E. White ed., *Contemporary Moral Problems*, 8th ed. (Belmont: Thomson Wadsworth, 2006), 484.
7. Lackey, "Pacifism," in, 487.
8. Lackey, "Pacifism," in, 489.
9. Jordan, *The Shadow Rising*, 420.
10. Jordan, *The Eye of the World*, 409.
11. Jordan, *The Shadow Rising*, 420, 415 respectively.
12. Bertrand Russell, "Pacifism and Modern War," in Gregory M. Reichberg, Henrik Syse, and Endre Begby eds., *The Ethics of War: Classic and Contemporary Readings* (Malden: Blackwell, 2006), 601.
13. There is much in this history that I cannot recount, and which explains interesting aspects of the Aiel's history. It's all contained in *The Shadow Rising*, chaps. 24–26.
14. See Lackey, "Pacifism," in, 488.
15. Gratian, "War and Coercion in the *Decretum*," in Gregory M. Reichberg, Henrik Syse, and Endre Begby eds., *The Ethics of War: Classic and Contemporary Readings* (Malden: Blackwell, 2006), 114.

16.  Saint Thomas Aquinas, "Just Wars and Sins Against Peace," in Gregory M. Reichberg, Henrik Syse, and Endre Begby eds., *The Ethics of War: Classic and Contemporary Readings* (Malden: Blackwell, 2006), 190.
17.  Robert Jordan, *The Dragon Reborn* (New York: Tom Doherty Associates, 1991), 8.
18.  Saint Augustine, "Just War in the Service of Peace," in Gregory M. Reichberg, Henrik Syse, and Endre Begby eds., *The Ethics of War: Classic and Contemporary Readings* (Malden: Blackwell, 2006), 72.
19.  Paul Weithman, "Augustine's Political Philosophy," in Eleonore Stump and Norman Kretzmann eds., *The Cambridge Companion to Augustine* (New York: Cambridge University Press, 2001), 240.
20.  Gregory M. Reichberg, "Jus ad Bellum," in Larry May ed., *War: Essays in Political Philosophy* (New York: Cambridge University Press, 2008), 13.
21.  Weithman, "Augustine's Political Philosophy," in, 247.
22.  Robert Jordan, *The Great Hunt* (New York: Tom Doherty Associates, 1990), 85.
23.  Aquinas, "Just Wars and Sins Against Peace," in, 182–183.
24.  Aquinas, "Just Wars and Sins Against Peace," in, 172.
25.  Jordan, *The Eye of the World*, 380.

# HUMANKIND IS MADE FOR UNCERTAINTY

**16**

# Un/Common Bonds: Ethics and Polyamory in *The Wheel of Time*

## Benjamin B. DeVan

When a fan asked James Oliver Rigney Jr.—also known as Robert Jordan—why his *Wheel of Time* protagonist Rand al'Thor—also known as the Dragon Reborn—first fell in love with and then married three women, he replied:

> Um, when I was much younger, before I met Harriet [Rigney's wife], I had two girlfriends simultaneously, who arranged my dating schedule between them, who was going to date me on which night. They chipped in together to buy me birthday presents and Christmas presents. You know, they just sort of shared me between them, you know. And they had been friends before, and I am not quite sure whether or not they made the decision they were both going to date me or not, on their own, before they first met me, it just came about. But I figured if I could manage two, surely Rand could manage three. Besides there are mythological reasons to have these three women involved with him.[1]

Rand and his sister-wives Aviendha, Elayne, and Min were not the only characters in *The Wheel of Time* who courted or desired or married more than one person at a time. Rand's fellow Aielman Gaul spoke of marrying two wives, Bain and Chiad, to make of them a triad due to each maiden's close friendship with the other.[2] Moving to one woman with multiple men, Aes Sedai Alanna Mosvani concurrently cavorted with her two warders Owein and Ihvon.[3] A saucy-eyed tavern singer in a presumptive "hell" lamented the scheduling limits for several swains:

> Now Jac gets an hour when the sky is clear,
> and Willi gets an hour when my father's not near.
> It's the hayloft with Moril, for he shows no fear,
> and Keilin comes at midday; he's oh so bold!
> Lord Brelan gets an evening when the night is cold.

> Master Andril gets a morning, but he's very old.
> Oh, what, oh, what is a poor girl to do?
> My loves are so many and the hours so few.[4]

Yet it does not appear as if all *Wheel of Time* characters prefer *polyamory*—meaning, many loves—or grouples, as it were, over couples. All known Novice or Accepted pillow-friends (with benefits!) in the White Tower were monogamous.[5] Rand feared he was a lecher for wooing three women at once, and Rand's "Wisdom" Nynaeve pronounced that he was worse than a lecher.[6] In the Amazon series, Rand's teenage crush Egwene—raised later to the Amyrlin Seat—is visibly startled by Alanna, Owein, and Ihvon, whereas in the books she accepts prospective couple-to-throuple Bael, Dorindha, and Melani, though she muses about the strangeness of their ways.[7]

Perrin and Andoran noble Elenia Sarand remind their would-be admirers or seducers that because they are married, they are off-limits. Perrin quotes an adage applicable to wedding two or more sister-wives: "'A jealous wife is like a hornets' nest in your mattress.' ... No matter how you twitched, you got stung."[8] Countless *Wheel of Time* couples, including Egwene and Gawyn, Morgase and Tallanvor, the Basheres, Siuan and Gareth, Egeanin and Bale, Moiraine and Thom, joyfully relinquish all previous and additional romantic bonds for full-hearted devotion to each other. Jordan's one-and-only wife Harriet McDougal Rigney demurred on the real-life applications of Rand's fictional polyamory: "I am not for it."[9]

## Is Monogamy or Polyamory Better?

Despite historical and cultural assumptions—in both the western lands of this world and *The Wheel of Time*—philosophers like Elizabeth Brake assert that polyamorous partnerships are healthier if polyamory promotes authenticity, inclusivity rather than exclusion, are in accord with human nature or orientation, and may be more sexually, relationally, and romantically fulfilling than monogamy. Brake appeals further to equity: "Perhaps those with less income, worse social skills, or unconventional looks—might have more access to sexual and romantic relationships."[10]

Reinforcing these notions are popular book titles like *The Ethical Slut*, *Multiamory*, and *Polywise*. In film, Stanley Kubrick's dystopian satire *Dr. Strangelove* imagined sexual polyamory not only as preferable but compulsory under circumstances such as after a nuclear war, when: "a sacrifice [is] required for the future of the human race. I hasten to add that since each man will be required to do prodigious ... *service* along these lines, the women will have to be selected for their sexual characteristics which will have to be of a highly stimulating nature."

Twenty-first-century streaming and television networks feature shows like *Sister Wives*. Meanwhile *The Bachelor* and its derivatives glamorize temporary romantic polyamory with one star chased by numerous suitors, though seasons regularly, perhaps ironically, consummate in a monogamous marital engagement. Robert Jordan insisted on the power of entertainment and *The Wheel of Time*'s viability for exploring these and other ethical matters: "Fantasy is an area where it is possible to talk about right and wrong, good and evil, with a straight face."[11]

How then do *moral philosophers* or *ethicists* who reason about what is good, beautiful, true, and just approach or evaluate decisions about whether or not to cultivate more than one beloved? This chapter argues that *it depends on which ethical framework a person or group uses*. Competing or overlapping ethical visions will be variously colored or tinted. Asking whether polyamory is morally forbidden, suspect, optional, commendable, or essential varies depending on which ethical lens or philosophical "looking glass" informs one's thinking.

## A Many Splendored Thing?

Before polishing and peering through ethical glasses, let us clarify the type of "many loves" we'll focus on. In ancient Greek (and Illian?) categories of love, *ludus* is playful flirting along the lines of Mat tossing silver at pretty ankles, or Maglin Madwen hinting with *double entendre*: "I could not help noticing what looks like a flute case sticking out of your man's bundle."[12] *Ludus* foreseeably foreshadows *eros*, the physical, emotional, romantic, or sexual passionate love that inflamed historic philosophers Abelard (1079–1142) for Héloïse, Dante (1265–1321) for Beatrice, Simone de Beauvoir (1908–1986) and Jean-Paul Sartre (1905–1980) for each other and polyamorously for others. *Ludus* blossoms into *eros* in *The Wheel of Time* when Egwene giggles about making love to her warder-husband Gawyn until he cries for mercy or Aviendha playfully instructs Rand to "bed me now."[13] *Mania* is obsessive "love," like Lanfear hungering for Lews Therin or Mat's fetish for his dagger. *Pragma* is practical, political betrothal calculated by individuals, families, societies, or nations. Relatives or state alliances may coordinate *pragma* marriages as "one of the only ways to become nobility," as Thom told Mat.[14]

*Storge* is simply affectionate or domestic familial love. As a metaphor, it grounds the last rites for Lan's people: "May the last embrace of the mother welcome you home."[15] *Phileo* or *philia* involves brotherly love or friendship beyond biological or adoptive family. Ancient Jewish wisdom in Proverbs 18:24 advised that there is a friend who sticks closer than a brother. Aristotle (384–322 BCE) would probably recognize Elayne Trakand as a pleasant, useful, good friend who paid not only her own but also her friends' debts under the proper conditions.[16] The Chosen or Forsaken—again depending on one's perspective—could hardly countenance *philia* or close friendships, not even on the order that Socrates dissects in Plato's *Symposium*.[17]

*Agape* or active goodwill is altruistic or sacrificial love that wills and works for the good of everyone in a kind of aspiring infinite polyamory in the optimal sense of each word. *Agape* is the principle behind the Yellow Ajah's "love to make things well, to fix that which is broken," and the significance of *Aes Sedai* as "servant of all."[18] It is Rand as an Arthurian messiah who, like Jesus, dies and is raised from death after defeating Shai'tan for the life of the world.[19] It is Perrin carrying a burden so that his friend need not bear it, Verin giving herself for the Light's sake as a literal but not genuine Darkfriend, and Faile saving the life of a woman she hated.[20] Moiraine warns that *agape* as compassion could nonetheless be acted upon foolishly.[21] We need ethics or moral philosophy, love of *wisdom*, to discern how to love wisely, since so many people, things, and causes, clamor for our time, energy, and attention.

## Eros Loving Wisely?

*Ludus, mania, pragma, storge, phileo,* and *agape* invite their own dilemmas, such as who to welcome as family, the prudence of orchestrating marriages, or flirting with friends. Here we supply a succinct primer on major moral philosophical traditions to advance the discussions around three subcategories of *eros*—romantic, sexual, or marital polyamory—the last labeled polygamy or plural marriage. These three resonant *eros* loves are not identical, but they stir up similarly thorny issues in the media, philosophy, and notorious "define the relationship" talks or DTRs. We will focus less on whether polyamory is psychologically *sustainable* toward two or more beloveds, nor if varieties should be *legal*, though these issues inform and are informed by ethics. Rather, we inquire primarily on whether polyamory is *justifiable* or *preferable* according to particular ethical or moral philosophies.

## Emotivism and Ethical Egoism

If a philosopher among the White Ajah or a philologist among the Brown inquired whether ethical *emotivists* should practice romantic, sexual, or marital polyamory, she would counsel the emotivist to attempt whatever bolsters the brightest emotions. Although analytic philosophers like Sevara Sedai would prefer more nuance—even if Min Farshaw would prefer less—emotivism, as its name implies, reduces ethics to the emotions our actions evoke.[22] We glow with glee at Bel Tine, and it is *good*, subjectively, at least to us. Someone else cries, "boo," or "boohoo," and whatever prompted that emotion is subjectively bad for them. A.J. Ayer (1910–1989) is one analytic philosopher who argued meticulously for emotivism.[23]

Deciding between monogamy and polyamory for the emotivist boils down to the hippy motto: "If it feels good, do it!" If your emotional fulfillment as Brake suggests is higher with one partner, stick with him or her. If you go giddy for a group of gals or guys, then go along with them. Still, such affairs are not so straightforward. Pragmatic polyamory might yield bigger bangs for emotional bucks in the getting-to-know-you stage of mate-marketing, while sexual and marital monogamy across a lifetime might in due course bloom lusher fruit.

Encompassing but not constraining to emotional highs, lows, and moods, *ethical egoism* expands our standards from nothing more than feelings to how "I" will benefit in the long run, no matter the feelings or vantages of anyone else! Ayn Rand (1905–1982) notoriously championed ethical egoism in *Atlas Shrugged*, a novel that exceeds *The Shadow Rising* in length.[24] The Darkfriend Liandrin offers Nynaeve a pinch of egoist charm before the latter braves the Aes Sedai arches: "If you are doing this for someone else you will fail. Do this for you or not at all."[25] If monogamy or polygamy scores more points for "me" in the long game, that is how "I," if I am an ethical egoist, will swing. Everyone else can go figuratively to Shayol Ghul!

An egoist might rejoin that respecting other people's feelings such as Brake's socially less desirables will also increase "my" well-being. Yet trekking this path bids social contract, utilitarianism, and other moral philosophies like those below to cut in on the mating dance if we bear in mind how esteeming others contributes to or is inseparable from our own good. Challenges linger for emotivists and ethical egoists. How do we *know* or accurately *predict* what is or will be most pleasurable or best for us ultimately? To break with Brake, I could mistakenly assume that multiple lovers will maximize my happiness when, in fact, one partner at a time in loving monogamous relationships would best facilitate my most fulfilling life. This problem of knowing or *epistemology* is not unique to the emotivist or egoist. Nevertheless, characters in *The Wheel of Time* skirting closest to strict egoism are Darkfriends, the Forsaken, and the Dark One. After thousands of years indulging her *mania* for Lews Therin and for power, the externally beautiful Lanfear became, "a woman who had never known [real] love, a woman who would not let herself know it … who could not choose a side other than her own."[26] Shai'tan's egoistic agenda was to provoke the egos of all people and nations to destroy each other so that: "I WILL MAKE A WORLD WHERE THERE IS NOT GOOD OR EVIL. THERE IS ONLY ME."[27]

## Cultural Relativism and Social Contract Theory

While ethical egoism prioritizes the perceived best for oneself, cultural relativism and social contract theory prize what a given culture or society expects from its citizens. To employ *Wheel of Time* geography, when in Tar Valon, do what Tar Valoners do! Rand's genealogical Aiel kin live in culturally polygamous environments. For cultural relativism, marital polyamory is justifiable for Aiel. Since Two Rivers natives marry one person at a time, all (except Rand!) in Emond's Field must on cultural relativist logic love monogamously. Relatedly, philosophers like Thomas Hobbes (1588–1679) beckon rational folk to consent to be governed by one society or another to foster peace and prosperity because mass egoistic emotivism leads to lives that are "solitary, poor, nasty, brutish, and short."[28] Social contracts in the form of laws protect us from each other, and societies punish us if we break them. Therefore, if the state forbids polyamory, avoid it. If not, contemplate it. If mandatory, do it. This begs questions about whether polyamory *should* be legal. The problem with cultural relativism is that it undermines societal growth unless moral progress is already built in or valued. If culture or popular opinion is the definitive ethic, then reforming or changing culture could be prohibited as unethical!

Like Elayne critiquing Galad, cultural relativism acknowledges ethical complexities for differing contexts, but spells trouble for arbitrating disagreements between cultures, as well as overlapping societies or subcultures like the Andorans and Seanchan.[29] British General Charles Napier warned those under his authority who petitioned to practice their custom of *sati* or *suttee*, ritually burning widows alive: "My nation has also a custom: When men burn women alive, we hang them."[30] Napier added that if locals practiced their custom under his jurisdiction, he would practice his as well. Who or what mediates which, if any, cultural rules, and norms prevail? Is there a clearer ethical lens than culture, custom, and tradition to break the stalemate between encouraging or allowing for monogamy, polygamy, or both in any given society or culture?

## Natural Law and Duty

St. Augustine of Hippo (354–430) in his reading of Cicero (106–43 BCE) wrote at the origins of what philosophers label "natural law" ethics when he declared that: "a law that is not just does not seem to me to be a law."[31] In natural law theory, physical reality and ethics are justly regulated by universal or scientific laws as firmer terrain than the laws of the land, whether or not we comprehend them comprehensively. Yet how do we intuit or gain access to universal laws? Our conscience provides insight into what is good, to our duty disclosed by what Immanuel Kant (1724–1804) christened, "the moral law within."[32] Debating polyamory and monogamy from these angles ideally summons lovers to the better angels of our nature, factoring in which competing ethical obligations are preeminent.

The South Asian philosophical epic the *Mahabharata* depicts a duty favoring polygamy grounded in the overriding natural obedience that royal offspring owe to their elders. In the *Mahabharata*, Arjuna the archer wins Princess Draupadi as his wife. When Arjuna escorts Draupadi home, his mother Kunti, unawares, tells Arjuna that he and his brothers must enjoy equally among them whatever Arjuna has won. Draupadi obediently marries all five brothers, alternating her conjugal boons for each individually one year at a time![33]

Genesis 29 in the Bible records another controversial story portraying partly duty-motivated polygamy. When Laban invokes custom for deceptively giving his eldest daughter Leah to Jacob as Jacob's wife, Jacob works for seven more years to gain his beloved Rachel as wife along with Leah—not necessarily due to culture—but as a duty to his father-in-law. How characters act in sacred narratives is not normative for the religious in every case, but these examples permit polygamy as a byproduct, mixed blessing, or lesser evil in honoring filial duty.

## Divine Command Theory and Religion

If ego, emotion, culture, society, epistemological access to natural law, or duty fail to suffice, does the Creator command or reveal intentions regarding polyamory? Via Jordan as *The Wheel of Time* Creator, the Pattern as Divine Providence grants Rand three wives who love him and love each other, pragmatically binding Rand to three kingdoms. But since Jordan was an Episcopalian who was influenced by Judaism, Christianity, and Islam in creating *The Wheel of Time*, it is worth asking what these religions teach about polyamory.[34]

A thorough study of world religions is beyond this chapter, but ethicists detect nascent clues in holy texts or scriptures. The Jewish Bible—aka the Old Testament—reports without endorsing marriages to more than one wife for Patriarchs such as Abraham and Jacob in Genesis, but reprimands philosopher-king Solomon for letting his numerous wives lead him astray (1 Kings 11). King David's polygamous marriage to Abigail, an intelligent diplomat, may be a rare example of judicious, if not fully praiseworthy, stately plural marriage in the Hebrew Bible (1 Samuel 25). On the other hand, Genesis 2:24, in speaking of the primordial parents Adam and Eve, advocates that a man shall leave his father and mother and be joined to his wife—in the singular, not wives in the plural—and together they two shall become one flesh.

This theme of one wife and husband becoming one flesh persists in the New Testament whenever Jesus and the Apostle Paul reference Adam and Eve in Genesis 2.[35] Paul adds that a married church elder should be faithful to his wife and manage his household well (1 Timothy 3). Loosely consistent with most kingdoms in *The Wheel of Time*, the New Testament implies but does not require potential remarriage to a different wife or husband if a former spouse dies or cheats or abandons or is unfaithful to the marital covenant.[36] Mathetes (100s–200s) wrote that *eros*-polyamorous Romans were scandalized by *agape*-polyamorous Christians who: "share a common table but not a common bed … they love all … and are persecuted by all."[37]

Turning to Islam, the Qur'an allows up to four wives and a parallel to captive *gai'shain* in Surah 4:3 and 4:24. At the same time, Muslim polygyny (two or more wives) is qualified by a husband's capacity to provide for up to four wives, even if treating them equally is unworkable (Surah 2:223–2:241, 4:129). Cadsuane Sedai in a country evocative of Arabia as the cradle of Islam cautioned in Arad Doman: "Give a man one cow, and he'd care for it with concern, using its milk to feed his family. Give a man 10 cows, and he was likely to think himself rich—then let all 10 starve for lack of attention."[38] Although Cadsuane's cattle analogy risks dehumanizing polyamory, her consequentialist logic is elaborated below.

## Consequentialism and Utilitarianism, Rights and Virtue

In the space that remains, let us briefly inspect polyamory with the associated philosophies of consequentialism, utilitarianism, rights, and virtue or character ethics. Consequentialism aims to maximize the good of long-term consequences for one person—as in egoism—or for many, as in Utilitarianism. Consequentialism is why the Aiel will not fight the Seanchan after Aviendha foresees doom if they do.[39] Jeremy Bentham (1748–1832) and John Stuart Mill (1806–1873) are the best-known utilitarian philosophers, but Francis Hutcheson (1694–1746) captures their exacting ethic: "*that action* is *best*, which procures the *greatest happiness* for the *greatest numbers;* and that *worst*, which, in *in like manner*, occasions misery."[40] The Aiel woman Mera suggests utilitarian merit in apportioning a polyamorous sister-wife to help manage a husband and children.[41] Utilitarianism is also why the aforementioned Gaul would marry Bain as a second wife to make Bain and Chiad happy, even though Gaul does not like Bain.[42]

Consequentialism and utilitarianism can be qualified by *universal rights* to prevent their excesses. On *rights* logic, thirteen or more Aes Sedai may crave to enslave Rand to alleviate their own anxiety, but Rand's right to autonomy outweighs thirteen (or more!) Aes Sedais's satisfaction in kidnapping and torturing Rand.[43] If, or when, hierarchical polyamory or forced nonconsensual monogamy violate people's rights to life, liberty, and the pursuit of happiness, they ought to be opposed rather than tolerated. Correspondingly, provocative social science supports consensual marital monogamy over polyamory. For example, the University of Virginia's Brad Wilcox collects a range of studies that show monogamous married couples are happier, healthier, wealthier, and more successful on diverse measures than single, divorced, widowed, or alternative relationships.[44] *Rights* ethics adds that we learn from history, where countless women, children, and men endured rights violations in harems, sexual slavery, and more for *eros, mania*, or *pragma* purposes. A resolute polyamorist will object that past abuses fail to disqualify suitably thriving polyamorous relationships in the present or future. And yet, recalling George Santayana (1863–1952): "Those who cannot remember the past are condemned to repeat it."[45]

Consequentialists consider outcomes, whereas virtue ethicists consider what sort of character we acquire if we hope, think, and act in specific ways, including why, how, and when one practices monogamy or polyamory. Rand charged Shai'tan: "It is not strength that beats you. It is nobility."[46] Integrity attracts mates such as Faile to Perrin in *The Wheel of Time*, and the Asha'man Androl to Pevara: "A pretty face was nothing compared to the type of *solidity* a woman like Pevara displayed."[47] For those aspiring to monogamy or polyamory, how will your ethical choices and lenses impact who you yearn to be? Aristotle wrote: "We become just by doing just acts, temperate by doing temperate acts, brave by doing brave acts."[48] So too, Benjamin Franklin (1705–1790): "If you would be loved, love and be loveable."[49] Robert Jordan concluded: "As far as my view on this, with Harriet, I have many more than three women, there are so many facets to her personality she quite often makes me dizzy, I am quite satisfied there. I seem to remember her saying to me, you do remember this is fantasy right? And I think it was an accident she was holding a carving knife to my throat, just coincidence, but I am not sure."[50]

# Notes

1. Robert Jordan in Matt Hatch, "DragonCon Report: Question 21" (Atlanta, Georgia, September 4, 2005), at https://www.theoryland.com/intvmain. php?i=204.
2. Robert Jordan and Brandon Sanderson, *A Memory of Light* (New York: TOR Books, 2012), 297.
3. *The Wheel of Time*, season 1, episode 4, "The Dragon Reborn"; season 2, episode 1, "A Taste of Solitude."
4. Robert Jordan, *Knife of Dreams* (New York: TOR Books, 2005), 275.
5. See references to pillow-friends in Robert Jordan, *New Spring* (New York: TOR Books, 2004), 45, 103, 174, 230; Robert Jordan, *The Path of Daggers* (New York: TOR Books, 1998), 52; Robert Jordan, *Winter's Heart* (New York: TOR Books, 2000), 308; Jordan, *Knife of Dreams*, 487, 517–518, 536–537; Robert Jordan and Brandon Sanderson, *The Gathering Storm* (New York: TOR Books, 2009), 200; https://wot.fandom.com/wiki/Pillow_friends.
6. Robert Jordan, *The Fires of Heaven* (New York: TOR Books, 1993), 363; Robert Jordan, *Lord of Chaos* (New York: TOR Books, 1994), 380, 530; Jordan, *Winter's Heart*, 284; Jordan and Sanderson, *A Memory of Light*, 120.
7. Jordan, *The Fires of Heaven*, 107–108; "A Taste of Solitude."
8. Robert Jordan, *The Shadow Rising* (New York: TOR Books, 1992), 645; Robert Jordan, *Crossroads of Twilight* (New York: TOR Books, 2003), 370; compare Jordan, *New Spring*, 209; Robert Jordan, *A Crown of Swords* (New York: TOR Books), 121; Jordan and Sanderson, *A Memory of Light*, 413.

9. Harriet O'Neal Rigney, in Hatch, "DragonCon Report."

10. Elizabeth Brake, "Is 'Loving More' Better? The Values of Polyamory," in Raja Halwani, Alan Soble, Sarah Hoffman, and Jacob M. Held eds., *The Philosophy of Sex: Contemporary Readings*, 7th ed. (Lanham: Rowman & Littlefield, 2017), 214.

11. "Robert Jordan Chats About His Wheel of Time Series," CNN, December 12, 2000, at http://www.cnn.com/chat/transcripts/2000/12/12/jordan.

12. Robert Jordan, *The Great Hunt* (New York: TOR Books, 1990), 260; Robert Jordan, *The Dragon Reborn* (New York: TOR Books, 1991), 283; compare Robert Jordan and Brandon Sanderson, *Towers of Midnight* (New York: TOR Books, 2010), 146.

13. Jordan, *Crossroads of Twilight*, 492; Jordan and Sanderson, *A Memory of Light*, 120; see also Jordan, *Winter's Heart*, 271.

14. Jordan and Sanderson, *Towers of Midnight*, 282.

15. Jordan and Sanderson, *A Memory of Light*, 181–212; *The Wheel of Time*, season 2, episode 4, "Daughter of the Night."

16. Jordan, *Crossroads of Twilight*, 302; Aristotle, *Nicomachean Ethics*, trans. W.D. Ross, Books VIII–XI, at https://classics.mit.edu/Aristotle/nicomachaen.html.

17. Robert Jordan, *The Eye of the World* (New York: TOR Books, 1990), 34; Jordan, *The Fires of Heaven*, 76; Jordan, *Knife of Dreams*, 147; Plato, *Symposium*, at https://classics.mit.edu/Plato/symposium.html.

18. "The Dragon Reborn"; Jordan and Sanderson, *The Gathering Storm*, 196–197.

19. Jordan and Sanderson, *A Memory of Light*, 171, 267, 811, 851; "Rand al'Thor Parallels," A Wheel of Time Wiki, at https://wot.fandom.com/wiki/Rand_al%27Thor/Parallels.

20. Jordan and Sanderson, *The Gathering Storm*, 598–605; Jordan and Sanderson, *Towers of Midnight*, 456; Jordan and Sanderson, *A Memory of Light*, 889.

21. Jordan and Sanderson, *A Memory of Light*, 254; compare 172.

22. Jordan, *A Crown of Swords*, 517–547.

23. A.J. Ayer, *Language, Truth, and Logic* (New York: Oxford University Press, 1936).

24. Ayn Rand, *Atlas Shrugged* (New York: Random House, 1957).

25. *The Wheel of Time*, season 2, episode 3, "What Might Be"; see also Nynaeve in Jordan and Sanderson, *Towers of Midnight*, 309–314.

26. Jordan and Sanderson, *A Memory of Light*, 267.

27. Jordan and Sanderson, *A Memory of Light*, 716.

28. Thomas Hobbes, *Leviathan* (London: Andrew Crooke, 1651), chap. XIII, at https://www.gutenberg.org/cache/epub/3207/pg3207-images.html.

29. Jordan and Sanderson, *Towers of Midnight*, 457.

30. William F.P. Napier, *History of General Sir Charles Napier's Administration of Cinde and Campaign in the Cutchee Hills* (London: Chapman & Hall, 1851), 35.

31. Saint Augustine, *On the Free Choice of the Will*, 1.55.11.33, trans. Peter King (Cambridge: Cambridge University Press, 2010), 10.

32. Immanuel Kant, *Critique of Practical Reason*, trans. Thomas Kingsmill Abbott (London: Longmans, Green & Co., 1909), conclusion at https://www.gutenberg.org/cache/epub/5683/pg5683-images.html#link2H_CONC.

33. One condensed version is Namita Gokahle, *The Puffin Mahabharata* (New Delhi: Puffin, 2009), esp. 48.

34. Robert Jordan, November 14, 2000, at https://www.theoryland.com/intvmain.php?i=123; Robert Jordan, June 1, 2007, at https://www.theoryland.com/intvmain.php?i=303.

35. Matthew 19:1–12; Mark 10:1–9; 1 Corinthians 6:12–20; Ephesians 5:25–33.

36. For example, Matthew 1, 5, 19, 22; 1 Corinthians 6–7; Jordan, *The Eye of the World*, 8; Jordan, *A Crown of Swords*, 547.

37. *The Epistle of Mathetes to Diognetes* 5, at https://www.newadvent.org/fathers/0101.htm.

38. Jordan and Sanderson, *The Gathering Storm*, 478.

39. Jordan and Sanderson, *Towers of Midnight*, 712–736; Jordan and Sanderson, *A Memory of Light*, 180.

40. Francis Hutcheson, *An Inquiry into the Original of our Ideas of Beauty and Virtue* (London, 1725), 181, at https://gutenberg.ca/ebooks/hutchesonf-inquiry/hutchesonf-inquiry-00-h-dir/hutchesonf-inquiry-00-h.html (emphasis original).

41. Jordan, *Lord of Chaos*, 385.

42. Jordan, *A Crown of Swords*, 102.

43. Jordan, *Lord of Chaos*, 636–639, 661–665, 682–683, 687–688.

44. Brad Wilcox, *Get Married* (New York: Broadside/HarperCollins, 2024).

45. George Santayana, *The Life of Reason* (New York: Charles Scribner's Sons, 1905), 284.

46. Jordan and Sanderson, *A Memory of Light*, 851.

47. Jordan and Sanderson, *A Memory of Light*, 673; Jordan, *The Path of Daggers*, 191; see also Jordan, *The Eye of the World*, 614.

48. Aristotle, *Nicomachean Ethics*, Book II, at https://classics.mit.edu/Aristotle/nicomachaen.html.

49. Benjamin Franklin, *Poor Richard's Almanac* (Philadelphia, November 1755), at https://founders.archives.gov/documents/Franklin/01-05-02-0136.

50. Robert Jordan, in Hatch, "DragonCon Report."

**17**

# Fear of the Beast Within: Perrin, Hopper, and Human–Animal Relationships

*Maja Griem*

Take care, Young Bull. The day of the Last Hunt draws near.
We will run together in the last Hunt.[1]

It is surprising that of all the characters in *The Wheel of Time*, Perrin Aybara can telepathically communicate with wolves. Perrin is calm, reflective, non-impulsive—a prime example of what philosophers would describe as a "rational human being." In contrast, nonhuman animals are generally thought to be impulsive, irrational creatures, driven by their immediate needs. These assumed differences between humans and other animals have been found in philosophy, anthropology, literature, religion, and culture in many parts of the world from ancient times onwards.[2] For instance, in the Bible, animals are described as inferior to humans. Similarly, in Buddhism, animals are thought to be unable to reach Nirvana.

As we'll see, Perrin's struggle with his connection to the wolves highlights two contrasting human views of animals. On the one hand, animals are seen as beautiful, majestic, and wise creatures, while, on the other hand, they are perceived as dangerous monsters, inferior in intellect.

## The Beast Within

Perrin Aybara—also known as Perrin Goldeneyes and named Young Bull by the wolves—is one of the so called *ta'veren* (which means a person intertwined with destiny) in *The Wheel of Time*. He is tall and strong, yet shy and calm. He contemplates before talking or acting, which is why others often assume he has a slow mind. Throughout the first book Perrin gains more and more awareness that he can telepathically communicate with wolves. It is ironic that Perrin becomes a wolfbrother because he is

*The Wheel of Time and Philosophy*, First Edition. Edited by Jacob M. Held.
© 2025 John Wiley & Sons, Inc. Published 2025 by John Wiley & Sons, Inc.

slow and thoughtful, whereas animals are perceived to be impulsive, irrational, and reactive.

Wolves have a human-like social structure, which makes them more appealing to us than other carnivores such as bears or cats, which live more solitary lives. In *The Wheel of Time*, wolves are even depicted as having partners and close family structures. Yet, the wolf has always been ambiguously depicted in stories. On the one hand, wolves can be described as wise and beautiful. On the other hand, wolves are seen as untamable beasts, like the Big Bad Wolf in European traditions. In fact, the farmers in Emond's Field fear wolf attacks, and see them as fierce predators, not amiable companions. In Roman mythology, the founders of Rome, Romulus and Remus, were adopted and fed by a she-wolf. The wolf was thus a symbol of religious importance, because without the she-wolf, Romulus and Remus would have died and Rome could not have been founded. This tradition also had an impact on the treatment of wild wolves compared to other large predators.[3] In addition, in some Native American traditions, the wolf's loyalty to its pack and its ferocity serves as a role model, teaching humans how to hunt.[4]

In Norse mythology, Fenrir, the most prominent wolf character, is a malevolent beast bound by the gods but destined to grow larger until his bonds will break during Ragnarök, when he will devour Odin. However, Odin also owns two loyal pet wolves, Geri and Freki.[5] Throughout European traditions, the image of the wolf has suffered greatly, leading to the eradication of the species in large parts of Europe. In Christian traditions, the wolf is often the counterpart to the image of the good shepherd (Jesus) leading and protecting the herd of sheep (true Christians).[6] Imagery of the wolf is partly influenced by the stereotype of the wolf in *Aesop's Fables* and *Grimm's Fairy Tales*, where wolves are depicted with human-like features and attributes and set up as antagonists. However, recent movies featuring wolves present more positive imagery, such as *The Jungle Book*, *Balto*, *Princess Mononoke*, or *Wolfwalkers*.

In *The Wheel of Time* book series, we encounter a similar ambiguity. On the one hand, Perrin fears becoming a wolf, an instinct-driven creature, and losing his human rationality. At first, Perrin is afraid and ashamed of his ability to communicate with wolves; he is reluctant to reach out to the wolves and hides his abilities and his golden eyes from others. This difference is magnified because Perrin is the most thoughtful of the *ta'veren* characters, always thinking carefully before speaking and acting. Furthermore, his physical strength and animality, notable when he loses his temper, highlights this contrast and his inner struggle. On the other hand, the wolves—and especially Hopper—are described as thoughtful, making their own decisions, and are even consulted for advice. The different ways wolves and becoming a wolf are described in the series reflect Perrin's inner struggle. The reader also sees this struggle play out as Perrin vacillates between the axe and the hammer. The axe represents killing, and the hammer represents peaceful work. However, it turns out that the hammer can be used for both work and killing—Perrin learns this from Hopper in *Tel'aran'rhiod*, the World of Dreams. Like an Aiel spear, the hammer is both a weapon of war and a valuable tool. A similar duality troubles Perrin. Despite his close relation to Hopper and the pack, he persistently struggles with the fear of becoming a wolf, the fear of the beast within.

## Struggling Against the Beast

The fear of becoming a wolf and losing his human identity is a great concern for Perrin as a wolfbrother. Perrin is afraid of communicating with the wolves and begins to hate himself for being a wolfbrother. Throughout the books, however, the wolves and being with them, running and hunting with them, retains an appeal. This ambivalence not only reflects Perrin's inner struggle, but also draws on the motif of humans being fascinated by nature and its beasts, despite also fearing them. So why would it be bad to become a wolf? And what does it mean to lose one's humanity?

The first wolfbrother Perrin meets is Elyas Machera, a man who was formerly a warder but now lives with his wolf pack. Elyas seems calm and wise, teaching Perrin about the wolves and introducing him to the pack. In stark contrast, another wolfbrother is mentioned who lost his ability to speak and communicate with humans and ran off into the wild, leaving his brother and family behind. The young man is described as insane, and this is the fate Perrin fears. He is afraid of losing his rationality and turning into a beast. The two different visions of becoming a wolfbrother create a stark contrast between a human being and a beast.

This contrast between rationality and aggression is one of the main motifs when it comes to the difference between humans and other animals in literature. In most philosophical traditions, emotions, such as anger, need to be overcome, or at least controlled, by rationality, something that supposedly only humans can do.[7] For example, in the *Phaedrus*, Plato (428–348 BCE) explains the three parts of the human soul (reason, spirit, and appetite) by using the image of a coachman (reason) who has to lead two horses (spirit and appetite).[8] Along these lines, in *The Eye of the World*, Elyas tells Perrin, "Think if you want to stay alive. Fear will kill you if you don't control it."[9] These words deliver the message that thinking is the means to stay alive and human, while strong emotions like fear must be controlled and should not take over the decision process.

However, studies conducted on apes, crows, and ravens—which are supposed to be the Dark One's eyes in *The Wheel of Time*—and other animals over the last twenty years suggest a continuity between human and non-human animal minds. Nonetheless, many contemporary philosophers still believe that rationality divides us from other species.[10] Evidence is mounting for rational choices, complex object manipulation, and innovative problem solving in other species. One example is Betty, a crow, who spontaneously formed a hook out of a piece of wire—a material she had never worked with before—to lift a bucket with food into her reach. Whether her behavior was insightful—driven by rationality—or just a behavioral disposition and part of her natural behavioral repertoire—driven by her current needs plus instinct—is still debated.[11]

Notably, in the *Wheel of Time* books, Jordan does not depict the wolves as highly aggressive or lacking intelligence. However, the wolves do have a simplistic "eye for an eye" ethics, mostly driven by instinct, although they can somehow talk to Perrin in a human-like fashion. Again, this parallels the ambiguity of humans and nature, as does Perrin's inner struggle. This is further expressed by the hatred he feels for his axe after he has killed with it. Intriguingly, Perrin's first contact with wolves and his first killing of a human (a Whitecloak) is immediately followed by the group meeting the *Tuatha'an*. The *Tuatha'an* follow the Way of the Leaf, a peaceful tradition in which they refrain from harming and killing others, even in the case of self-defense. Here, Perrin's wish for peaceful actions grows stronger and he thinks about giving up on the axe and fighting altogether. In the end, however, many of the *Tuatha'an* are killed, and Perrin always decides to fight again.

## Hopper: The Wolf as a Guardian Animal

Perrin has a special connection to Hopper, a wolf who is especially anthropomorphized. Hopper is part of the wolf pack journeying with Elyas, and he and Perrin appear to be soulmates from the beginning. Hopper can (telepathically) talk to Perrin, although it is often hard to understand wolves because of strong differences in their art of communication and their distinct desires and rationality. Hopper is described with human-like feelings (such as sorrow, grief, and love) and acts calmly based on rational choices. The connection between Perrin and Hopper is interesting, because of the frequent shifts between who is acting rationally and who is acting emotionally. Subverting expectations about humans and animals, Hopper often takes the lead in the relationship. Indeed, most of the time, Hopper makes his own decisions (for example, when he jumps to be killed by Whitecloaks), and Perrin even asks for Hopper's advice and opinion. After Hopper's death and his passing into the Wolf Dream (which is what the wolves call *Tel'aran'rhiod*), he becomes a guardian animal for Perrin. More so than other humans, wolfbrothers have a strong connection to the World of Dreams. *Tel'aran'rhiod* itself has many similarities to the Australian aboriginal concept of the dreamtime. Much as the World of Dreams in *The Wheel of Time* is inhabited by the Heroes of the Horn and wolves, Australian aboriginal dreamtime is inhabited by heroic, ancestral individuals and linked to totemic animals.

Hopper appears in *Tel'aran'rhiod* and saves Perrin by snapping him out of the Wolf Dream when Perrin accidentally meets the Forsaken in the World of Dreams. Hopper later guides Perrin to a safe place where he witnesses a meeting between Lanfear and Ba'alzamon (two of the Forsaken). Perrin also learns details about Darkhounds (dog-like creatures sent by the Dark One to hunt down his enemies) from Hopper, who refers to them as Shadowbrothers. When Faile, a woman who is dear to Perrin, is held captive in *Tel'aran'rhiod*, Perrin enters the Wolf Dream to save her. Hopper accompanies and guards him throughout this journey until Perrin finally rescues Faile. Later in the books, Hopper becomes Perrin's mentor, teaching him how to find the balance between his human and wolf selves and how to manipulate the Wolf Dream—by which parts of the real world can also be manipulated due to the strong connection between these worlds. Perrin also has dreams that are somehow related to future happenings in the story, very much like a shaman might consult a guardian animal in the spirit world to see the future.

## From the Big Bad Wolf to a Guardian Animal

Perrin's inner struggle against the beast within him and his fear of losing his rationality is underlined by his connection to wolves. Most wolves he encounters are only slightly anthropomorphized and support him by killing other humans without regret or any kind of conscience, thereby reflecting parts of the ferocious beast side of the coin. Hopper, though, plays the role of wise guardian animal. As Perrin struggles to make peace with the beast within, so must we all. Our scientific understanding of animals continues to advance and to demonstrate that humans are not as sharply separated from wolves and other animals as we once thought. If we open our eyes and our hearts, we can recognize the rationality of animals and we can embrace the beast within.[12]

## Notes

1.  Robert Jordan, *The Shadow Rising* (New York: TOR Books, 1992), 86.
2.  See for example, Urs Dierauer, *Tier und Mensch im Denken der Antike* (Amsterdam: Grüner, 1977); Immanuel Kant, *Anthropology from a Pragmatic Point of View*, ed. and trans. Robert Louden and Gunter Zoller (Cambridge: Cambridge University Press, 2010); Hilary Thompson, *Novel Creatures: Animal Life and the New Millennium* (London: Routledge, 2018); James Serpell, *In the Company of Animals: A Study of Human–Animal Relationships* (New York: Cambridge University Press, 2003); Margo DeMello, *Animals and Society: An Introduction to Human–Animal Studies* (New York: Columbia University Press, 2012).
3.  Mika Rissanen, "Was There a Taboo on Killing Wolves in Rome?," *Quaderni Urbinati di Cultura Classica* 107 (2014), 125–147.

4. "Wolves in Native American Culture," Wolf Song Alaska, at https://www.wolfsongalaska.org/chorus/?q=node/179 (last accessed July 2024); Brandy R. Fogg, Nimachia Howe, and Raymond Pierotti, "Relationships Between Indigenous American Peoples and Wolves 1: Wolves as Teachers and Guides," *Journal of Ethnobiology* 35 (2015), 267.

5. Hélène A. Guerber, *Myths of the Norsemen: From the Eddas and the Sagas* (Mineola: Dover Publications, 2003).

6. Garry Marvin, *Wolf* (London: Reaktion Books, 2012).

7. Platon, *Timaios*, trans. Thomas Paulsen and Rudolf Rehn (Stuttgart: Reclam, 2009), e.g. 41e–42e.

8. Michael Erler, "Platon: Affekte und Wege zur Eudaimonie," in Hilge Landweer and Ursula Renz eds., *Klassische Emotionstheorien: Von Platon bis Wittgenstein* (Berlin and New York: De Gruyter, 2008), 24.

9. Robert Jordan, *The Eye of the World* (New York: TOR Books, 1990), 429.

10. Giacomo Melis and Susana Monsó, "Are Humans the Only Rational Animals?," *The Philosophical Quarterly* 74 (2024), 844–864.

11. Christian Rutz, Shoko Sugasawa, Jessica E.M. van der Wal, Barbara C. Klump, and James J.H. St. Clair, "Tool Bending in New Caledonian Crows," *Royal Society Open Science* 3, 160439.

12. I would like to thank my colleague Eline Kuipers for her encouraging and helpful feedback on my work.

# 18

# Gendered Souls and Bodies: Hylomorphism and the *Saidin/Saidar* Distinction

*Julie Loveland Swanstrom and Caitlynn Fletcher*

[*The Wheel of Time*] is a world of balance and the world of yin and yang and the strength you always have to have.[1]

Differences that need to be balanced abound in Robert Jordan's world, but the Amazon series showrunner Rafe Judkins thinks that gender in particular needs balance.[2] Unlike other fantasy series—we're looking at you, Tolkien—women play a huge role in *The Wheel of Time*. Originally quite forward thinking, the male/female gender binary pairing like men accessing *saidin* and women accessing *saidar* now feels a bit dated in some ways. Even Judkins, who loves Jordan's works, questions how gender operates as he adapts of *The Wheel of Time*.[3]

Like light and dark, women can't exist without men. We don't mean that in a rom-com sense where weak women need men to save them from the crushing weight of loneliness. It's a biological reality for humans generally—our reproductive processes need sperm and an egg along with a uterus. But other realities beyond the biological may be at play in *The Wheel of Time* that help guide how gender can be understood. Perhaps gender roles, like biological sex, are essential realities. That's what the ancient philosopher Aristotle (384–322) seems to think, as we'll see below. Things could be even more complicated. Maybe what we think of as "biological reality" for human beings depends not only on physical stuff like cells but also something metaphysical like a soul. Both Aristotle and the early modern philosopher Descartes (1596–1650) embrace views like this. For Judkins to play with gender in *The Wheel of Time*, understanding humans as bodies with souls but without essential gender roles would give him the best sort of playground.

*The Wheel of Time and Philosophy*, First Edition. Edited by Jacob M. Held.
© 2025 John Wiley & Sons, Inc. Published 2025 by John Wiley & Sons, Inc.

## *Saidin/Saidar* Gender Essentialism

Women and men access the One Power differently. Moiraine, Nynaeve, Egwene, Aviendha, and Elayne access *saidar* by surrendering to the power, and Rand and Logain access *saidin* by dominating it.[4] Gender essentialism explains how men and women are fundamentally different, having different characteristics and abilities. Aristotle theorizes how male and female animals (humans included!) have inherent differences: males are hotter, more active, more intelligent, more decisive, more trustworthy, and more powerful than women, who in comparison are colder, passive, dumber, indecisive, deceptive, and weaker. Since these differences can be seen in any species, from tigers to beta fish to humans, he concludes that males and females are just different.[5] Rand's struggle to control the One Power follows Aristotle's descriptions of male/female differences quite nicely: he feels like *saidin* is a raging, powerful torrent that he must control. No matter how cunning or crafty Moiraine, Egwene, and Elayne might be, they must passively submit to *saidar*.[6] Being healed with *saidin* feels warm, but being healed with *saidar* feels cool.[7] Just as Aristotle would predict, men are stronger channelers than women. When comparing the strength of channelers, the strongest female channelers (Lanfear, Semirhage, and Alivia) are equivalent to the seventh strongest male channeler.[8] The Aes Sedai challenge many of Aristotle's expectations: they are active and calculating but also deceptive, even despite Artur Hawkwing's three rules that limit their powers and attempts to elevate their trustworthiness.[9]

The use of the One Power varies by gender in vaguely Aristotelian ways. Women can't help Rand learn to channel, not even the great Moiraine, Egwene, or Elayne! He needs a male teacher, be it False Dragon Logain in the Amazon series or the Forsaken Asmodean in the books.[10] Rand's and Logain's weaves can't even be seen by women, which is how Logain can surprise Moiraine, Kerene, Liandrin, and Alana.[11]

If Aristotle can claim that men are hot and dry while women are cool and wet, then some of the gender essentialist traits that exist in *The Wheel of Time* seem a bit less odd. Cats are for women, and dogs are for men: cats show up at Aes Sedai encampments, but the Black Tower is surrounded by dogs.[12] Aristotle has earth, air, water, and fire as his primary elements, and *The Wheel of Time* adds spirit, too. Just as Aristotle assigned particular properties to men (dryness and heat) and to women (wetness and cold), male and female channelers have different abilities and strengths in different elements. Men were most commonly strong in Earth or Fire while women were strong in Air and Water (and Spirit was rarely anyone's strength). As usual, Nynaeve overachieves by using all five elements to heal.[13] Egwene and Elayne both show strength in Fire and Earth, using those powers to create *cuendillar* and *ter'angreal*.[14]

## Halima's Hylomorphism

Some characters are gender complicated, such as Balthamel. A notorious womanizer, Balthamel has his soul put into a woman's body by the Dark One. As if this weren't already confusing, the female-body-with-Balthamel's-soul is named Aran'gar but is under cover as Halima. For the sake of conversational ease, let's call this individual Halima. Halima continues to channel *saidin* rather than now channeling *saidar*.[15] Halima provides a fairly straightforward case to ask whether your soul or body determines if you'll channel *saidin* or *saidar*. We say "fairly straightforward," though, because sometimes it seems like the Dark One has rules entirely of his own. But let's assume that Halima can tell us about that soul/body–*saidin*/*saidar* connection. Halima's soul must determine whether Halima channels *saidin* or *saidar*. Halima's soul is essentially, and perhaps Aristotelianly, male.

Halima shows that the soul is particularly significant for using the One Power. Our friend Aristotle thought that any living entity was composed of a soul and a physical body, a view called hylomorphism. Rather than being spooky or spiritual things, the soul is an organizing principle for the matter, providing shape, function, and purpose to the body. The soul informed the matter by giving the matter its peculiar form, and soul (or, for non-living things, form) cannot exist without matter.[16] Beings of the same type, such as birch trees, would each have a birch tree soul, cats would have a cat soul, and humans a human soul.

Because of the close relationship between the type of soul a being has and how the being is categorized, medieval philosophers following Aristotle begin to associate his use of "soul" with "essence." Aristotle roots a number of our human abilities in our soul, particularly the ability to sense, move (especially in response to what we sense), think, and imagine.[17] In the soul-matter hylomorphic union, the soul acts while the matter is acted upon. Here Aristotle means to describe the world rather than evaluate it.[18] But later thinkers focus on our ability to think as the key marker of humans, believing the "active" part of the human—the soul—to be better or more important than the passive, material part. One stop in this transition of "soul" to "essence" occurs in the work of medieval philosopher Ibn Sina (980–1037) (or Avicenna for the Latin speakers). He came up with a thought experiment about a "flying man" to help analyze the soul. Imagine someone popping into existence, fully matured, inside of a sensory deprivation chamber, something vaguely reminiscent of Rand's void. The sensory deprivation bubble prevents the flying, or floating, man's awareness of his body at all. The floating man would still have some awareness of himself, which means for Ibn Sina that the soul must be distinct from the body.[19] If we can be aware of ourselves without our senses, then our souls can't be made of the kind of stuff that is felt by senses; souls must be immaterial.[20] René Descartes goes so far as to say that the soul is the part of a person that is most real. Descartes, the "I think, therefore I am" guy, claims that his ability to think is evidence that he exists even under extreme circumstances, like if he had a soul but not a body. Cartesian dualism means that bodies, while not mere illusions, are lesser than the supernatural wisp of the soul.[21] Descartes' soul can, at least theoretically, be separated from matter, and the soul itself has graduated to be the essence of each person. Descartes' version of hylomorphism, adapted from Aristotle, helps us understand Halima. Why could Halima channel *saidin* despite Halima's female body? The soul within Balthamel must explain this: as the soul of a man, Halima's soul can only contact *saidin*. Balthamel thinks, therefore he channels *saidin*. Gender and soul reveal how the One Power can be accessed, at least in Jordan's books.

## Body and Balance

Body matters, too, or else Nynaeve, Elayne, and other channelers couldn't be temporarily cut off from the One Power by sleepwell root or forkroot in their drinks.[22] Even mighty Moghedien is susceptible, for Nynaeve doses her with forkroot in *Tel'aran'rhiod*.[23] A channeler's abilities can also be limited by pregnancy, like what Elayne occasionally experienced when pregnant with Rand's twins. But after giving birth, a channeler's usual abilities come right back.[24]

The physical component of channeling has been emphasized in the Amazon series. Child Valda offers a grizzly reminder of how Aes Sedai use hand gestures while channeling: he simply removes the hands of any Aes Sedai whom he captures. Valda gloats to Egwene that these hand gestures aren't technically needed.[25] Perhaps if someone lost a hand in an accident, they could learn a new way to make those weaves, but they won't be able to instantly. Something less shocking than dismemberment matters, too, since Moiraine's stab from a Trolloc temporarily halts her ability to channel.[26] Channeling isn't entirely physical, but it isn't entirely about someone's soul, either, which is what we'd expect with hylomorphism like that of Descartes.

Hylomorphism may tie to a type of balance in *The Wheel of Time*. It can contribute to the notion of balance, especially if we follow medieval philosopher St. Thomas Aquinas (1225–1274). Instead of saying that the human soul is somehow the real self like Descartes implies, Aquinas says that the union of soul and body together makes a person.[27] Soul alone can't do that; Aquinas tells us plainly that a human soul without a body would merely maintain the barest, passive existence of a person rather than being the real person.[28] If a channeler needs her body and her soul together, then the union of body and soul brings balance to these disparate components of a human, just like Aquinas would predict. Balthamel/Aran'gar/Halima is an odd case, since Balthamel had his soul saved by the Dark One.

Seemingly as a punishment, Balthamel's soul was put in the body of a woman; oh, the poor dear! By having Balthamel's soul shoved into a woman's body, Balthamel is supposed to feel unbalanced and unnatural, though the Father of Lies—always a trustworthy source!—insists that Balthamel will adjust.[29] Balthamel/Aran'gar/Halima can channel in a woman's body, but they can't channel the way a woman usually would. Something is off about the soul and body union in Halima! For other characters who haven't had their souls ripped from their original bodies and shoved into a differently sexed body—one of the many things regarding soul–body configuration that Aquinas does not discuss outright—the body and soul together seem to tell us reliably whether that character will channel *saidin* or *saidar*. (At least in the books.)

## Body + Soul = Hero

Birgitte Silverbow, Hero of the Horn herself, has a soul–body connection that, while weird, is maybe more ordinary than Balthamel/Aran'gar/ Halima … not that that's hard. As one of the Heroes of the Horn, Birgitte appears when someone has blown the Horn of Valere to aid the Light.[30] Because she protected Nynaeve from Moghedien in the world of dreams, *Tel'aran'rhiod*, Birgitte is expelled from *Tel'aran'rhiod* by Moghedien. Elayne bonds Birgitte as her warder in order to save Birgitte's life.[31] As Elayne's warder, Birgitte continues to forget the details of her previous lives to the point where all she can remember at the end is her own current existence.[32] After she is killed in the Last Battle, she returns when the Horn of Valere is sounded.[33]

As odd as it is that Birgitte loses her memory, hylomorphism can help us understand why this happened: her soul ended up in the wrong body, or rather, a body that wasn't supposed to be hers. Like with Halima, Birgitte's body that popped into existence when she was thrown out of *Tel'aran'rhiod* wasn't a body ready and able to house her soul. The body that housed her soul upon the Horn being sounded was the right sort of body, and it would allow her to retain the memories from her previous incarnations. Birgitte needs the right sort of body in order to use the full abilities of her soul, which follows Aquinas's expectations. One soul can only be united to one body: because the soul–body union makes people distinct, Birgitte needs her own body in order to retain herself.[34] The distinct person Birgitte needs her own unique soul along with her unique body for her soul to be able to exercise its abilities.[35] Aquinas even thinks that memory is a power residing in the soul![36]

Birgitte's appearance and that of her beau, Gaidal Cain, show how the particularities of a body might be important. Always reincarnated together, Birgitte and Gaidal have certain characteristics: Birgitte is blond, athletic, and uses a silver bow; Gaidal is muscular, short, and ugly.[37] Their souls are housed in bodies with these sorts of characteristics, so general body configuration and specific body properties seem to matter. Birgitte and Gaidal's soul–body relationship fits with hylomorphism. The soul–body connection, and thus balance, is preserved.

## Black, White, and Gray

White and black make up the two sides of the yin–yang and are associated with women and men respectively. If the goal is balance, then maybe the blend of white and black should represent the embodiment of balance. The Gray Men might be such people. The Gray Men are tools of the Dark One, and they have no souls in their bodies because they gave them to the Dark One.[38] By the rules of hylomorphism, they're missing part of themselves, part of what makes up a normal human: their souls. Wolves—and their wolfbrother, Perrin—can smell them, but others cannot.[39] Rand kills one but only because of the Gray Man's poor hygiene: he stinks so badly that Rand can locate him![40] Yet, the Gray Men, despite being gray, aren't a balance between black and white—they aren't anywhere close. Because the Gray Men are missing part of what makes them a person, they don't even seem to be a part of regular existence anymore.

Despite how Jordan (and Sanderson) used binaries—body/soul, *saidin/saidar*, male/female—and centered female characters in the narrative, binary pairs with regard to gender limit gender expression. The "more binary and less binary" representations of gender across the wide variety of cultures in *The Wheel of Time* were "pushing the envelope a lot for the genre at the time" and can be adjusted today. Judkins specifically considered gender essentialism "where men act one way and can access one part of the magic and women another."[41] The Dragon could be male or female![42] Gendered connection to the elements can be removed.[43] Female channelers don't have to be cat ladies.[44] Traits that Jordan associated with one gender lose that association under Judkins's guidance. Commitment to balance doesn't have to look exactly like the gender roles in Jordan's original works.

One binary manifested in gender essentialism is gone—Judkins simply removes gendered traits and roles in the Amazon series—but what puzzles us is the *saidin/saidar* distinction. No matter how Judkins adjusts aspects of gender essentialism, a key aspect of balance in Jordan's story is the association of *saidin* with men and *saidar* with women. How can Judkins claim to be breaking "outdated" binaries but preserve this fundamental gendered distinction?

We think the tools that helped us understand balance in the first place can help explain why *saidin* and *saidar* remain connected to gender. Gender essentialism is out. Hylomorphism, that tool that helped us see how crucial soul–body connection and balance is for Jordan's story, might get Judkins out of the pickle in which he finds himself. To see how, let's create a new character: Jain Farstrider Doe.

## Jain Doe, the Hylomorphic Hero

Jain Doe's soul isn't gendered. This is one of Judkins's prime adjustments in his attempt to leave gender essentialism behind. Since the soul seems to be the part of a human that determines what kind of access Jain has to the One Power, then Jain's soul must determine a leaning toward *saidin* or *saidar*. Which way Jain's soul leans must also be independent of gender.

Jain still needs a body in order to channel. The Gray Men remind us that Jain must have a soul–body connection to be balanced. Jain's body doesn't determine whether Jain channels *saidin* or *saidar*—again remember the unforgettable Balthamel/Aran'gar/Halima. If Jain's body mattered for the *saidin/saidar* capacity, then this would just be another type of gender essentialism, one of the body rather than the soul.

Balance is key for Judkins and for Jordan, so how can Jain's soul determine whether Jain channels *saidin/saidar* without the *saidin/saidar* connection being based on gender (in the soul or the body)? We think a biological fact about balance in human beings explains why *saidin* and *saidar* are correlated to gender. Roughly half of the human population is female and the other is male, and a small percentage of people are intersex or transgender (or both). If those whose souls just happen to lean toward *saidin* end up in male bodies (or are transgender men), then this would naturally align with an existing kind of biological balance. The same is true for those whose souls lean toward *saidar*: if they end up in female bodies (or are transgender women), then the number of people who use *saidar* will remain in balance with the general human population. The sex/gender association that we experience between *saidin* and *saidar* is just a convenient way of achieving something like balance due to biological realities. For these correlations to exist, we don't need gender essentialism. The biological reality that Jain needs a soul (which isn't gendered but may lean toward either *saidin* or *saidar* or neither) and that Jain needs a body (which will have some sort of sex configuration) means that Jain will have some sex/gender. Correlation between *saidin* and men or *saidar* and women acknowledges these biological realities and piggybacks on the basic sex balance that is already replicated in biology.

What about people who are intersex? Or people who identify as nonbinary? Or other ways that people identify regarding gender that might not have been on Jordan's radar thirty-some years ago? The best part of the balanced-sex *saidin/saidar* corollary is that the hylomorphic but not gender essentialist understanding of *saidin/saidar* means that flexibility and openness exists here that didn't explicitly exist in Jordan's original conception. Not every manifestation of the One Power in *The Wheel of Time* follows a cleanly constructed division between *saidin* and *saidar*. Wolf kin, people like Perrin Aybara or Elyas Machera, can be male or female.[45] The Dark One has a power rooted in himself, the True Power, that isn't correlated to gender at all (but is locked to His Chosen).[46] Removing the gender essentialist connection between the soul and *saidin/saidar* more accurately reflects the variety of powers in *The Wheel of Time* and the variety of humans in the world. Regardless of Jain's body construction or gender identity, Jain has a chance to have a connection to power.

Using hylomorphism, we can explain how Judkins can strip the soul of gender but maintain balance with *saidin/saidar*. Body and soul together constitute a person. The biological realities of reproduction in humans lead to a fairly even sex balance in the population, a mere convenience to which *saidin* and *saidar* correlate. The Wheel weaves body and soul together without constraining *saidin/saidar*, particular strengths, or unique abilities to sex/gender. This rich tapestry of humanity better represents the complex and beautiful pattern of the Wheel and our world.[47]

# Notes


1. Preeti Chhibber, "The Wheel of Time's Showrunner Isn't Sweating the Game of Thrones Comparisons," *Polygon*, November 18, (2021), at https://www.polygon.com/interviews/22788333/wheel-of-time-amazon-showrunner-adaptation-interview.
2. Chhibber, "The Wheel of Time's Showrunner Isn't Sweating the Game of Thrones Comparisons."
3. Rob Bricken, "Adapting the Wheel of Time for TV Is an Epic All Its Own," *Gizmodo*, November 10, (2021), at https://gizmodo.com/adapting-the-wheel-of-time-for-tv-is-an-epic-all-its-ow-1848026456.
4. *The Wheel of Time*, season 1, episode 1, "Leavetaking."
5. Aristotle, *Generation of Animals*, 765b10–35, in Jonathan Barnes ed., *The Complete Works of Aristotle* (Princeton: Princeton University Press, 1984), 1134–1135; Aristotle, *History of Animals*, 608a19–608b15, in Jonathan Barnes ed., *The Complete Works of Aristotle* (Princeton: Princeton University Press, 1984), 948–949.
6. Robert Jordan, *The Shadow Rising* (New York: TOR Books, 1992), 145–155.
7. Robert Jordan and Brandon Sanderson, *A Memory of Light* (New York: TOR Books, 2012), 621.
8. Chris Lough, "The Wheel of Time Companion: Strength Chart of Major Channelers," *Reactor Magazine*, October 27 (2015), at https://reactormag.com/the-wheel-of-time-companion-strength-chart-of-major-channelers.
9. Robert Jordan, *The Great Hunt* (New York: TOR Books, 1990), 335–336; *The Wheel of Time*, season 1, episode 2, "Shadow's Waiting."
10. *The Wheel of Time*, season 2, episode 3, "What Might Be"; Jordan, *The Shadow Rising*, 972–973.
11. *The Wheel of Time*, season 1, episode 4, "The Dragon Reborn."

12.  Robert Jordan, *Knife of Dreams* (New York: TOR Books, 2005), 121; Robert Jordan, *Winter's Heart* (New York: TOR Books, 2000), 62–63.

13.  Robert Jordan and Brandon Sanderson, *Towers of Midnight* (New York: TOR Books, 2010), 447.

14.  Jordan, *The Great Hunt*, 597.

15.  Jordan, *Knife of Dreams*, 540–542.

16.  Aristotle, *On the Soul* 412b10–413a10, in Barnes ed., *The Complete Works of Aristotle*, 657–658; Aristotle, *Categories*, 2a12–34, in Barnes ed., *The Complete Works of Aristotle*, 4–5.

17.  Aristotle, *On the Soul*, 427a18–430a9, 679–683.

18.  Aristotle, *On the Soul*, 430a10–430a26, 684.

19.  Ibn Sina, al-Shifa': *al-Tabfiyyat* (Physis); *al-Nafs* (Psychology), ed. G.C. Anawati and S. Zayid (Cairo, 1975), I, 1, p. 13, in Michael Marmura, "Avicenna's 'Flying Man' in Context," *The Monist* 69 (1986), 387. The translation is provided by Marmura.

20.  The floating (or flying) man thought experiment could be to further clarify the nature of the soul, or it could also presage something like Descartes' ideas about the link between thinking and existing. If you're interested, see Peter Adamson, *Philosophy in the Islamic World, vol. 3 of A History of Philosophy Without Any Gaps* (New York: Oxford University Press, 2016), 133–139, especially fn1.

21.  René Descartes, "*Meditations on First Philosophy*, trans. John Cottingham, Robert Stoothoff, and Dugald Murdoch," in *The Philosophical Writings of Descartes, Volume II* (New York: Cambridge University Press, 1984), 14, 17.

22.  Robert Jordan, *The Fires of Heaven* (New York: TOR Books, 1993), 218; Jordan, *Knife of Dreams*, 164.

23.  Jordan, *The Fires of Heaven*, 951.

24.  Robert Jordan, *Crossroads of Twilight* (New York: TOR Books, 2003), 425–426.

25.  *The Wheel of Time*, season 1, episode 5, "Blood Calls Blood."

26.  "Leavetaking"; "The Dragon Reborn."

27.  Saint Thomas Aquinas, *Commentary on Aristotle's De Anima*, 2.1.234, trans. Kenelm Foster and Sylvester Humphries (New Haven: Yale University Press, 1951); Aquinas, *Summa Contra Gentiles*, II.57.3, 5, 15, trans. James F. Anderson (Notre Dame: University of Notre Dame, 1975), 169, 172; Aquinas, *Summa Theologiae* I.75.4. response, trans. The Fathers of the English Dominican Province, at https://www.newadvent.org/summa.

28.  Aquinas, *Summa Theologiae* I.77.8 response. Aquinas addresses this question since Aquinas thinks that death means the separation of soul from body but also believes in the future resurrection of humans where souls are united to bodies once more.

29.  Robert Jordan, *Lord of Chaos* (New York: TOR Books, 1994), 70–72.

30.  Jordan, *The Great Hunt*, 659–662.

31.  Jordan, *The Fires of Heaven*, 553–555.

32.  Jordan and Sanderson, *A Memory of Light*, 682.

33.  Jordan and Sanderson, *A Memory of Light*, 814.

34.  Aquinas, *Summa Contra Gentiles* II.83.34, 283.

35.  Aquinas, *Summa Contra Gentiles* II.83.35, 284.

36.  Aquinas, *Summa Theologiae* I.79.7 response.

37. Robert Jordan, Harriet McDougal, Alan Romanczuk, and Maria Simmons, *The Wheel of Time Companion: The People, Places, and History of the Bestselling Series* (New York: TOR Books, 2015), 29–30, 68.

38. Robert Jordan, *The Dragon Reborn* (New York: TOR Books, 1991), 692.

39. Jordan, *The Dragon Reborn*, 504.

40. Jordan, *Lord of Chaos*, 566.

41. Bricken, "Adapting the Wheel of Time for TV Is an Epic All Its Own"; Chhibber, "The Wheel of Time's Showrunner Isn't Sweating the Game of Thrones Comparisons."

42. "Leavetaking"; Bricken, "Adapting the Wheel of Time for TV Is an Epic All Its Own."

43. Though keeping the color schema (black for *saidin*, white for *saidar*), characters seem able to use whatever element is useful in the moment, such as Moiraine using earth to fight the Trollocs, Alana detonating the ground against Logain's Dragonsworn, or Verin lighting her warder's blade on fire to save Moiraine from a Myrddraal ("Leavetaking"; "The Dragon Reborn"; *The Wheel of Time*, season 2, episode 1, "A Taste of Solitude").

44. "Leavetaking."

45. Robert Jordan, "TOR Questions of the Week Part II," Theoryland, January 25, 2005, at https://www.theoryland.com/intvmain.php?i=6.

46. Robert Jordan, *A Crown of Swords* (New York: TOR Books, 1996), 412.

47. Julie Loveland Swanstrom is grateful to the Augustana Research and Artist Fund for a grant supporting work on this project.

# Epilogue: A Portion of Courage

Often, if not always, when writing there are ideas left on the cutting room floor. These are ideas that might not fit with the current project, or ideas not well enough constructed to warrant a place in the finished piece, or which lack adequate philosophical grounding to merit a place in a professional publication. But often these flashes of insight, these tidbits, are catalysts for further thinking, even if it requires a bit of courage to send into the ether ideas not fully developed. While working on a project like *The Wheel of Time and Philosophy* there are invariably such insights and ideas, often triggered by a particularly poignant quote. (I'm sure many readers can recall several impactful quotes from memory. I'd guess several are already beginning to recite: "Death is lighter than a feather …") But what to do with these ideas if there is no obvious place for them in a structured essay? I offered to collect them and paste them into an Epilogue. I offered every author the chance to choose a quote from the series that they found particularly poignant and provide a short excursus. This was an opportunity to say what hadn't been said in their chapter, or what might not have an outlet elsewhere. Not all authors chose to contribute. What follows is what was provided from those that did; just a small portion of their wisdom, offered, perhaps, with a portion of courage.

## Roderick Cooke

And these southlanders think Trollocs are myths, and Myrddraal a gleeman's tale. … It seemed the only way. … Better the Shadow, I thought, than useless oblivion, like Carallain, or Hardan, or … . It seemed so logical, then.[1]

My chapter in this collection focuses on the philosophy of storytelling in *The Wheel of Time*, and on Jordan's stance toward transmission of stories

*The Wheel of Time and Philosophy*, First Edition. Edited by Jacob M. Held.
© 2025 John Wiley & Sons, Inc. Published 2025 by John Wiley & Sons, Inc.

between eras, both in our own world and in his fictional land. But the above quote, which as many readers will quickly recognize constitutes Lord Ingtar Shinowa's last words before sacrificing himself to atone for his service to the Shadow, opens a parallel perspective on storytelling.

"History" and "story" are similar words for a reason; they both come from the Greek and Latin term *historia*, and many other languages (French *histoire*, German *Geschichte*, for instance) also use the same word for both concepts. Ingtar, baring his soul to Rand, explains that the specter of historical oblivion, in the form of his nation Shienar's deeds and memories being swallowed up by an uncaring, forgetful world, drove him to become a Darkfriend. Robert Jordan, and characters such as Thom Merrilin, are primarily interested in how stories are passed on, and how they change in the (re)telling. However, through a character like Ingtar, Jordan also makes room for the other side of the coin: the existential fear that can take hold of a person, or even a culture, if they believe that their story, their *historia*, will disappear, and the tragic choices that such people can make.

As Ingtar says outright, until his final epiphany and redemption, being a Darkfriend seemed a rational choice, one driven not by self-interest but by a sense of patriotic duty gone far astray. National survival, at any cost, was for a long time preferable to becoming one of the dead and forgotten nations that litter old maps of the Westlands. Ingtar's inclusion in the series shows that Jordan's interest in the topic, and his exploration of the ethical dimensions of storytelling, was multifaceted. It inverts not only the views of a character like Thom, but also those of Ishamael, who was Ingtar's master for years despite the latter believing him to be the Dark One himself. Ishamael famously joined the Shadow for philosophic reasons, the belief that its victory was inevitable, and would bring the erasure of all human existence, and thus of all storytelling, forever, as he craved. Ingtar, seeing less clearly into his master's nature, was tricked into the same choice for the opposite motivation.


## Benjamin B. DeVan

An argument must have opposition if it is to prove itself, my son. One who argues truly learns the depth of his commitment through adversity. Do you not learn that trees grow roots most strongly when winds blow through them?[2]

In this metaphor from *A Memory of Light*, Covril communicates to Loial why she argued against the Ogier fighting in the Last Battle despite her holding the opposite conviction. Her confidence that arguments, like people, strengthen through struggle pervades the history of philosophy. Master Kong Qui (c. 551–479 BCE), also known as Confucius counseled: "Walking among three people, I find my teacher among them. I choose what is good in them and follow it, and that which is bad and change it."[3] Hebrew wisdom counseled: "Iron sharpens iron, and one person sharpens the wits of another."[4] The *Rig Veda* invited: "Let auspicious ideas come here to us from all sides."[5] And, the New Testament: "The testing of your faith produces perseverance."[6] To faithfully riff on Socrates (c. 470–399 BCE), the unexamined argument is not worth retaining.[7]

What about medieval and modern thinkers? One need not be Catholic to play devil's advocate. The Muslim philosopher al-Kindi (c.801–873) maintained: "We should not be ashamed to acknowledge truth and to assimilate it from whatever source it comes to us ... there is nothing of higher value than the truth itself; it never cheapens or abases him who reaches for it, but ennobles and honors."[8] Correspondingly, John Milton (1608–1674) insisted: "Give me the liberty to know, to utter, and to argue freely according to conscience. ... Let her and Falsehood grapple; who ever knew Truth put to the worse, in a free and open encounter?"[9]

Alex Shand (1832–1907) reiterated a Proverb above in recognizing that "mind clashes with mind, and sparks of brilliant intelligence are set flying, as from the sharp contact of flint striking upon steel."[10] Martin Luther King Jr. (1929–1968) commended considering enemy perspectives: "We may indeed see the basic weaknesses of our own condition, and if we are mature, we may learn and grow and profit."[11] Michael J. Buckley (1931–2019) proposed clashing disagreements could even cultivate community! "One of the ways in which human beings can come together is to fight."[12] Finally, philosopher William J. Abraham (1947–2021) advised: "The best way forward in adjudicating claims is to allow particular, positive claims and their particular appropriate defeaters to proceed without prejudice or restriction."[13]

Seneca (c. 1 BCE–65 CE) wrote that there is no easy way from the earth to the stars.[14] Will our philosophy proceed accordingly? Thomas Paine (1737–1809) intuited one reason why it must: "What we obtain too cheaply, we esteem too lightly."[15] Pressured like Paine in *The Crisis*, Rand in *The Wheel of Time* realized on Dragonmount that in every challenge is a thread to weave a better life.[16] Francis X. Clooney elevated the same approach for competing arguments: "There need not be any fear of what we might learn, there is only the Truth that sets us free."[17]


## Jacob M. Held

Just because fate has chosen something for you instead of you choosing it for yourself doesn't mean it has to be bad. Even if it's something you are sure you would never have chosen in a hundred years.[18]

Min says the above to Perrin in the context of a story about a woman and her arranged marriage. It is obviously relevant to Perrin and the other *ta'veren. The Wheel of Time*, all things considered, is a story about fate, and so many of the characters often lament that they aren't making choices for themselves; they're being driven by external forces, and if only they were in complete control, then their lives would be much better. Many of us often think this way. We regret past choices, unchosen circumstances, and decry the lack of options currently available to us. We bellyache that our lives are not our own; if only we'd had better moral luck, clearer foresight, greater control ... This attitude, aside from being counterproductive, is also ignorant. It assumes that we control the outcomes of our choices and actions, as if were we to have more control over our lives we could've assured ideal results. It assumes we are omniscient in terms of all viable possibilities and how each one would redound to our benefit. It assumes that if only we could steer our lives without any external interference, they would be perfect. The corollary is that anything in one's life that is not perfect must, therefore, be the result of an external influence frustrating our otherwise perfect plans.

But, we are not perfect as is. Humans develop over time in response to challenges, not of our choosing, but endemic to our condition as part of a disordered world. Nor do we know ourselves as well as we think we do. Introspective knowledge is not always accurate; we are not transparent to ourselves. We can be, and often are, mistaken about what is best for ourselves. If we were infallible in this regard psychologists and therapists would be out of jobs, justifiably. Nor do we often appreciate the circumstances within which we find ourselves. What we consider deviations from our plans, obstacles, or hinderances, don't sidetrack us from an otherwise perfectly planned life of guaranteed satisfaction, they define life, and we define ourselves through our responses. Min's tale reveals a profound understanding of the nature of human life. It recalls a lesson from Epictetus (c. 50–135):

> What kind of man do you suppose Heracles would have been if it hadn't been for the famous lion, and the hydra, the stag, the boar, and the wicked brutal men whom he drove away and cleared from the earth? What would he have turned his hand to if nothing like that had existed? Isn't it plain that he would have wrapped himself up in a blanket and gone to sleep? He would surely have never become Heracles if he had slumbered the whole of his life away ...[19]

Mat, Perrin, Rand ... us, we all lament missed opportunities, current struggles, and foreseeable derailments from intended plans. We often wish life were other than what it presently is, but this is not evidence that fate is cruel, or that our lives are less than they might otherwise have been. Instead, this attitude demonstrates a failure to appreciate the role we play in defining our lives as given. It shows a lack of gratitude for the opportunities that are present and, in general, a failure to affirm life, with all its high and lows. With Nietzsche, let us "learn more and more to see as beautiful what is necessary in things, then [we] shall be ... those who make things beautiful ..."[20]

## Kenneth Pike

But men often mistake revenge and killing for justice. They seldom have the stomach for justice.[21]

So declares Nynaeve al'Meara, sparing the lives of captured *sul'dam* by sentencing them to the slavery they once inflicted on others. The idea that moral reasoning admits a gender divide is not original to *The Wheel of Time*. For example, Annette C. Baier (1929–2012) famously suggested that "men's" moral theory privileges the logic of contractual obligation, where a "woman's theory" of moral reasoning would instead center on nurture or care.[22]

Whether gender essentialism is true in our world, it is clearly true in the text of *The Wheel of Time*. The differences between *saidin* and *saidar*, and the persistence of gender across multiple lifetimes (even when reincarnated into a body of a different sex), makes that clear. It is unsurprising, then, for Nynaeve to perceive a gender binary in moral judgment. What the men in her life *might* find surprising is that she regards their tendency to "mistake" vengeance for justice as *soft*. Readers, likewise, may see this passage as an insight, not into gendered justice, but into the abrasiveness of Nynaeve's personality.

But I think this passage best illustrates how an ethics of care can, at times, result in far harsher judgment than an ethics of obligation. C.S. Lewis (1898–1963) once observed that "The robber baron's cruelty may sometimes sleep, his cupidity may at some point be satiated; but those who torment us for our own good will torment us without end for they do so with the approval of their own conscience."[23] Lewis was writing on tyranny, but not everyone who torments us for our own good is our enemy, or a tyrant. Nynaeve never hesitated to torment others for their good. When she drops Lan in Saldaea after extracting his promise to accept anyone who wishes to accompany him on his way to Tarwin's Gap, this torments him greatly. Lan felt obligated to kill, and to die, in pursuit of vengeance. Nynaeve's ethics of care imposed a weightier burden.

## Michel-Antoine Xhignesse

The oak fought the wind and was broken, the willow bent when it must and survived.[24]

This quote is, of course, a transparent reference to Aesop's fable of the oak and the reeds. In Randland, it is applied to gender dynamics in particular: men are said to think of strength or power as requiring them to resist change, and so find that they break themselves against it. Women, meanwhile, are said to adapt with changing circumstances; as a result, they offer less spectacular displays of their power, but also ensure its endurance across time. This is reflected, of course, in real-world gender socialization, as well as in their different approaches to accessing the One Power: men *seize saidin*, while women *embrace saidar*.

It also clearly characterizes Randland's political situation after the Breaking, where women occupy dominant roles in the power hierarchy, but do not rely on that power to govern, preferring subtle political maneuvers instead. This is particularly true of the White Tower, though much of the un-Powered world is likewise ruled by women, and reflects a similar commitment; think of Mayene or Andor, for example. Meanwhile, the "oak" kingdoms, such as Shienar and Cairhien, relied on their might and eventually found themselves cast down by events. Similarly, Rand thinks that he must be hard to defeat the Dark One, and is constantly reminded by those around him, notably Cadsuane, that although steel is hard, that hardness makes it brittle.

So much for literary analysis. But what I find much more interesting is simply the fact that this fable—among others—is woven into the texture of Randland in the first place. It is just one of many passing references to the events, literature, and mythology of our own world, and yet another way of driving home the point that Randland is supposed to be a version of our own world. That we recognize so much of our world lurking behind Randland is no accident of lazy worldbuilding; the parallels are deliberate, and help to establish our world as part of Randland's background.

# Notes


1. Robert Jordan, *The Great Hunt* (New York: TOR Books, 1990), 552–553.
2. Robert Jordan and Brandon Sanderson, *A Memory of Light* (New York: TOR Books, 2012), 195.
3. Confucius, *The Analects*, 7.21, translated in e.g. Dr. Purushothaman, *What Confucius Said* (Kerala, India: Centre for Human Perfection, 2014), 27.
4. Proverbs 27:17 (NRSV, updated ed.).
5. Stephanie W. Jamison and Joel P. Brereton, trans., *The Rigveda: The Earliest Religious Poetry of India, Volume 1: South Asia Research* (New York: Oxford University Press, 2014), 221.
6. James 1:3 (NIV).
7. Plato, *The Trial and Death of Socrates: Euthyphro, Apology, Crito, Death Scene from Phaedo*, 3rd ed., trans. G.M.A. Grube, rev. John M. Cooper ed. (Indianapolis: Hackett, 2000), *Apology* 38a, 39.

8.  Al-Kindi in Seyyed Hossein Nasr, *Philosophy from Its Origin to the Present*, Vol. 136 (New York: State University of New York Press, 2006), 288.

9.  John Milton, *Aeropagitica, edited with introduction and notes by John Wesley Hales* (Oxford: Clarendon Press, 1874), 50–52.

10. Alexander Innes Shand, *Half a Century: Or, Changes in Men and Manners*, 2nd ed. (Edinburgh: William Blackwood & Sons, 1888), 62.

11. Martin Luther King Jr, *The Trumpet of Conscience* (Boston: Beacon Press, 2010), 29.

12. J Michael, *Buckley, At the Origins of Modern Atheism* (New Haven: Yale University Press, 1937), 34.

13. William J Abraham, "Eschatology and Epistemology," in Jerry L Walls ed., *The Oxford Handbook of Eschatology* (New York: Oxford University Press, 2008), 588–589.

14. Megara in Lucius Annaeus Seneca, *Hercules Furens*, trans. Frank Justice Miller (Cambridge: Harvard University Press, 1917), line 437, at https://www.theoi.com/Text/SenecaHerculesFurens.html.

15. Thomas Paine, "The American Crisis, No. 1," Philadelphia, December 19, 1776, at https://americainclass.org/sources/makingrevolution/war/text2/painecrisis1776.pdf.

16. Robert Jordan and Brandon Sanderson, *The Gathering Storm* (New York: TOR Books, 2009), 758–760.

17. Francis X Clooney, *Comparative Theology: Deep Learning Across Religions Borders* (Oxford: Wiley Blackwell, 2010), 165, referencing John 8:32.

18. Robert Jordan, *The Dragon Reborn* (New York: TOR Books, 1991), 25.

19. Epictetus, "Discourses," in *Discourses, Fragments, Handbook*, trans. Robin Hard (Oxford: Oxford University Press, 2014), 17.

20. Friedrich Nietzsche, *The Gay Science with a Prelude in Rhymes and an Appendix of Songs, trans. Walter Kaufmann* (New York: Vintage Books, 1974), 223.

21. Robert Jordan, *The Great Hunt* (New York: Tom Doherty Associates, 1990), 548.

22. Annette C Baier, "What Do Women Want in a Moral Theory?" in *Moral Prejudices: Essays on Ethics* (Cambridge: Harvard University Press, 1994), 1–17.

23. C S Lewis, "The Humanitarian Theory of Punishment," in Walter Hooper ed., *God in the Dock: Essays on Theology and Ethics* (Grand Rapids: William B. Eerdmans, 2014), 318–333, 324.

24. Robert Jordan, *The Fires of Heaven* (New York: TOR Books, 1994), 617.

# Index of Terms and Names

Printed and bound by CPI Group (UK) Ltd, Croydon, CR0 4YY

19/08/2025

14720467-0001